Modernizing China's Industries

Dedicated to
Robyn, Lygia, Jill and Marilyn

Modernizing China's Industries

Lessons from Wool and Wool Textiles

Colin G. Brown, Scott A. Waldron and
John W. Longworth

The University of Queensland
Brisbane, Australia

Edward Elgar
Cheltenham, UK • Northampton, MA, USA

Published by
Edward Elgar Publishing Limited
Glensanda House
Montpellier Parade
Cheltenham
Glos GL50 1UA
UK

Edward Elgar Publishing, Inc.
136 West Street
Suite 202
Northampton
Massachusetts 01060
USA

A catalogue record for this book
is available from the British Library

ISBN 1 84376 591 8

Printed and bound in Great Britain by MPG Books Ltd, Bodmin, Cornwall

Contents

Figures

Tables

Boxes

Images

Preface

Our first encounter with the Chinese wool textile industry came through a large, intensive research project that ran from 1989 to 1993. That project was concerned with an economic investigation of Chinese wool production, marketing and processing. The wool textile industry was extremely fluid at the time and very much in a process of transition. In response to a series of fiscal reforms many small, early-stage processing facilities were being established by agencies of local governments which had no prior experience in these activities. Large State-owned mills – which were effectively mini-communities – were seeking ways to address looming problems especially in connection with their worker welfare obligations and waste treatment. Institutional turf battles were regularly being waged (such as between the Ministry of Agriculture and the Ministry of Commerce, and between the Ministry of Foreign Affairs, Economic Relations and Trade, and Chinatex). The traditional agribusiness and marketing giant, the Supply and Marketing Co-operative system, was seeing its marketing empire threatened by other government agencies as it lost its sole-procurement rights. State Farms dominated the top end of the fine wool market and were seeking ways to develop further and take advantage of their leading position. Flirtations, largely unsuccessful, with new marketing channels such as wool auctions were being made. Local governments were flexing their growing autonomy in several areas, but the central government decisively re-exerted its influence on regular occasions.

The research team followed the fortunes of the wool textile industry throughout the 1990s, while at the same time examining the transition occurring in other Chinese industries through a series of research projects. However it was not until another large intensive research project from 2000 to 2004 that we were able to focus our attention on the wool textile industry again. On this occasion, the research centred on examining ways of improving the viability of wool textile mills, which at the time were in dire straits. Our research was from a whole-of-industry perspective and involved an examination of the domestic and overseas supply chains for wool and the market for textile products. This project enabled us to return to many of the same regions, organizations, enterprises and marketing channels that we had investigated a decade or more earlier.

Despite having followed the path of the industry in the intervening period, after closer reinvestigation, we were amazed by the changes that had taken place and were occurring. Some segments of the industry, such as wool marketing, had gone from the extreme of a single cumbersome, monolithic agency to a fragmented and uncoordinated segment involving a very large number of small entrepreneurial dealers. In other industry segments, large State agencies – though often in a very different form – prevailed. For example the fine-wool growing State Farms had now delegated many of the sheep-raising activities and control to households living on the farm. Furthermore, and perhaps in contrast with the stated intentions of the industry reforms, there had been a significant downgrading of their breeding programmes and hence a decline in the quality of the wool produced on State Farms to service the premium fine-wool markets. Almost all the small unskilled processing facilities initiated by local governments in response to the fiscal reforms had failed to stay the distance, but so too had many of the larger State-owned mills. Other mills were in the process of changing alliances – either as a result of strategic decisions or under coercion – and were desperately seeking ways to modernize their management and analytic skills to match new investment and technology upgrades. The central government was taking a more facilitative macro-guidance role while local government influence was being exerted more through their indirect involvement in local enterprises than via direct policy initiatives.

Our reflection on the changes and modernization occurring in the wool textile industry over the 15 years from 1989 to 2004 suggested that a detailed micro-level analysis of the pressures on the industry participants, and how they have responded to these pressures, would shed a great deal of light on the problems and opportunities arising from the economy-wide transition occurring in China. An in-depth study of a particular industry would highlight many facets of the process of transition not evident from the more common macro-level studies based on aggregate empirical modelling.

This book therefore provides a detailed micro-level investigation of industry modernization and the process of transition in China as seen through the window of the wool textile industry. We do not argue that the wool textile industry provides all the answers – indeed the path of industry transition will be unique for each industry. Nevertheless there are several features about the wool textile industry that make it a particularly relevant case. In particular, the industry has deep roots in the Central Planning era but has experienced strong and turbulent growth in the reform era. It comprises diverse industry participants that span a long production and marketing chain which raises many issues of industry-wide development and co-ordination. There are strong domestic market connections in terms of wool inputs and wool textile outputs, but the industry also relies heavily on a rapidly changing global wool and wool textile industry.

To conduct research of this type however can be a monumental task, especially in China, as it requires detailed interviews with a wide variety of industry participants who are geographically dispersed and time constrained. The information and analysis in this book has been assembled from a number of research projects involving the China Agricultural Economics Group at The University of Queensland. However special reference must be made to the research project mentioned earlier that spanned the period 2000 to 2004 and which was concerned with the viability of Chinese wool textile mills. This project was funded by the Australian Centre for International Agricultural Research. Details about this project, the earlier ACIAR-funded wool industry project conducted in the 1989 to 1994 period, and other related projects can be found on the China Agricultural Economics Group website at http://www.nrsm.uq.edu.au/caeg. We are indebted to the Australian Centre for International Agricultural Research for their ongoing financial support of research in this area.

The research undertaken between 2000 and 2004 involved collaboration with the Chinese Research Center for Rural Economy. We gratefully acknowledge the many researchers from the Research Center for Rural Economy who have been involved in this project and especially the Director, Ke Binsheng, who took the initiative and sought to involve the Research Center for Rural Economy in the project. Professor Ke also provided many valuable insights and inputs at various stages in the project. In addition special acknowledgement must be made of Zhao Yutian who demonstrated his formidable organizational and leadership skills in guiding the project and organizing the interviews among the diverse group of industry participants. We have also benefited enormously from Yutian's academic and research skills in unravelling the mysteries of complex problems, and from his entrepreneurial and analytic skills in devising practical approaches to progressing the finding of solutions to problems facing the industry. The development of many arguments in the book owes much to Yutian's ideas and analysis. It takes gifted and well-organized researchers like Zhao Yutian to bridge the gaps between government officials, industry officials, enterprise managers and academics.

Apart from Zhao Yutian and other researchers at the RCRE, we would like to express our deep gratitude to Li Wei (Lanzhou Sanmao – for facilitating our understanding of the technical aspects of wool processing), Ben Lyons (University of Queensland – for his insights on Sino-Australian wool trade), and Professor Li Ping (China Agricultural University – for her understanding of the Chinese approach to financial and managerial accounting), who have all been heavily involved in the research. Although these researchers have contributed much to the ideas in the book, we stress that they are in no way responsible for any errors or omissions it may contain.

The research could not have been possible without the support and involvement of the industry itself. Information on which the book is based came from fieldwork and interviews over an extended period involving hundreds of industry participants from herders, State Farm managers, wool dealers, local officials, enterprise managers, production and technical managers, enterprise accountants and information technology staff, central-level officials, overseas traders, customs officials, inspection and testing officials and many others. Special mention must be given to a number of mills – who will remain anonymous here to preserve their confidentiality – that the research team spent many days with and with which ongoing analysis is occurring. All industry participants provided a frank, informed and open exchange of views, and contributed much to ideas on how the industry should move forward as well as being open to suggestions and seeking advice on how to make this happen. Indeed, if for no other reason than this entrepreneurial and positive spirit among industry participants, the industry is on the path of successful transition.

Although every endeavour has been made to check the accuracy of the information contained in the book, the speed and nature of industry transition means that the situation – and the information that describes the current state of affairs – can and will change rapidly. Indeed the book is all about understanding the drivers for change rather than presenting a snapshot of the industry at a particular point in time. Readers seeking precise information on a particular organization or enterprise need to check these details at the time of their inquiry, with the book providing a useful guide on where to source the information and what other related information should also be sought.

Conducting the research and organizing the ideas into a book of this nature is one thing, but preparing the manuscript to a camera-ready copy (CRC) ready for printing is quite another. In connection with this task, we are deeply indebted to Stephanie Cash. This is now the fourth major book – not to mention numerous other major reports and articles – that Stephanie has been responsible for preparing as a CRC manuscript. Her contribution extends well beyond preparing the technical manuscript. Apart from her English language skills, Stephanie's ability to (subtly) highlight our inconsistencies, to suggest ways of communication and presentation, and to overlook or tolerate our impossible deadlines and sometimes disorganized approaches are greatly appreciated.

Finally, none of the research or production of the book would have been possible without the support of our families. The many months of fieldwork in China are only the tip of an iceberg of the many hours spent in analysing the information and in reporting it in forums such as this book. We are deeply grateful to our families for the support of these activities and their sacrifices and contribution towards them.

Colin Brown
Scott Waldron
John Longworth
February 2005

1. Mega-forces and Mega-consequences

China's economic liberalization programme (1978 to present) has been under way for almost as long as China operated under a strict Central Planning regime (1949 to 1978).[1] It is hardly surprising therefore that China's economic transition programme is well advanced. Nowadays for the vast majority of industries, market rather than administrative signals determine who produces how much of what, how outputs are sold and inputs procured, and at what prices. State marketing and trade monopolies have been dismantled, subsidies for State-owned Enterprises wound back, ownership transition firmly entrenched, and administrative institutions reformed. Thus the foundations for an irreversible transition from a command economy to a more market-driven system have been solidly laid.

China's incremental reform process has generated tremendous growth and change, all without the major upheavals of the "big bang" transition of the former Soviet Union. On a lesser scale however it has thrown much of the economy into what is commonly referred to in China as a disorganized or chaotic (*luan*) state. Local economic agents do not always act in a way consistent with the long-term well-being of their unit, their industry or society as a whole. Markets are volatile, fragmented and uncoordinated.

While not seeking to turn the clock back by reinstating strict Central Planning, the Chinese government continues to play a major role in almost all sectors of the economy. However the intervention occurs in increasingly subtle ways and within a new framework of economic governance. Government agencies are moving towards playing a more facilitative rather than coercive role. They are limited to setting the macro-environment and establishing structures that provide services to economic agents. Within this institutional setting, often referred to as "capitalism with Chinese characteristics", the market is primarily responsible for regulating economic activity.

The devolution of economic decision-making powers poses enormous challenges for industries, enterprises and households. They must first survive the full onslaught of powerful new external forces unleashed through the transition process. Amidst intense and immediate day-to-day pressures, economic agents must also proactively modernize and plan for the long-term future. At the most fundamental level, economic agents must somehow find the resources – especially time, skills and vision – to undertake these longer-term tasks. On a more systematic level, this requires micro-level changes in management structures and processes within the economic units, and close coordination between units across industry sectors and across national and international boundaries. Until recently these forms of coordination have been hindered by administratively established boundaries that economic agents have had only limited experience in traversing.

Viewed as a multi-stage and multidimensional process, China's economic transition still has a long way to go. Most attention has focused on the first phase of transition of macro-level ownership and administrative reforms. A second phase of technological upgrading is also well advanced. These two phases are crucial in the overall transition process, but not sufficient in themselves. China has yet to tackle seriously the essential third phase of the transition to a modern market economy. This third phase involves a series of micro-level reforms and measures aimed at improving the way enterprises manage their internal and external environment, coordinate with other industry participants, and go about making their economic and other decisions. The obstacles to, and the opportunities offered by, the successful tackling of this third phase of transition are examined in this book through the window of the Chinese wool textile industry.

1.1 TRANSITION FROM CENTRAL PLANNING TO MARKET ECONOMY

Some aspects of the complex transition process for China's industries are captured in the simplified diagrammatic representation in Figure 1.1. It contrasts the relationships and management of industries under the Central Planning era (left hand side of the diagram) with that of the current, more market-oriented era (right hand side of the diagram). The solid arrows in the diagram represent the different forces pressing on economic agents in the two eras. The six mega-forces impacting on economic agents in the current era are briefly discussed in Section 1.2.

Economic agents experienced a different set of external pressures in the Central Planning era. Furthermore the forces were interpreted by the State administrators, translated into decrees and plans, and passed down through vertical line bureaus to economic agents for implementation. That is, the State played a key role in the operations of the economic agents (enterprises and households) as well as broader industries and sectors.

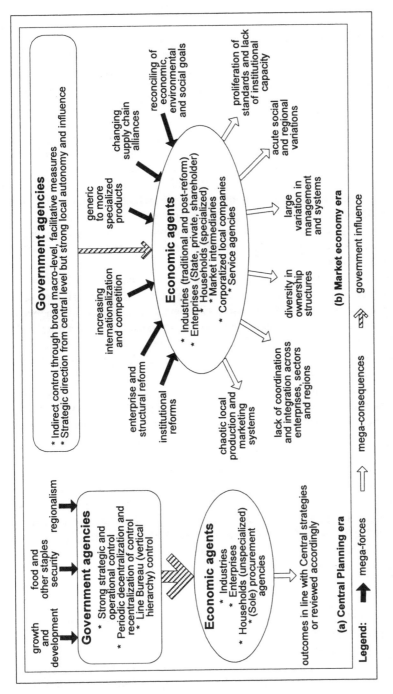

Figure 1.1   Contrasting the Central Planning era with the market economy era

(a) Central Planning era

Government agencies
* Strong strategic and operational control
* Periodic decentralization and recentralization of control
* Line Bureau (vertical hierarchy) control

growth and development   food and other staples security   regionalism

Economic agents
* Industries
* Enterprises
* Households (unspecialized)
* (Sole) procurement agencies

outcomes in line with Central strategies or reviewed accordingly

(b) Market economy era

Government agencies
* Indirect control through broad macro-level, facilitative measures
* Strategic direction from central level but strong local autonomy and influence

changing supply chain alliances   reconciling of economic, environmental and social goals

generic to more specialized products

increasing internationalization and competition

enterprise and structural reform

institutional reforms

Economic agents
* Industries (traditional and post-reform)
* Enterprises (State, private, shareholder)
* Households (specialized)
* Market intermediaries
* Corporatized local companies
* Service agencies

proliferation of standards and lack of institutional capacity

acute social and regional variations

large variation in management and systems

diversity in ownership structures

chaotic local production and marketing systems

lack of coordination and integration across enterprises, sectors and regions

Legend: ➤ mega-forces   ⇨ mega-consequences   ➡ mega-consequences   ⇨ government influence

3

Through an incremental and not yet complete transition, relationships in industries have come to resemble those outlined on the right-hand side of the diagram. Government still wields influence on the industry, but indirectly through broader macro-settings including legal settings and service provision. Consequently economic agents more directly experience the pressures of external influences and forces.

The combination of rapid structural reforms with the emergence of powerful, new, economic mega-forces has led to a high-pressure situation in which industries have been shaken up in unexpected and, at times, unintended ways (Section 1.2). The mega-consequences of industry transition – including "chaotic" (*luan*) local production and marketing systems and large variations in profitability, modernization and management of enterprises – are highlighted by the hollow arrows at the bottom of the diagram. The mega-consequences are overviewed separately in Section 1.3 and are a major focus throughout the book.

So-called "chaotic" industry situations also occurred in the Central Planning era. During this period the central government periodically released power to localities or local agents to stimulate stagnating local economies. When economic and political activities were deemed too disorderly or chaotic, the central government re-exerted power over economic decision making. These periodic *fang-shou* cycles of decentralizing and recentralizing control were a feature of the era.

The methods government used to re-exert control during the Central Planning era are now much less of an option. They place too heavy a burden on State coffers, are politically problematic to implement, and are contrary to international commitments and domestic expectations. Even if the government sought to reintroduce Central Planning-type measures on a widespread basis, they would be ineffective given the extent to which transition has proceeded and the relative power and nature of external forces currently impacting on industry participants. Thus the government – in unison with economic agents – must seek new ways to bring order from the chaos. After taking full account of the intricacies and forces facing economic agents and industries in the book, the concluding chapter offers some recommendations about what might be required.

1.2 MEGA-FORCES DRIVING CHINA'S ECONOMIC TRANSITION

The future and fortunes of economic agents and industries are intertwined and, in both cases, determined by their capacity to deal with the forces or pressures created by the process of economic transition. Some of these forces impact upon specific industries, but there are a number of developments in the economic, political, social and market environments that exert a profound impact across a broad range of industries. An overview of some of these key pressures or "mega-forces" follows.

1.2.1 Institutional Reforms

China's economic transition has been underpinned by a series of administrative reforms. Specialized economic departments with direct control over State-owned Enterprises and agencies have all but been abolished. They have been replaced by "macro-control" departments that implement macro-policies, which impact upon industries in a less discriminatory way (Waldron et al. 2003, Part B).

The pressures exerted by institutional reform manifest themselves in various ways. First, industry participants are now less subject to direct administrative control, either through decree or ownership links. Second, industry development plans and deliberate coordination efforts are no longer led by administrators, but by individual industry participants, or not all. Third, administrative reforms have reduced the artificial boundaries that existed between economic sectors. This final point has especially important implications for the third phase of the economic transition process emphasized in this book.

China's economic reform process has closely followed institutional lines organized on a sectoral basis. That is, rather than having jurisdiction over entire vertically organized industries, government departments controlled segments of particular industries such as processing, international trade, agricultural procurement and agricultural production. Reform measures have been applied to these industry segments in different and often uneven ways. For industry transition, as illustrated by the wool textile industry in this book, the uneven application of reforms can create enormous pressures on different segments of the industry to move in different directions.

1.2.2 Enterprise and Structural Reforms

Administrative reform is inextricably related to enterprise reform. Specialized economic departments have been abolished and forced to divest themselves of their state-owned enterprises and agencies. However as mentioned above, the role of the State varies by economic sector, or industry segment.

In general the reform of all enterprises has been implemented incrementally through a series of laws (such as bankruptcy, merger, company and taxation laws), programmes (such as shareholderization programmes and capacity cutbacks) and institutional reforms (such as the elevation of State Asset Management Commissions). The result for enterprises is that they have fewer non-commercial obligations, are less subject to administrative decree, less eligible for subsidies and favourable policies, and operate under harder budget constraints. The market now primarily determines what and how enterprises market outputs, process products and purchase inputs. This has had an indirect – though not necessarily pervasive – effect on the "nuts and bolts" systems of operating an enterprise including finance, accounting, information, human resource, storage and distribution systems. By any reckoning, enterprise reform is a powerful force for change.

These forces have affected different enterprises in different ways. Some have adjusted and prospered, some struggle to keep afloat and others have not been able to survive. The different impacts depend on the characteristics the enterprise brought into the enterprise reform process as well as the enormous variation of the process itself. There are major differences in the reform paths of State-owned Enterprises, Township and Village Enterprises, State marketing agencies, State trade agencies and enterprises with other ownership structures and functions. Reforms also differ by region (where those in developed eastern areas generally have a better chance of successfully reforming) and vertical administrative level (where reforms have been implemented and impact unevenly). As mentioned above, there are also differences by industries and sectors.

Structural and ownership elements of the enterprise reform process are well under way and could be expected to enter the advanced stage in the not too distant future. Enterprises will emerge on a roughly equal footing. Many enterprises are converging toward shareholder companies, although there is enormous diversity within these structures. With continued diversity across all ownership types, debate arises about the relationship between ownership and productivity (Steinfeld 1998; Weitzman and Xu 1994). This book shows that across many sectors, each enterprise type – including State-owned Enterprises and State trading agencies – have their own strengths and weaknesses.

Thus macro-level ownership and structural issues will become less important as the broader enterprise reform proceeds. Enterprises compete fiercely with each other based on their own strengths and weaknesses and on their capacity to face the set of pressures outlined below. Their ability to do so will be determined predominantly by the micro-level systems that they put in place and – somewhat ironically given the increasing competition – their capacity to coordinate with other industry participants. How enterprises in the wool textile industry are responding to these forces and challenges is a focus of this book.

Image 1.1   Fabric store in Wangfujing Street: 1990

This fabric store in busy Wangfujing Street in Beijing is a hive of activity in 1990. (Note cashier in top left corner who receives payment by a string pulley system.) The store, which has since been demolished and replaced by a modern shopping centre, contrasts markedly with retail outlets such as that shown in Image 1.2. The pace of change and diversity in industry structures calls for a detailed, micro-level form of analysis.

1.2.3   Increasing Internationalization and Competition

Many industries in China rely heavily on imported raw materials and also export significant proportions of their final outputs. Thus growing internationalization will continue to exert a massive force on China's economic transition process.

In this context, much has been made of China's accession to the World Trade Organization. Accession has encouraged a move towards the lowering of tariffs and elimination of import quotas, the provision of better access to overseas markets, and the introduction of more foreign competition. However in the same way that ownership and structural change represents only one part of the broader enterprise reform process, World Trade Organization accession represents only one part of the broader internationalization process – and a small part at that. Industry participants must now change management practices to operate effectively in the increasingly sophisticated and internationalized environment.

Relative factor endowments have enabled Chinese firms to manufacture some products at a lower cost or in a better form than suppliers from other countries. Increasing internationalization requires that these firms be in a position to make the most of their comparative advantages by tailoring their input procurement, output, product selection and production systems to maximize these advantages. This can be problematic given that relative factor endowments and input and output markets change continuously. Firms must capture any ephemeral advantages if they are to survive in the longer term, and be flexible enough to adjust when market conditions move against them.

Greater internationalization can raise the level and change the form of exposure to risk. Many of the risks associated with operating in overseas markets relate to changing market access arrangements, changing consumer preferences and other changes in the business environment. Successfully competing in overseas markets requires a full understanding of these changes and markets. The informal and ad hoc risk management processes previously employed fall well short of the risk management that is such an integral part of operating successful and competitive international firms.

At the same time, the blind pursuit of export markets at the expense of opportunities afforded by a rapidly growing domestic market is as inappropriate as ignoring the opportunities created by increasing internationalization. Successful strategies involve market segmentation, which may include multiple segments of both the export and domestic markets. Thus increasing internationalization is more about choices – management strategies and decisions that need to be made in an environment of a wider selection of product markets, source of inputs, and manufacturing processes.

As if adapting management practices to the forces of internationalization is not challenging enough, China also needs to proactively consider its longer-term and strategic role in international industries. Despite the fact that China accounts for a high proportion of world output in many industries, relatively few large Chinese enterprises or company alliances have established, for example, international brand names, vertically integrated international structures, or strong and informed input purchasing positions. These types of issues will need to be considered if China's international role is not to be confined to one of a passive processor as the "world's factory". The wool textile industry illustrates well the important point that all aspects of industry transition in response to internationalization require increased coordination across sectoral, administrative and national boundaries.

Image 1.2   Baoxiniao garment store in Changzhou: 2004

Modern, well-presented and expensive retail outlets such as the Baoxiniao outlet in Changzhou City are part of the streetscape of large and mid-sized cities throughout China. Large garment makers such as Baoxiniao have hundreds of chain stores, many of which are operated under franchise arrangements.

1.2.4   Shift from Generic to More Specialized Products

Many industries in China have developed on the basis of cost advantages in producing generic, low-value products for an undifferentiated domestic mass market. Features of the manufacturing systems servicing this sector are repeat orders from regular customers, standard and readily available inputs, minimal product design, and selling from stock rather than producing to order. Using such production and management systems, China demonstrated its ability to rapidly expand the output of generic products throughout the 1980s and 1990s across a wide range of industries.

In the early stages of reforms in the 1980s, the influx of market entrants and rapid increase in production covered previous unmet demand for low-quality products. Lucrative returns could be obtained from volume production using low-cost production systems. However the initial lucrative returns and relative simplicity of production systems – supported in various ways by government – led to a surplus in many low-value products. Increasing consumer orientation in domestic and global markets has exacerbated the problems of surplus products and capacity in low-value markets.

Consumers and intermediate customers are now much more specific, not only about biophysical product attributes, but also about quality assurance, source of materials and product safety. Products must meet specified requirements just to gain access to some international markets and high-value domestic markets. This increasing specification drives a wedge between the prices of the generic and specified products.

The glut of low-value products and the knock-on effect on prices have meant that generic production systems based on passive traditional management systems are no longer a sustainable option. Even enterprises that adopt a cost-focused strategy must adjust to changing market conditions by for instance making optimal inputs choices to control costs. However most enterprises – especially those with good technical capacity and relatively high cost structures – are acutely aware of the need to move up value chains and access premium markets.

Tailoring production and management systems to manufacture specific products for specific customers and markets is an enormous task and requires a fundamental rather than incremental shift for many enterprises. Because of the additional costs involved and the production of more specific products that cannot be viably sold on mass markets, the risks are high. As demonstrated in the wool textile industry, firms able to make these reforms and cope with the added risks will surge ahead in a less crowded industry and rapidly growing markets.

1.2.5   Changing Alliances in Product Supply Chains

One of the consequences of moving from low-value to higher-value markets or from generic to more tailored products is a lengthening of the marketing chain. For low-value generic products, small-scale production often revolves around households integrated or coordinating across the stages of straightforward input procurement, low-technology processing, and wholesaling in physical market places. For larger-scale enterprises, more sophisticated marketing and processing tasks are vertically integrated within the organizational unit, or organized through direct and informal arrangements.

Higher-value and more specialized products change the nature of these arrangements. First, they lengthen the marketing chain either through further product transformation or through increased services such as quality assurance, information provision, or after-sales service or advice. Second, they increase the complexity of the marketing tasks involved. The complexity either takes the tasks out of the feasible realm of households and small enterprises, or means that specialized firms perform the specific task more efficiently.

As will become evident in the case of the wool textile industry, changes in product requirements necessitate high levels of coordination, either within the enterprise (vertical integration) or between industry participants including intermediaries (market integration). The form of integration adopted depends on the relative transaction costs, which will vary with developments in institutional arrangements, marketing services, technology and consumer preferences.

1.2.6 Reconciliation of Economic, Social and Environmental Goals

In the pursuit of rapid economic growth and development, social and environmental impacts have often been overlooked in China. However awareness is growing about the need to balance these impacts with the economic aims of industry development. These issues are largely a matter of public policy but have an impact and require the cooperation of industry participants.

Economic transition has bought about massive social change. Many people have been able to take advantage of the new opportunities while others have not, either because of their failure to adapt or for structural reasons outside the control of the individual. The gap between the gainers and losers could be expected to continue to widen as transition continues. Some specific reasons why this might happen can be identified through an analysis of industry transition in the context of mega-forces outlined above.

The influx of market entrants into burgeoning industries over recent decades created opportunity for entrepreneurs and workers alike. More recent enterprise restructuring has curbed this growth, and indeed resulted in net employment losses in many industries. This has occurred not only in State-owned Enterprises saddled with surplus workers and welfare obligations. Smaller enterprises have buckled under the pressure of the mega-forces outlined above and have been targeted by government policy aimed at closing small, polluting firms that are largely responsible for producing surpluses of low-value products. The plethora of households that run market stalls, small trade operations and cottage industries have felt and will continue to feel the pressure of industry modernization. Through the many industries that source raw materials from agricultural production and mineral extraction, internationalization will impact negatively upon many millions of rural households.

Responsibility for finding long-term solutions for these social problems lies largely with government, but other industry participants also have an important role to play. The need to develop existing and new industries for the redeployment of unemployed or underemployed labour is of course another major stream of China's economic transition process, but is proving difficult in many areas. Institutional systems to support and facilitate coordination across regional boundaries and between smaller participants – small enterprises (versus large enterprises), market integration (versus vertical integration) and primary production systems – are underemphasized in China but may have a significant positive social impact, even given the power of larger mega-forces.

China's massive environmental problems in nearly all industries are also coming under scrutiny. In some cases, the means of addressing the problems have been absolute. Polluting companies have been shut down or are precluded from some international markets. Other less absolute measures include fines, certification and pricing schemes. Because the implementation of environmental regulations is highly uneven and the costs of non-compliance low, most enterprises continue to trade off the costs against revenues. However as the measures are tightened and become more uniform, enterprises will need to adapt through new technologies, processing methods, products and management practices.

Both social and environmental imperatives must ultimately be incorporated into industry structures, including those of the wool textile industry. The road to achieving this however will be long and difficult. The main obstacles are the differing objectives, capacities and incentives of industry participants, including central government, local government, large enterprises, smaller enterprises and households. Thus economic transition involves much more than a well-defined drive toward efficiency, internationalization and moving up value chains. It also must address the consequences for different industry stakeholders, or who gets what out of the transition.

1.3   MEGA-CONSEQUENCES OF CHINA'S ECONOMIC TRANSITION

It is widely believed that increasing market liberalization that exposes economic agents directly to economic forces will generate more efficient and progressive industries better equipped to face future challenges. From a historical perspective, this holds in the case of China. However if observers were to take a snapshot at present, it would be hard to discern industries that are gearing up for future challenges in a proactive and coordinated way. Rather, industry participants often act individualistically, speculatively, passively and through informal means. As already mentioned, one of the terms commonly used in China to describe this state of affairs is *luan*, which means disorder or chaos. The industries, and participants within them, are searching for ways to move to the next phase of transition.

The primary focus of Chapters 4 to 8 of this book is to compare and contrast the path of transition for different economic agents and sectors of the wool textile industry, and to make some sense out of what appears on the surface to be a chaotic and complicated situation. As a prelude to this description and analysis, this section seeks broadly to categorize some of the mega-consequences of industry transition as highlighted by the hollow arrows at the bottom of Figure 1.1.

1.3.1 Chaotic Local Production and Marketing Systems

One feature of industry transition has been to open up markets and production to a much wider group of economic agents. In the 1980s, State-owned Enterprises were joined by a plethora of smaller Township and Village Enterprises and household enterprises with lower cost structures and more flexible operations. Previous sole procurement agencies and distribution giants with enormous advantages in distribution and ongoing political networks have been swamped and outcompeted by a plethora of small traders. Former State trading agencies have lost their monopoly positions, have been split into smaller entities and now compete with non-State traders.

Many of these new market entrants are small, unsophisticated operations that target low-value markets on the basis of cost competitiveness. In the early stages of reform, managers were often well-connected entrepreneurs rather than professional managers with a long background in the industry or in commercial operations. Together these participants have contributed to the fragmentation of marketing and production systems. As will be outlined in Chapters 4 to 8, the impacts of the fragmentation can be profound in areas such as information flows, price volatility, product quality and assurance, and the cost of providing marketing services.

The proliferation of new market entrants has facilitated economic opportunities for many enterprises and households, and has played an important role in diversifying many local economies, which is especially important in rural and remote areas. Some rationalization of uncompetitive enterprises is inevitable and indeed already happening. Otherwise the challenge is to develop more systematic and coordinated enterprises and industries.

Image 1.3   Modern Dandinghe Garment Factory in Wenzhou

World Trade Organization accession and increasing globalization have pressured many garment makers in Wenzhou to increase scale and modernize to meet the new competitive challenges and to take advantage of new international opportunities. The transformation of these essentially private companies from humble beginnings has been remarkable. However these enterprises will need to continue to adapt to a rapidly changing market environment.

1.3.2   Lack of Coordination and Integration

A related consequence to the fragmented industry structures is the lack of coordination and integration within industries. The lack of integration can occur at a number of levels. There may be little feedback of consumer and user preferences to producers, or between other participants in the marketing–processing chain. Spatial integration may also be low with local markets operating independently of developments occurring in other regions. Furthermore there may be poor integration between different products and even between different forms of a product.

Much of the poor integration stems from incomplete information flows arising from the fragmented industry structures. The fragmented structures are not conducive to coordinating industry activities, both from the perspective of the logistics of organizing a large number of diverse industry participants, and in terms of a concordance of interests. However institutional arrangements – for information, contracts, standards and inspection – could also be better provided to facilitate accuracy and reduce transaction costs. These systems have now literally fallen into disuse in many industries and sectors, partly because they are not economically justifiable in low-value markets. The dismantling of specialized economic units (government units with sectoral jurisdiction) has led to little institutional capacity to deliver services to industry and promote industry coordination. In this regard, administrative reforms have thrown the "institutional baby out with the bathwater". Thus subsequent institutional reforms will need to be targeted at building institutions – government, semi-government or non-government – that are suited to the market economy, including those that have the capacity to integrate industries such as wool textiles, provide valuable services to industry participants, and protect and enhance social benefits.

1.3.3 Large Diversity in Enterprise Structures

Compared with the discrete number of well-defined ownership structures in the Central Planning era – and even in Western economies – ownership and management structures in China are now highly diverse. Some of the main structures include State-owned Enterprises, State-controlled enterprises, collectives, shareholder companies, private enterprises and foreign-invested enterprises. Each category has its own set of subclassifications, governance structures and financing arrangements. The histories and systems that enterprises bring into the transition process are also of consequence. Older, larger and more established State-owned Enterprises hold some advantages in terms of enterprise systems, technical levels, reputations and customer bases that must be seen against disadvantages such as inflexibility and non-commercial obligations. The converse holds for the newer entrants.

In most industries and economic sectors in China, enterprises also span a very large scale or size continuum. Many of the large enterprises – such as State-owned Enterprises, State marketing or trading agencies – have been joined by newer enterprises such as Township and Village Enterprises and foreign-invested enterprises some of which now rank as amongst the largest in their respective industries. Industries that have long been subject to liberalization measures however are dominated by small industry participants, including small private enterprises, Township and Village Enterprises and households not registered as enterprises.

The diversity that exists in Chinese enterprise structures – in terms of ownership structures, scale and degree of integration – does not necessarily in itself hinder industry development. Indeed the diversity may facilitate balanced development. In the "anything goes" environment, any organization that can muster the necessary resources is actively encouraged by policymakers. Furthermore there is some evidence to suggest that some convergence is taking place toward for example shareholder structures.

Nonetheless, the diversity of enterprise structures does complicate tasks for policymakers. Different types of enterprises are subject to different registration procedures, legal environments, tax and accounting systems. The diversity complicates statistical collection and reporting as well as membership and jurisdiction in various industry institutions.

1.3.4   Variations in Management Systems and Outlooks

The management systems of State-owned Enterprises in China are also still strongly influenced by Central Planning systems which, in one way or another, remain pervasive. Managers are often still accustomed to waiting for orders in a passive manner and procuring inputs through long and well-established channels. In this case, much of the focus is on managing processing decisions within the enterprise or, more specifically, the political and human environment in which these processes take place. Managers were – and still are – appointed by local government. These appointments are based not just on their management skills, but also on their political and technical credentials. Thus much of their job is to communicate with government and, in particular, manage the large hierarchy of supervisors, technicians and workers.

Another major task of managers was to report to higher administrative levels – in terms of revenues to be passed up, commodity flows and inventories, and State resources (such capital, equipment and facilities) used. The skills of managers under Central Planning systems remain useful today and have been adapted in different ways to the contemporary era. Nevertheless there is still a large gulf between these traditional management practices and those of modern managers elsewhere.

In addition to management systems that can be traced directly to the Central Planning era and are of most relevance to State-owned Enterprises, other culture-bound management issues arise. Much of the chaos that exists in Chinese industries comes from informal management and exchange mechanisms. Political and interpersonal relationships (*guanxi*) and credit or trustworthiness (*xinyong*) have been instrumental in all aspects of business in China, including sourcing inputs and marketing outputs. As the number of transactions increases over longer distances and with more anonymous partners, these personalized forms of exchange are no longer by themselves reliable or efficient means of regulating exchange. This is reflected in the high incidence of disputes, reneging on contracts and debts, and other inappropriate business practices. Thus more formalized arrangements –

including well-defined contracts, precise standards and objective measurement – are required to "standardize" the market.

Enterprise management is often conducted under Confucianist, top-down structures where high-level managers take responsibility for a wide range of operational decisions, rather then delegating the decisions to specialists within or outside the enterprise. These structures mean that decisions are made on an intuitive basis rather than through systematic research or more "scientific" means. Although such management forms also have advantages such as flexibility and quick reaction time, they have contributed to industry disorder and can not keep pace with the increasing complexity of enterprise management.[2]

Another broad aspect of enterprise management in China is that managers often adopt a short-term or speculative approach to management. The myopic approach partly relates to the need to capitalize on periods of stability and opportunities, to a relatively brief experience in market economy systems, and to tenure situations where State-owned Enterprises and Township and Village Enterprise managers are appointed for only a matter of a few years. "Short-termism" features prominently in many developing and transitional economies. Systems are needed to enable and encourage more strategic, long-term and sustainable decision making.

The issues raised above are well recognized in China and are in the process of being addressed in many industries including wool textiles. However the implementation of solutions to these problems has been highly variable and, especially in the case of trustworthiness, the weak link can break the industry chain. Although primary responsibility lies with the enterprises, government and industry bodies have an important role to play in terms of regulation and service provision.

1.3.5 Acute Social and Regional Differences

The mega-forces outlined above have generated opportunities for many industry participants, which are generally thought to have knock-on effects for other participants in the industry (through industry integration) and the country (through increased regional integration). The effects of transition however have often been very uneven. Some industry participants have forged ahead, while others have buckled under the weight of competition, internationalization and the need to adjust to new consumer demands. Industry rationalization has also been abrupt due to the high number of new industry entrants in the 1980s and early 1990s. During exit or restructuring, enterprises have had to shed large workforces. The social effects of this restructuring process vary by region, such as when inland mills lose out to east coast mills. For eastern areas of China, there are often alternative industries where capital and employment can be taken up, while the same alternatives are less common in western China. The increasing income and regional differences in China are another element of the chaos in the transition process that is illustrated well through geographically diverse industries such as wool textiles.

Image 1.4   Wool market in Lixian County of Hebei Province

The consequences of industry transition have not always been predictable or orderly, with fragmented industry structures and rapidly changing economic fortunes of industry participants. Furthermore the transition to a market-oriented system has not always been a linear path to increased product quality or move to higher-value segments. Here a small dealer collects wool destined for one of the many scours in the Lixian area. The outside storage on dirt and rudimentary grading of the wool limits it to lower-value markets. Nonetheless, a large proportion of China's coarse and semi-fine wool ends up at these markets and is a particularly vibrant part of the overall industry compared with some other higher-value segments that have faced stagnation and pressure to restructure.

1.3.6   Proliferation of Standards, Regulations and Information

Economic standards, regulations and information are integral to market-oriented development. There has been considerable effort devoted to developing standards, to the extent where there has been a proliferation in the post-reform era. Nonetheless issues arise over whether they have been managed in an orderly way.

One such example relates to environmental regulations. Environmental regulations are promulgated on a general level (such as water discharge standards for industry), for particular activities (such as wool scouring or cattle slaughtering), for resource use (such as grassland utilization) or for inputs (such as feed and veterinary products). In addition there are often multiple environmental and food certification schemes, while local government also has a large degree of discretion in formulation of regulations. Industry standards also tend to be simply layered on top of each other as the need arises, which leads to significant replication.

Statistical information for the same items is often collected through different systems with different statistical criteria. On top of this, a large and growing number of organizations – ranging from government departments to associations to companies – provide an enormous amount of industry information in printed form or through the internet. However the quality of the statistical information is mixed, while the overlapping sources of information can lead to conflicting data.

The problems outlined above have occurred primarily because institutional structures have failed to keep pace with the growth and fragmentation of industry structures. The fragmentation of production and marketing structures – with the entry of large numbers of small and diverse industry participants outlined above – makes it costly and logistically difficult to enforce regulations, to inspect commodities according to industry standards and to collect information in a systematic way. The costs of building institutional capacity to conduct these tasks have proven prohibitive. This is especially the case given the downsizing of most government departments, and that replicated and overlapping institutional structures remain. These issues constitute another layer of chaos in China's economic transition.

1.4 INVESTIGATING TRANSITION THROUGH THE WOOL TEXTILE WINDOW

Understanding and unravelling the complexities of China's transition process and its consequences is a major challenge. Economy-wide or sector-wide studies and macro-level empirical modelling – while serving a specific purpose – gloss over many of the nuances of the transition process that lie at the heart of their comprehension.[3] In contrast, this book captures the nuances through a detailed investigation of how transition has proceeded in a particular industry, namely the wool textile industry.

Section 2.1 in Chapter 2 cites several compelling reasons why the wool textile industry provides a useful case study of industry transition in China. It is part of the broader textile industry in China that has been used as a vehicle to usher in enterprise and broader economic reforms from the late 1990s. As one of the numerous consumer good industries in China, the wool textile industry raises issues common to a broad sector of the economy. [4] Furthermore while transition has not progressed as far in some strategic and staple industries such as energy, infrastructure, grains and cotton, the wool textile industry may be a harbinger and provide lessons for subsequent transformation of these strategic industries. The wool textile industry straddles both eras of Figure 1.1, having deep roots in the Central Planning era but also undergoing strong but turbulent growth during the market economy era. The industry is also highly internationalized and comprises diverse industry participants that span a long production and marketing chain. Furthermore they must orient toward a garment and fashion market that is diverse, fast changing and notoriously fickle.

To reveal the transition process and its consequences, the book is organized in the manner highlighted in Figure 1.2. A feature of Figure 1.2 is the window on the wool textile industry that is used to investigate and reveal insights about the broader process of economic and industry transition in China. Chapter 2 sets the scene for this wool textile industry window by describing key features of the industry pertinent to the subsequent analysis. A discussion of broader institutional structures and changes in Chapter 3 provides further context and background.

Readers interested in broad insights about and lessons from industry transition in China, without having to immerse themselves in details of the wool textile industry in Chapters 4 to 8 of the book, will still gain much from a reading of Chapters 1 and 9. These chapters are integrally linked through a series of major themes.

Chapters 4 to 8 reveal details of the transition process and its consequences for different segments of the wool textile industry. Chapter 9 then seeks to make some sense of the transition process and much of the chaos associated with it. Section 9.1 does so by examining China's economic transition process as a series of phases in which the first phase of administrative and ownership reform and the second phase of technological modernization are well advanced but where the third phase, which involves the transition of operational and management practices, lags behind. Based on this assessment of where industry transition is at, Sections 9.2 and 9.3 discuss ways of smoothing this third and final phase of the transition in the light of the current political, economic, market and international environment. Suggestions about how to progress transition in a more orderly manner may prove useful for

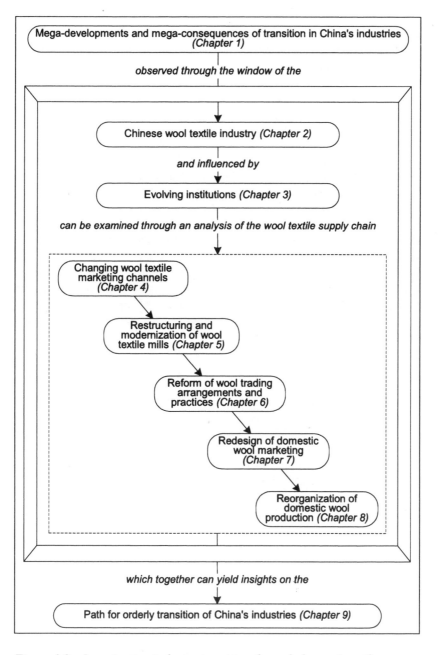

Figure 1.2 Investigating industry transition through the wool textile window

other industries that have not yet proceeded as far with the transition process as the wool textile industry.

To understand fully the nuances of industry transition and the logic behind the assessment and recommendations presented in Chapter 9, readers should venture into the series of detailed analytic chapters that examine transition in different segments of the wool textile industry. The chapters are organized in such a way as to facilitate an understanding of how transformation in any one industry segment can impact upon, or be dependent upon, transformation in other segments. Specifically the chapters follow a path along the supply chain, starting with a discussion of wool textile users and wool textile marketing channels in Chapter 4. The demands of these wool textile users such as garment makers are met by processing mills (Chapter 5) who occupy a prominent position in the whole wool textile supply chain. The processing mills use both imported and domestic wool. Thus an analysis of wool trade in Chapter 6 examines issues associated with the international wool supply chain for Chinese wool textile mills, while Chapter 7 (domestic wool marketing) and Chapter 8 (domestic wool production) examine the domestic wool supply chain. Although Chapters 4 to 8 provide a useful statement of where transition is at in the Chinese wool textile industry and in each of its segments, their primary purpose is to draw broader insights about industry transition in China in general.

NOTES

1   The distinction between a Central Planning and market-oriented era is less clear cut than implied by this chronological distinction. Central Planning mechanisms were and still are used in the post-1978 liberalization period, while the pre-1978 period was punctuated by periods when the use of market-like instruments was common.
2   A large body of literature addresses issues associated with Chinese business culture and management including Redding (1990) and Schak (1995).
3   Many studies adopt an economy-wide approach, including Zhang and Lloyd (2001), Liew (1997), Chai (1997), Hannan (1998) and Kwan and Yu (2005). Other studies such as Groenewold et al. (2003), Chen and Shi (2004), Tong (2002), and Laurenceson and Chai (2003) adopt a sectoral approach, while other studies address specific issues such as internationalization (Wei et al. 2002), accounting systems (Ji 2001), enterprise types (Chen, H.Y. 2000; Steinfeld 1998), and regional issues (Qi 2001). Some publications such as Zhang (1992) and Lu and Wong (2003) use industry case studies but examine the industry from a more macro perspective than that employed in this study.
4   Other consumer good industries include industries involved in the manufacture of paper, bicycles, white goods, items of daily use, consumer electronics and motorcycles.

2. Wool Textiles and Industry Transformation

Fathoming the intricacies of industry transition and modernization in China is a daunting task. Furthermore investigation of the operational and managerial transition referred to in Chapter 1 as the third phase of the transition process calls for a detailed, micro-level industry analysis. In this book the analysis of industry transition is conducted through the window of the wool textile industry. This chapter provides a concise discussion of selected aspects of the wool textile industry pertinent to understanding this window on the transition process.

There are several dimensions to the discussion. First, as a basis for understanding technical terms that appear elsewhere in the book, the different market segments and processing systems – including the numerous processing stages – in the wool textile industry are briefly outlined. Second, the relevance of the case study in terms of the textile industry's prominence in industry restructuring in China, the relative importance of wool in Chinese textiles, and the importance of China in the global wool textile industry are revealed. Third, in order to appreciate the transition issues of most concern to the wool textile industry, several key aspects of the industry are presented including the broad structure of the industry, the nature of the supply chains and marketing channels for wool inputs and wool textile outputs, and the trends in prices and markets.

2.1 WOOL TEXTILES AS A CASE STUDY

Although the book draws on examples from various industries, the main focus is on the wool textile industry. A priori, the wool textile industry may seem a rather obscure choice. Yet as briefly argued in Chapter 1, there are several compelling reasons why the wool textile industry provides a fascinating case from which to gain an understanding of how Chinese industries are being transformed.

An investigation of the wool textile industry offers not just an analysis of a single industry but instead an analysis of a number of closely related industries. As outlined in Section 2.2, the wool textile industry contains a long marketing chain comprising wool producers, wool marketers, early-stage processors (including scourers and topmakers), later-stage processors (such as spinning and weaving mills) and garment makers. All of these industry participants operate in different segments, experience different pressures and have proceeded down various transition paths. Yet their fortunes are all intertwined. In addition some enterprises are integrated over multiple industry segments. Thus the wool textile industry allows an examination of why closely related industry segments proceed down different transition paths, along with the implications of the different paths for the broader industry.

Wool textiles form part of a broader textile or fibre industry with various levels of substitution between fibres occurring at a number of stages in production, marketing and processing. The cross-industry linkages reveal how, if transition or policy measures are viewed in isolation of what is happening in other fibre markets, unintended or unforeseen adverse or perverse effects can arise.[1]

The wool textile industry is a long-established industry in China with ties extending back before the formation of the People's Republic. But it is also an industry greatly affected by the post-Mao reforms, experiencing massive growth in the 1980s and a turbulent period since then. The mix of long-established enterprises, which carry some form of political or economic legacy, combined with the plethora of new, post-reform entrants presents the possibility of various transition paths.

With its strong trading links, the Chinese wool textile industry reveals various insights into globalization and increasing international competition. Table 2.1 and Section 2.5 highlight the overwhelming dominance of China in the global wool textile industry in terms of the production and trade of wool textiles and as a user and importer of wool inputs. Another way of interpreting the information in Section 2.5 is that China must constantly seek ways to maintain or improve its international competitiveness and find effective ways of facilitating the smooth flow of wool into and wool textiles out of China.

Although relying heavily on overseas markets, China has an enormous domestic market for wool textiles along with a large domestic wool growing industry. Thus choices and assessments have to be made regarding the relative opportunities afforded by overseas and domestic markets. Furthermore domestic wool production, and its connection with the development of the politically sensitive pastoral region, raises the spectre of local government intervention influencing industry transition.

Table 2.1   *Importance of China in the global wool textile industry*

Indicator	Period	Value	World rank (% of world total)	
Wool production				
- sheep population	2002-03	139 million	1	(14)
- greasy wool production	2003-04	314 kt	2	(15)
- wool production (clean equivalent)	2003-04	157 kt	3	(13)
Wool trade				
- imports of raw wool (clean equivalent)	2002	192 kt	1	(29)
Wool textile production				
- consumption of wool (clean equivalent) by wool textile industry	2002	368 kt	1	(30)
- wool tops	2002	150 kt	1	(31)
- yarn production (of wool and other fibres) by wool textile industry	2002	473 kt	1	(24)
- woven fabrics (apparel and non-apparel; of wool and other fibres) by wool textile industry	2002	368 kt	1	(45)
- woven apparel fabrics (of wool and other fibres) by wool textile industry	2002	486 000 m^2	1	(30)
- production of blankets (of wool and other fibres) of wool textile industry	2002	493 000 m^2	1	
Wool textile trade				
- import of scoured wool	2003	48 kt	1	(22)
- export of scoured wool	2003	15 kt	4	(6)
- import of wool tops	2003	30 kt	2	(18)
- export of wool tops	2003	22 kt	4	(10)
- import of synthetic tops	2002	30 kt	1	(20)
- import of worsted yarns	2003	33 kt	1	(24)
- export of worsted yarns	2003	37 kt	1	(28)
- import of woollen yarns	2003	4 kt	6	(5)
- export of woollen yarns	2003	17 kt	1	(23)
- import of woven wool fabrics (apparel and non-apparel but excluding blankets)	2002	73 million lineal metres	1	(38)
- export of woven wool fabrics (apparel and non-apparel but excluding blankets)	2002	50 million lineal metres	1	(45)
- exports of wool blankets	2002	3 kt	1	(30)

Source: IWTO (2004).

Wool and wool textiles are highly differentiated products with many attributes that influence product design and manufacturing costs and which in the case of wool can be influenced by climatic and biological conditions. The differentiation provides opportunities to tailor products and manufacturing processes, but also requires management skills and supply chains to service these specialized systems. Thus the wool textile industry provides some insights as to how China's industry modernization and transition process can cope with these more precise manufacturing systems.

Wool textiles are a volatile industry with wool textile output and wool input price relativities changing dramatically over short periods of time (see Section 2.9). The garment and fashion industry is notoriously fast changing and fickle, and participants all along the supply chain need to be able to respond quickly. How enterprises modernize their systems, especially with respect to risk management, to cope better with these fluctuations is crucial to their success in the new economic environment. Furthermore government measures to facilitate long-term transition need to be formulated in an environment of short-term volatility.

Although wool textile manufacturing is considered a low-technology industry, there is a rapid and steady stream of new technologies emerging. Mills are under constant pressure to modernize equipment and processes in order to remain competitive and secure access to particular market segments. In terms of industry transition, this raises questions about research and development, technology transfer, information and extension provision, financing, and mechanisms to assess the viability of new technology or equipment.

While an investigation of wool textiles reveals many facets of industry transition in China, an awareness of the key aspects of the industry is needed in order to interpret and understand the lessons that emerge. A concise overview relevant to an analysis of industry transition is provided in the remaining sections of the chapter.

2.2   WOOL PROCESSING SYSTEMS AND STAGES OF PROCESSING

Getting wool from a sheep's to a human's back involves a whole series of processing stages as highlighted in Figure 2.1. Two main systems operate, namely a worsted system – which uses finer, longer-staple, higher-quality wool to produce apparel items such as suitwear, fashion fabrics and lightweight knitwear – and a woollen system – which uses coarser, shorter wool to produce bulkier apparel items such as most knitwear, tweeds and flannels as well as upholstery, carpets and blankets. The main difference in the processing occurs at the topmaking stage where in worsted processing the wool fibres are combed to align the fibres in a parallel manner to form a sliver or top, whereas in woollens processing, the sliver or top is formed from a "card" of interlaced fibres. Thus the worsted and woollens systems use different wool inputs and produce very different products for different segments of the market.

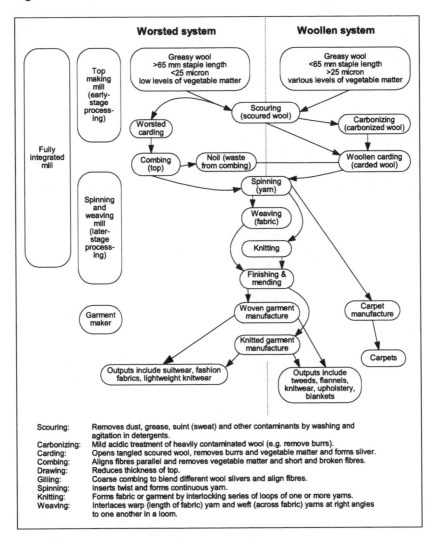

Figure 2.1   Wool processing systems

Wool textile mills can be either worsted mills or woollen mills, depending on whether they produce or use combed or carded tops. The left-hand side of Figure 2.1 also reveals that wool textile mills can specialize in processing stages. In particular, a distinction arises between early stage processors (involving some or all processes up to making wool tops such as scouring, combing, carding and carbonizing) and later-stage processors (associated with spinning, weaving, knitting, and finishing and mending). Some mills may be specialized in a single processing stage (such as a scouring plant or finishing mill) while other mills integrate over all stages from scouring through to finishing and sometimes even into garment making.

2.3   TEXTILES AND INDUSTRY RESTRUCTURING

The textile industry has been at the forefront of industry restructuring in China. As a core industry in the economic development of the People's Republic, the textile industry was governed by its own ministry. The contribution of the textile industry to overall output and employment attracted considerable attention because changes within the sector had macro-impacts of interest to central planners. The size of the sector has also meant that the government has sought an orderly transition of the industry.

A diversity of enterprises makes up the wool textile sector as outlined in Section 2.6. However many textile mills have been large State-owned Enterprises with substantial workforces and that contributed in other ways to the local economy. Furthermore the long history of these mills left them with a legacy of a large proportion of retired workers who drew their retirement income and welfare from the mill itself. Thus the scope of textile industry restructuring extends well beyond the direct activities of the mill. The large debts these State-owned Enterprise mills have incurred, partly as a result of inherent inefficiencies and partly as a result of other non-production related commitments, made them a prime candidate for reform and an initial target of industry reforms and restructuring. Wool textile mills were well represented among these large, loss-making State-owned Enterprises in the broader textile industry.

The textile industry has also been at the forefront of changes in global and regional comparative advantage. Shifting global comparative advantage has resulted in textile production, over an extended period of time, moving from Europe and North America to East Asia (including China) and to other parts of Asia. Shifts in regional comparative advantage in textile production have also occurred within China as new industries have emerged and factor endowments and returns changed. Thus the textile industry is in a constant state of flux in response to economic growth as demand patterns and supply conditions change. Although various measures have been employed by other (developed) countries to ameliorate adverse adjustment impacts within the textile industry, these powerful economic forces ultimately determine the direction of the industry. Textile industry transformation in China is not insulated from these forces.

Realignments and changing comparative advantages in the world textile industry have led to changing and emerging opportunities in export markets; especially following World Trade Organization accession and reform of the Multi-Fibre Arrangement. Yet these export markets and opportunities are volatile. A major challenge in aligning the textile industry to future developments therefore is building flexibility into the transformation process.

2.4   IMPORTANCE OF WOOL IN CHINESE TEXTILES

Wool textiles account for only one of a number of textile industries in China including cotton, synthetic fibre and silk textiles as well as textile machinery. Indeed, within textile industry forums and the policy arena, wool textiles can be overwhelmed by the larger cotton and synthetic textile industries.

The total value of textiles increased from Rmb598.6 billion in 1995 to more than Rmb1000 billion in 2002; of which wool textiles accounted for Rmb64 billion or 6.4 per cent.[2] In contrast, cotton textiles accounted for 32 per cent of the overall textile industry, and synthetic fibres 11 per cent (CNTIC 2003).Wool's share of the textile industry grew during the 1980s and the first half of the 1990s but fell during the second half of the 1990s and early 2000s (EBACTI 2000, p. 4). For instance wool textiles' share fell from 9 per cent in 1995 to 7.6 per cent in 1998 and 6.4 per cent in 2002.

Each of the textile sectors operates within different spheres of influence. Cotton textiles are integrally linked with long-held imperatives to clothe the population and with domestic cotton production, an important agricultural crop throughout many regions in China. Thus restructuring in the cotton textile industry ties in with debates over agricultural sector adjustment. The domestic synthetic fibre industry has expanded rapidly under the guise of support for import replacement. Development of the wool textile industry has also partly been supported on the basis of developing an integrated wool industry in some remote and industrially undeveloped pastoral regions.

The small size of the wool textile industry relative to cotton and synthetic fibre textiles means that it has often been left to its own devices in textile industry restructuring. That is, compared to large strategic industries such as cotton, the wool textiles industry has been overlooked or has not received the same degree of support in the process of capacity reduction, State-owned Enterprise reform and general industry restructuring.

2.5   IMPORTANCE OF CHINA IN THE GLOBAL WOOL TEXTILE INDUSTRY

Despite the relatively small size of the wool sector in the Chinese textile industry, China dominates virtually all aspects of the global wool textile industry (IWTO 2004). Evidence of this dominance appears in Table 2.1 where the right-hand column of the table indicates China's world ranking and share of world totals. China's importance extends across the range of wool textile products and intermediate products from wool tops through yarn, woven apparel products and blankets. In all cases, China is the world's largest producer with an overwhelming share of world production of between 25 and 45 per cent.

The importance of wool textile production extends to the trade sector. China dominates the trade in wool textiles with the exception of wool tops and woollen yarns – although it still remains an important player in these segments. China acts as both a significant exporter and importer of wool textile products, with the trade flows servicing different segments of the market. The net import of wool fabrics that service China's large garment making industry also stands out in the trade statistics in Table 2.1.

On the wool input side, China accounts for 30 per cent of global wool imports and represents the main customer for key wool producing and trading countries such as Australia and New Zealand. Well over half of the wool used by the wool textile industry comes from overseas. Nevertheless China has a large domestic wool production sector in its own right. In 2002, China had the world's largest sheep flock and second-largest greasy wool production. This share increased throughout the 1990s as China's sheep numbers and wool production increased at the same time as they were rapidly declining in Australia. However as indicated at various stages throughout the book, a huge variation arises in wool types. In this context it is especially important that the most sophisticated and high-value end of the wool textile industry – the fine wool worsted sector – relies heavily on imported rather than domestic wool.

2.6   STRUCTURE OF WOOL TEXTILE PROCESSING

To gain an overview of the structure of the wool textile processing sector in China, this section draws upon information on individual mills contained in the *Almanac of China's Textile Industry* (EBACTI 2000). The size unit for these statistics is spindle number, which represents only one indicator (albeit a most important indicator) of industry structure.

2.6.1 Overview

China had around 3.8 million wool spindles at the end of the 1990s, an eightfold increase on the 1970s, and thirtyfold rise compared with the early 1950s. By 2001, wool spindle numbers had dropped to 3.6 million. More than one-half of the current spindles were introduced in the 1980s, of which around 15 per cent were imported spindles. Another one-third of the spindles were established in the 1990s. The drive towards modernization in the 1990s meant that a much higher proportion (25 per cent) of the spindles established were imported spindles than was the case in the 1980s. Almost one-half of the spindles were combing spindles, 15 per cent carding spindles and 36 per cent knitting spindles. At the end of the 1990s, around one-sixth of the total spindles were in Township and Village Enterprises, most of which were concentrated in locations in Jiangsu, Hebei, Shandong and Zhejiang Provinces. However as outlined in Chapter 5, massive changes in ownership and governance structures make some of the figures and classifications used in these statistics less meaningful.

2.6.2 Size Distribution

The Chinese wool textile industry developed in a way that resulted in great diversity in the size of operations. Historically there were a relatively small number of large State-owned mills that each operated many thousands of spindles. Fiscal reforms in the 1980s spawned a plethora of small mills throughout China. For instance Xinjiang saw the establishment of many small woollen mills, each with only a few hundred spindles, and Hebei saw the emergence of many small hand-knitting mills, while a proliferation of county-level wool scours occurred in Inner Mongolia. Although the industry is undergoing substantial restructuring and modernization, the diversity remains.

To reveal the diversity of sizes within the industry, Figure 2.2 plots the proportion of all wool spindles in China in mills at or below a particular size (numbers of spindles). One-half of all the wool spindles in China are in mills with less than 10 000 spindles, while 10 per cent of the spindles are in mills with more than 30 000 spindles. Translating this into number of mills (not shown in Figure 2.2), one-eighth of the mills account for half of all processing capacity. Indeed the largest nine mills account for 11 per cent of China's wool spindle capacity. Conversely, the smallest half of mills account for only 10 per cent of China's wool spindles. Ongoing industry modernization and rationalization has resulted in the closure of many small mills, but it has also taken its toll on the larger mills.

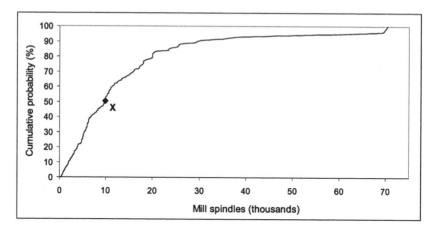

Note: The horizontal axis refers to the number of spindles (combing, carding or knitting) at an
         individual mill. The vertical axis represents the proportion of all wool spindles in China
         that belong to mills with a particular number of spindles or fewer. To interpret this curve,
         consider point **x** which shows that half of all spindles (50 per cent) in China are in mills
         with 10 000 spindles or fewer.

Source: EBACTI (2000).

*Figure 2.2   Cumulative probability distribution of mill spindle numbers:
             1999*

Thus a good deal of diversity remains among Chinese wool textile mills.
Large mills operate very differently and draw on different input supply and
distribution outlets than small mills, and also vary in their ability and the way
they cope with changing market environments.

2.6.3   Spatial Distribution

Although wool textile mills are distributed across the country, concentrations
of mills occur in areas such as the Yangzi River Delta (including Shanghai,
southern Jiangsu and northern Zhejiang). Table 2.2 highlights the relative
importance of provinces in terms of their proportion of China's total wool
spindles and wool textile outputs. A snapshot of the industry in selected key
provinces appears in Figure 2.3.

At a provincial level, Jiangsu dominates wool textile production with
around one-third of all spindles in China. Shandong has the next highest
proportion of spindles (10 per cent of spindles in China) while Hebei,
Shanghai, Zhejiang and Guangdong each have around 6 to 7 per cent of
spindles. Most other provinces each account for fewer than 3 per cent of total
spindles. Combing spindles are concentrated in Jiangsu (34 per cent),

Table 2.2 Proportion of China's wool spindles and output by province: 1999

Province	Spindles				Output	
	Total	Combing	Carding	Knitting	Hand knitting yarn	Wool fabric
			— % of all China —			
Anhui	2.0	1.6	3.1	2.1	0.4	0.5
Beijing	2.4	3.3	2.3	1.9	0.9	3.7
Chongqing	0.6	0.7	1.3	0.2	0.1	0.0
Fujian	0.5	0.9	0.0	0.7	1.3	0.2
Gansu	2.0	2.9	2.9	1.1	1.5	2.4
Guangdong	6.2	5.3	8.4	4.4	7.3	5.1
Guangxi	0.3	0.0	0.2	0.4	0.0	0.0
Guizhou	0.2	0.0	0.3	0.4	0.1	0.0
Hainan	0.4	0.0	0.1	0.0	0.0	0.0
Hebei	7.3	2.0	5.9	15.9	36.3	2.0
Heilongjiang	0.5	1.8	2.1	2.8	0.0	0.7
Henan	2.5	2.7	4.9	2.5	1.6	1.7
Hubei	2.7	3.7	1.4	2.3	1.0	1.2
Hunan	0.6	0.5	0.9	0.6	0.1	0.0
Inner Mongolia	1.8	2.1	0.5	0.5	0.3	1.6
Jiangsu	31.1	34.1	22.3	36.3	28.8	49.7
Jiangxi	0.8	0.7	1.5	0.6	0.1	0.5
Jilin	1.1	1.7	1.3	0.4	0.2	1.7
Liaoning	2.9	3.5	4.4	1.5	0.5	1.4
Ningxia	0.5	0.4	1.1	0.8	0.1	0.0
Qinghai	0.8	1.1	1.5	0.2	0.2	0.2
Shandong	9.5	2.5	2.3	1.0	13.1	6.2
Shanghai	6.8	8.0	12.9	16.1	1.4	6.5
Shaanxi	0.5	9.9	11.1	3.6	0.1	0.4
Shanxi	1.5	0.6	0.8	0.5	0.2	0.5
Sichuan	0.3	0.4	0.8	0.2	6.8	0.6
Tianjin	2.3	3.4	2.3	1.4	0.9	2.0
Xinjiang	3.5	6.2	2.9	1.2	0.3	3.7
Yunnan	0.2	0.0	0.2	0.2	0.0	0.0
Zhejiang	6.6	5.2	3.9	3.6	3.1	7.7

Source: EBACTI (2000).

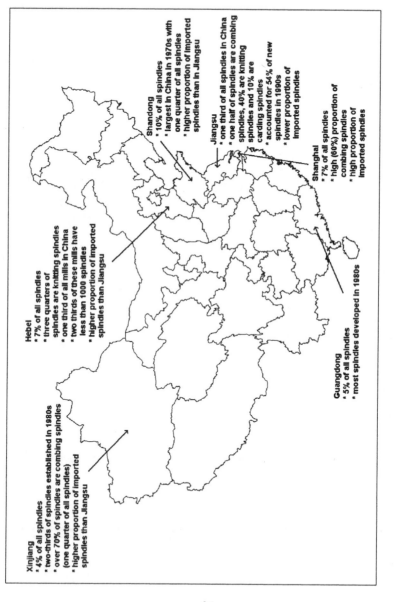

Xinjiang
* 4% of all spindles
* two-thirds of spindles established in 1980s
* over 70% of spindles are combing spindles (one quarter of all spindles)
* higher proportion of imported spindles than Jiangsu

Hebel
* 7% of all spindles
* three quarters of spindles are knitting spindles
* one third of all mills in China
* two thirds of these mills have less than 1000 spindles
* higher proportion of imported spindles than Jiangsu

Shandong
* 10% of all spindles
* largest in China in 1970s with one quarter of all spindles
* higher proportion of imported spindles than in Jiangsu

Jiangsu
* one third of all spindles in China
* one half of spindles are combing spindles, 40% are knitting spindles and 10% are carding spindles
* accounted for 54% of new spindles in 1990s
* lower proportion of imported spindles

Shanghai
* 7% of all spindles
* high (60%) proportion of combing spindles
* high proportion of imported spindles

Guangdong
* 5% of all spindles
* most spindles developed in 1980s

Figure 2.3   Snapshot of wool textile industry in selected key provinces

Shanghai (8 per cent) and Shandong (8 per cent), with carding spindles centred on Jiangsu (20 per cent), Shandong (11 per cent), Shanghai (10 per cent) and Guangdong (7 per cent). Knitting spindles are most pronounced in Jiangsu (35 per cent), Shandong (16 per cent) and Hebei (15 per cent). Hebei's strong links with much of the domestic coarse wool production (see Box 5.4 in Chapter 5) make it a vibrant part of the broader wool textile industry.

Spindle numbers reflect only part of the regional distribution of the industry. Mills vary in their level of capacity utilization and the efficiency with which they use the capacity. In Table 2.2, the proportion of national spindles appears alongside the proportion of China's wool textile output in 1999. In that year in terms of hand-knitting wool, almost two-thirds of production came from Hebei (36 per cent) and Jiangsu (29 per cent) alone. Most of the remainder came from Shandong (13 per cent) and Guangdong (7 per cent). Jiangsu dominated wool fabric production with half of all production. The next tier of provinces – Zhejiang, Shanghai, Shandong and Guangdong – each produced only around 6 per cent of wool fabric production.

The concentration of wool textile processing in southern Jiangsu, Shanghai and northern Zhejiang occurs in a largely contiguous geographic region. However differences in ownership structures and modes of development do vary by province. Beijing has fewer spindles than Shanghai, but has the same orientation to the worsted system. The long-established, large mills of Beijing and Shanghai are under enormous pressure both in terms of pressure on land use and pressure to meet the exacting environmental measures of these municipalities, with many of the Beijing mills virtually ceasing operations in the early 2000s.

The difference between regional proportions of spindle numbers and wool textile outputs is again dominated by Jiangsu. Although Jiangsu has around one-third of all spindles, it accounts for an even higher proportion of wool fabric production, suggesting higher rates of utilization and mill efficiency than elsewhere. Some provinces that increased spindles rapidly during the 1990s (such as Liaoning, Anhui and Henan) now have a disproportionately low share of output, indicating that many of their mills are underutilized. Municipalities such as Shanghai and Tianjin are also disproportionately represented in wool textile output relative to their spindle numbers. Although capacity utilization is only one factor in industry rationalization, mills with low levels of utilization will come under increasing pressure to close or change the nature of their operations.

In the wool-producing pastoral areas, wool textile processing was encouraged as apart of a mercantilist "self-produce, self-process, self-sell" policy. Wool textile mills were seen as leading the development of an integrated wool industry of benefit to numerous sheep herders long before this notion became popularized in the agro-industrialization policy of the 1990s and 2000s. Some industrial centres in the pastoral region such as Lanzhou also based their industries upon wool textile production. Thus sizeable industries developed in wool production areas although they never become substantial compared to the processing industry on the east coast. Most of the spindles – more than two-thirds for Xinjiang and Inner Mongolia but only 44 per cent for Gansu – were established in the 1980s. The other feature of spindles in pastoral provinces is that most of them are combing spindles (over 70 per cent for Xinjiang and Inner Mongolia and 55 per cent for Gansu).

The problem for the pastoral region occurred when much of the official support to develop the wool textile industry was wound back. The advantage for east coast mills in being close to import suppliers, overseas customers and shipping infrastructure, and the local government support provided to industries in the eastern regions, outweighs any of the benefit of proximity to domestic wool production for the pastoral production mills. Furthermore the geographic dispersion and fragmented nature of domestic wool production and marketing, and the switch from fine wool to semi-fine and coarse wool, makes it difficult to obtain large homogenous lots from nearby suppliers. As industries and populations develop in municipalities on the east coast, higher labour, land and other opportunity costs have forced some movement out of wool textile processing. However the shift has been to less-developed but still favourably located centres in east coast provinces rather than to western regions. The spindle reduction programme targeted spindles in the western regions and compounded the relative decline in wool textile processing in pastoral areas. Consequently many pastoral region mills have faced severe adjustment problems. Section 5.6 highlights recent developments to align the more efficient up-country mills (such as Chifeng City No. 2 mill and Lanzhou Sanmao) with mills on the east coast.

The push to develop fine wool production in pastoral provinces in the late 1980s (Longworth and Williamson 1993) may have been consistent with the development of worsted mills in the pastoral regions. However political support for fine wool production has since waned. Herders now find raising sheep for mutton and coarse wool more financially rewarding. Consequently more and more wool from pastoral areas is coarse and semi-fine wool unsuitable for worsted processing (see Chapter 8). The lack of suitable locally grown fine wool is putting increasing pressure on worsted (combing) spindles in pastoral areas.

2.7 RAW MATERIAL SUPPLY

Wool – either as greasy wool to integrated mills or as wool tops to spinning and weaving mills – is the major input to wool textile processing. The type of wool determines the kind of textiles that can be produced. Thus changing access to the various types of raw wool features prominently in the transformation of the whole wool textile industry. The following section briefly highlights key aspects about the wool supply chains with a detailed discussion of the imported wool supply chain in Chapter 6 and the domestic wool supply chain in Chapter 7.

2.7.1 Large but Low-quality Chinese Wool Production

China is one of the world's largest wool producers with an estimated 139 million sheep in 2002/03 and 314 kilotonnes (kt) of greasy wool in 2003/04 (IWTO 2004). The number of sheep and the amount of wool grown rose markedly during the 1990s despite the degraded state of the rangelands on which most of the sheep were raised. Much of the wool produced however is coarse wool suitable only for carpet production or woollen processing.

Official Chinese statistics cite a production in 2002 of 112 kt of fine wool (37 per cent of total wool in China) and 195 kt of semi-fine and coarse wool (63 per cent of total wool).[3] However Longworth and Williamson (1993, Chapter 4) argued that even in the late 1980s and early 1990s, very little of the "fine wool" in the official statistics was suitable as an input to Chinese worsted mills. Because the emphasis has shifted away from fine wool production in many areas, the proportion of fine wool that would be suitable for processing through the worsted system is likely to be even less than in the early 1990s.

Thus while China has a large domestic wool production, only a small proportion of this wool is suitable for higher-value worsted processing. Chapter 8 analyses developments in domestic fine wool production as well as efforts to develop fine wool production systems, while Chapter 7 examines the marketing channels that have emerged to supply worsted mills with better-quality, domestic, fine wool.

2.7.2 Reliance on Imported Wool

Despite the scale of domestic wool production and efforts to upgrade domestic fine wool production and marketing, the Chinese wool textile industry relies heavily on imported wool in the form of greasy wool, scoured wool, carbonized wool or wool tops. As shown in Table 2.1, imported wool accounts for over 55 per cent of the wool input to Chinese wool textile mills, with a large proportion used in higher-value worsted production. Readily available and smooth access to imported wool is becoming a crucial part of industry modernization and transformation. A critique of the supply pathways for imported wool appears in Chapter 6.

Most of the wool imported comes to China as greasy wool (Figure 2.4). The exception occurred in the late 1980s when severe import restrictions impacted most heavily upon imports in the form of greasy wool. The proportion of greasy wool in total wool imports was no higher in the early 2000s (around 60 per cent) than it was in the first half of the 1980s. For most of the 1980s and 1990s, wool tops accounted for around 20 per cent of all imports. The main tops imported include very fine wool and high-quality tops which Chinese topmakers have experienced difficulties in producing in the past, as well as very coarse wool tops that Chinese topmakers – who primarily use fleece wool – have difficulty manufacturing in competition with overseas topmakers. The relocation of overseas topmakers to China in recent years as outlined in Section 5.7 (Chapter 5) can be expected to reduce the proportion of imported wool brought in as wool top. The proportion of scoured, carbonized and other wool imports rose during the second half of the 1980s but subsequently declined through the 1990s.

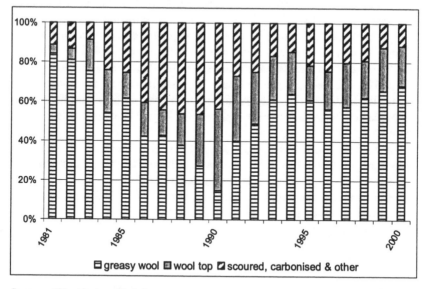

Source: China Customs Statistics.

Figure 2.4   Wool imports by type: 1981 to 2000

2.7.3 Complementarity of Domestic and Overseas Wool

In strategic discussions over the direction of Chinese wool and wool textile industries, including ongoing bilateral and World Trade Organization negotiations in 2004, the issue of the competitiveness of overseas wool with domestic Chinese wool regularly arises. In general, Chinese mills support unfettered access to overseas wool as a key input to their manufacturing systems. Conversely, elements within the Ministry of Agriculture and other organizations raise concerns about the impact of importing wool on the domestic wool growing industry. The evidence in general indicates that imported wool does not compete with domestic wool and that some important complementarities arise.

The essence of the argument is as follows. The quality of the vast majority of Chinese wool falls well short of, say, Australian wool. Even the very best wool grown in China (namely State Farm wool marketed through Chinese auctions) is shorter, less sound, has lower clean yields, and is a more heterogeneous fleece than Australian wool.[4] Although some attributes depend on sheep and wool management, and so are potentially able to be improved, many relate to the harsh physical conditions of China's pastoral region on which the sheep are raised. The severely degraded state of China's rangeland also imposes a severe constraint on fine-wool sheep numbers and fine-wool output. Longworth and Williamson (1993, Section 4.3.2) point out that on a clean scoured basis China produced only one-thirteenth of the amount of wool of 25 microns or less grown in Australian in 1991, and present rigorous evidence that China does not have the resource base to significantly expand its production of this type of wool. Furthermore while official policy has historically been to encourage the raising of fine-wool sheep, as outlined in Chapter 8, many of the economic incentives are for herders to produce dual-purpose meat and coarse-wool sheep.

Not only are the Chinese wool growing industry and some overseas industries not directly competitive, there are also some important complementarities. The poor quality of domestic wool can create problems for mills located in the pastoral region. The long-term viability of these pastoral region mills and their ability to compete with other Chinese mills on a level playing field depends on their access to better-quality imported wool for at least part of their supplies. When access to imported wool was restricted in the late 1980s and early 1990s, Chinese mills did not use more of the lower-quality and relatively more highly priced local wool as intended, but instead switched to synthetic fibres.

The potential switch to synthetic fibres and associated declining share of wool in overall textile production may lessen the Chinese government's resolve to support a large domestic fine-wool and wool textile industry in pastoral areas. For wool to maintain its strategic importance and enhance its consumer acceptance in China, mills producing for the domestic market must gain access to better-quality wool and process this wool efficiently. Thus it is in the interest of the wool industries in China and overseas for industry transition and modernization to improve the quality and processing of domestic wool in China and to encourage the use of and smooth access to imported wool.

2.8   TEXTILE OUTPUTS

Wool is used to produce a wide variety of intermediate and final wool textile products. Although this book focuses on wool fabrics, it is worth identifying broad trends in all of these products.

2.8.1   Types of Products [5]

Developments in the production of wool fabrics, blankets and knitting yarn appear in Figure 2.5. Between 1949 and 1979 the data series followed similar patterns, reflecting the stability of the product mix during the planning era. As firms have become more responsive to market price developments since the late 1970s, the data series have exhibited a much greater divergence.

Blanket production grew the fastest of all three types of products during the 1980s. Low-value products such as blankets were feasible for many mills established during the fiscal reforms of the 1980s. Blanket production peaked in the late 1980s, became extremely volatile over the 1990s, and fell in the late 1990s to the beginning of the 2000s. Blankets traditionally were made primarily from pure wool, but by 2002 pure wool blankets accounted for just 1.5 per cent of all blanket production, down from nearly 10 per cent in 1997. The vast majority of blankets (69 per cent in 2002) contain acrylic fibres (which may or may not also contain a wool blend), and 16 per cent are pure synthetics without any wool inputs.

Knitting yarn has been the least volatile of all the series. Nonetheless it also experienced a rapid rise in the second half of the 1980s and the first half of the 1990s. Production subsided in the late 1990s before returning to mid-1990s levels by 2002. Knitting yarn was traditionally mainly in the form of hand-knitting yarn made from wool and wool blends. By 2002, hand-knitting yarn made up only 18 per cent of the total knitting yarn segment, down from 36 per cent in 1997. Thus growth in the knitting yarn sector has occurred in machine-knitting yarn, which in 2002 accounted for 66 per cent of all knitting yarn, up from 41 per cent in 1997. Machine-knitting yarns use wool and synthetic blends to a greater extent than hand-knitting yarns. Consequently

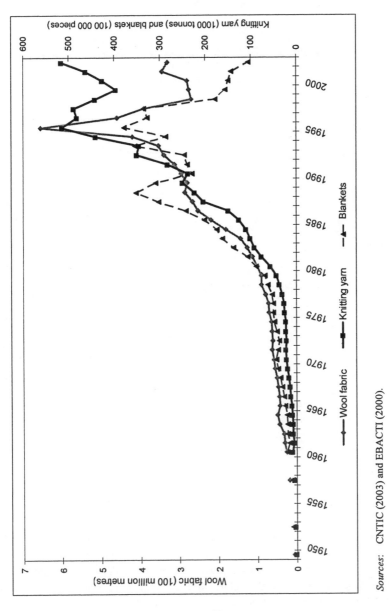

Sources: CNTIC (2003) and EBACTI (2000).

Figure 2.5   Chinese fabric production by fibre type: 1949 to 2003

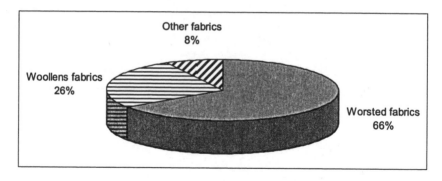

Source: CNTIC (2003).

Figure 2.6   Chinese wool fabric production by type: 2002

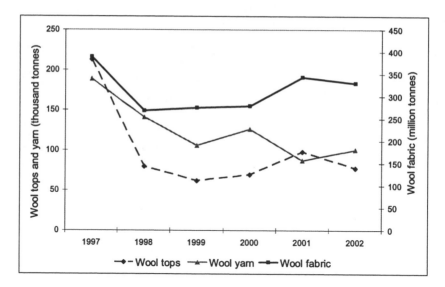

Source: CNTIC (2003).

Figure 2.7   Wool tops, wool yarn and wool fabric output: 1997 to 2002

the importance of pure synthetics as an input into knitting yarn has increased, from 39 per cent in 1997 to 62 per cent in 2002. This has not been at the expense of pure wool as an input into knitting yarn, which has maintained its share of around 17 per cent. Rather, the percentage of wool blends has dropped from 39 per cent in 1997 to 19 per cent in 2002.

2.8.2   Customer Base

In any given month, large and medium-sized wool textile mills may process scores of product orders from a diverse group of customers. Furthermore while there are mills that service either the domestic market or export market only, many mills service both markets. Although export markets are crucial to the Chinese wool textile industry especially in some high-value segments, an increasingly affluent and sophisticated domestic market has been behind much of the growth in the wool textile industry since the 1970s.[6] Indeed many of the volatile swings in the industry, such as that which occurred in the late 1980s, resulted from changes in domestic demand.

Despite the different buyers, some similarities arise in the mill customer base for export and domestic markets. Mills supplying the export market tend to have a few major and regular buyers supplemented by a large number of smaller, more opportunitistic orders. These export customers look for assurances that Chinese mills can supply the relevant quality in a timely and reliable manner and so seek to develop longer-term relationships with "trusted mills". Conversely the transaction costs of developing these longer-term relationships mean that mills will also focus their efforts on a select number of customers. While these core buyers are an important part of the overall mill strategy and profitability, mills also rely upon a large number of smaller customers. Relative to the regular large customers, the smaller orders are less stable and involve considerably more risk. Taking better advantage of this more lucrative but riskier end of their customer base requires mills to analyse and manage these orders more carefully.

Because of the importance of the domestic wool textile market and because it has generally received less attention in Western textile circles than export markets, the domestic market is analysed in detail in Chapter 4. The analysis reveals that large garment makers deal directly with mills but only with a small group of selected mills. Institutional buyers traditionally have been major customers for many mills and provided stable, though modest, returns. Beyond these large customers, the domestic wool textile marketing channels fragment into a plethora of small customers and sales outlets. Premiums may be associated with orders from these customers, but servicing them requires more management inputs and entails higher risks. Thus in the quest for improved profitability, mills require management and information systems that enable them to cope better with smaller, more lucrative, but potentially riskier orders.

2.9   PRICE DEVELOPMENTS

The transition from a Centrally Planned or command economy to a more
market-driven economic system requires industry participants to be more
responsive to market developments. Figure 2.8 presents monthly prices for
selected greasy wool and wool tops over the 1996 to 2002 period, while
Table 2.3 presents yearly average prices for these selected wools in the top
half of the table and monthly seasonal indices in the lower half of the table.
Several features stand out from a perusal of Figure 2.8 and Table 2.3.

First, wool and wool top prices exhibit extreme volatility. Price changes of
around 20 per cent within a few months occur at various points in the time
series. The implications for wool textile mills are profound because wool
input costs form the majority of overall costs.[7] They generate wide swings in
mill profitability that the mill must have the financial wherewithal to cope
with. Furthermore mills must have information and management systems that
provide the capability and flexibility to evaluate and implement different
wool input combinations as price relativities change. The previous
environment of generic orders produced by using "standard" wool input
combinations has not prepared Chinese mills well to develop these
information and management systems. Thus volatile prices are a major driver
for change in mill operations but, at the same time, pose major difficulties for
mills in that transformation.

Second, a seasonal pattern in prices emerges with higher prices in the June
to August period and lower prices in the December to February period.
However, the variation is relatively small and swamped by the variation
across years. Thus while mills need to be aware of the seasonal variation and
incorporate it into their management and purchase decisions, it does not pose
the same challenge that the variation in prices across years does.

Third, premiums between different types of wool or wool top vary through
time. For instance the variation in prices between 60-count[8] Australian wool
top and 70-count Australian wool top declined from around Rmb40/kg in
2000 to less than Rmb10/kg in 2002. A formal integration analysis of these
prices has been conducted and the methods and results reported in Brown et
al. (2005). The main findings from that analysis of relevance to this book
included: tops made from Australian wool exhibit little co-integration with
tops made from Chinese wool; Australian wool tops combed in China are
highly co-integrated with equivalent wool tops combed in Australia; higher-
count Australian wool tops (70s and above) are not highly co-integrated with
tops of lower count; some co-integration occurs between Australian 60-, 64-
and 66-count wool tops; and greasy wool prices appear related to some wool
top prices although in a less than perfect manner.

Table 2.3   Yearly and seasonal variation in selected greasy wool and top prices in China: 1996 to 2002

	GA66	TA60	TA64	TA66	TA70	TC64	TC66
(a) Yearly average prices (Rmb/kg)							
1996	51.85	56.88	62.09	67.95	78.71	52.85	60.66
1997	56.83	53.87	59.36	70.86	82.30	47.27	53.48
1998	43.09	47.75	51.07	59.83	75.23	40.80	47.02
1999	40.55	45.56	47.37	53.56	75.37	36.44	40.63
2000	41.29	43.00	45.25	53.75	79.41	37.02	42.79
2001	39.09	43.74	45.44	50.13	71.68	36.93	40.79
2002	54.89	60.46	62.35	63.99	70.74	43.25	49.13
Variation	17.74	17.46	17.10	20.73	11.56	16.41	20.03
(b) Monthly seasonal indices (Rmb/kg)							
January	-0.88	-0.81	-0.84	-0.58	-0.92	0.07	0.35
February	-0.14	-0.21	-0.03	-0.33	-0.05	0.31	0.44
March	-0.11	0.42	0.20	-0.31	-0.82	-0.17	-0.02
April	-0.32	0.02	-0.06	-0.83	-1.06	-0.32	-0.43
May	-0.24	-0.32	-0.82	-0.78	-0.73	-0.65	-0.37
June	0.80	0.01	-0.51	0.10	0.66	-0.25	-0.07
July	1.37	0.37	0.54	1.39	2.03	-0.01	0.18
August	0.87	0.33	0.48	0.91	1.21	0.01	0.09
September	0.18	-0.14	0.15	0.25	-0.05	0.07	-0.13
October	-0.75	-0.11	0.22	0.04	0.23	0.02	-0.34
November	0.12	0.44	0.54	0.49	0.06	0.52	0.20
December	-0.90	0.01	0.13	-0.36	-0.55	0.39	0.09
Variation	2.27	1.25	1.38	2.22	3.08	1.17	0.86

Note: The codes for the various greasy wool and wool top types are: GA66 (66-count greasy Australian wool); TA60 (60-count Australian wool top); TA64 (64-count Australian wool top); TA66 (66-count Australian wool top); TA70 (70-count Australian wool top); TC64 (64-count Chinese wool top); TC66 (66-count Chinese wool top).

Source: Derived from data provided by Nanjing Wool Market.

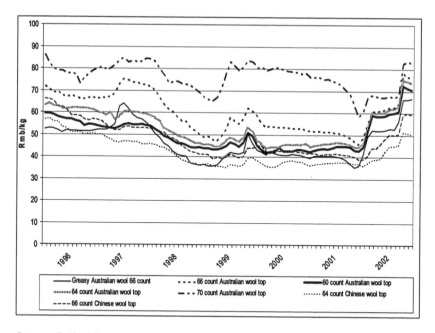

Source: Derived from information provided by Nanjing Wool Market.

Figure 2.8 Prices of selected greasy wool and tops: 1996 to 2002

NOTES

1 For example the Chinese government imposed import restrictions on wool in the late 1980s partly in response to rising domestic raw wool stocks brought about by a declining domestic demand. Unable to access imported raw wool, mills substituted not into the low-quality, relatively high-priced domestic raw wool but instead into synthetic fibres.

2 The official Chinese statistics for the value of output in the textile industry include the garment sector as well as synthetic fibre production. Thus the 6.4 per cent for wool textiles represents its proportion of value within this broader textile industry. As a proportion of the value of natural fibre textile industries (such as the cotton and silk textile industries), wool textiles account for over 13 per cent.

3 For official statistical purposes, in China fine wool is classed as 25 micron and less in fibre diameter.

4 See Longworth and Brown (1995, Section 8.3.1) for a comparison of the attributes of wool presented for sale at Chinese auctions in 1991 with the average for the whole Australian wool clip in 1991.

5 Official textile almanacs (EBACTI 2000) focus on the aggregate output of wool fabrics, blankets and knitting yarn, for which data is available from 1949. Other data sets (NTIBSC various years) provide a more disaggregated breakdown of these items, and are presented in this section for the years 1997 to 2002. These reports also have data on wool yarn and wool tops. Only three of the products – wool fabrics, wool yarn and wool tops – use wool for the majority of their inputs.

6   The domestic export orientation depends on the stage of output. For example despite the overwhelming size of the Chinese wool textile sector, it is a net importer of fabrics, with exports being in the form of finished garments. Conversely much of the recent expansion in wool top processing capacity in China has been associated with a relocation of overseas topmakers to China to supply wool top to other countries.

7   Greasy wool inputs can account for around 80 per cent of all costs for topmaking mills, while wool top inputs can be more than 50 per cent of costs for spinning and weaving mills.

8   Count is the standard indicator of wool fineness (or fibre diameter) in the Chinese typing system, where 60-count wool is coarser than the 70-count.

3. Evolving Institutions

Institutional reforms have underpinned the transformation of Chinese industries. The withdrawal of government in the post-reform era has created an institutional vacuum especially in the area of service provision. Government, semi-government or non-government units are still in the process of developing structures that enable them to deliver high-quality services to industry. Efforts to transform these structures and the obstacles they face are the major issues addressed in this chapter.

Within the wool textile industry, various institutions play important roles depending upon the industry segment and the economic activity under discussion. Figure 3.1 provides an overview of the key players in the Chinese wool textile industry at present. Figure 3.2 highlights some of the changes that have occurred in selected institutions.[1] More detailed diagrams and discussion of the institutional changes that have taken place in particular industry segments may be found in the chapters that follow. This chapter aims to paint a "big picture" of the institutional settings that impact upon the industry as a whole and to highlight some common features and inter-relationships of the institutional reform within different industry segments.

3.1 GOVERNMENT ADMINISTRATIVE UNITS

Throughout the Central Planning era and into the early reform era, powerful government departments controlled production and exchange in various segments of the industry. Several inefficiencies of the central planning system were well recognized including that intra-industry coordination and integration was truncated as different government departments controlled different industry segments.[2]

Administrative reforms have been a major plank of China's broader economic reform programme. In the 1990s administrative reforms sought to abolish government departments with "economic" functions (that is, control over industries); distribute economic decision making to economic actors (enterprises); sever ownership links between government and enterprises; and downsize government. Having largely achieved these objectives especially at

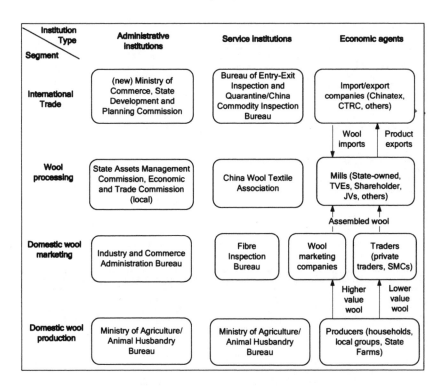

Institution Type Segment	Administrative Institutions	Service Institutions	Economic agents
International Trade	(new) Ministry of Commerce, State Development and Planning Commission	Bureau of Entry-Exit Inspection and Quarantine/China Commodity Inspection Bureau	Import/export companies (Chinatex, CTRC, others)
			Wool imports ↕ Product exports
Wool processing	State Assets Management Commission, Economic and Trade Commission (local)	China Wool Textile Association	Mills (State-owned, TVEs, Shareholder, JVs, others)
			Assembled wool
Domestic wool marketing	Industry and Commerce Administration Bureau	Fibre Inspection Bureau	Wool marketing companies / Traders (private traders, SMCs)
			Higher value wool ↕ Lower value wool
Domestic wool production	Ministry of Agriculture/ Animal Husbandry Bureau	Ministry of Agriculture/ Animal Husbandry Bureau	Producers (households, local groups, State Farms)

Figure 3.1   Simplified chart of the current structure of the Chinese wool textile industry

the central level of government, more recent rounds of reforms in the 2000s switched emphasis toward deepening the reform of the State-owned assets management system, improving the "macro-control" system and pushing forward reform of the distribution system.[3] The discussion below outlines the ways these reforms have been implemented in the wool textile industry.

3.1.1   Demise of Specialized Economic Units

Administrative reforms impacted most upon the so-called "specialized economic departments" that had direct jurisdiction over particular industries or, more commonly, industry segments. Some of the main changes of relevance to the wool textile industry are captured in Figure 3.2.

The first specialized economic department to be reformed in 1993 was the Ministry of Textiles Industry. In a series of reforms, the ministry was downgraded to become the Textile Industry Bureau under the State Economic and Trade Commission, before taking on a semi-government affiliation as the

Segment	1980s and early 1990s		Early 2000s	
	Affiliation	**Function**	**Affiliation**	**Function**
Wool production	State Farms (under the *Ministry of Agriculture*, and *Production and Construction Corps*, and local government)	Primary production and other activities	Notionally still under the *Ministry of Agriculture* or *Production and Construction Corps* but relaxation of production dictates, depending on administrative level of farm	Primary production and other activities
Wool marketing and scouring	*(Old) Ministry of Commerce*	Administered the *Supply and Marketing Co-operatives*	*Internal Trade Division* (under former *State Development and Reform Commission*)	Limited
	Supply and Marketing Co-operatives	Monopoly wool procurement and marketing agency	Central level conglomerate with local and largely independent subsidiaries	Compete on open market; diminishing role
Wool processing/ mills	*Ministry of Textiles Industry*	Ownership of textile mills, industry planning, control of *China Textile Resources Company* for wool imports	*Textiles Industry Association* (under *State Assets Management Commission*)	Industry coordination, representation (severed ownership links with mills and *China Textile Resources Company*)
	State-owned mills, under *Ministry of Textiles Industry* and local government	Fill plans and product orders from government institutions	Under *State Asset Management Commission*, local government, with ownership reform	Compete on open market, profit motives and act according to local objectives and incentives
Pricing	*Price Bureau* (under *Ministry of Planning*)	Pricing of wool and other commodities	*Price Department* now under *State Development and Reform Commission*	Price monitoring
Wool imports	*Ministry of Foreign Economic Relations and Trade* which became *Ministry of Foreign Trade and Economic Co-operation*	Control of Chinatex, import quota management	*Ministry of Foreign Trade and Economic Co-operation* absorbed into a new *Ministry of Commerce (Central level)*	Trade policy; severed ownership links with Chinatex
	Chinatex (under *Ministry of Foreign Trade and Economic Co-operation*), *China Textile Resources Company* (under *Ministry of Textiles Industry*)	Wool import monopoly/State agencies	Central level conglomerate with local and largely independent subsidiaries	No longer have import monopoly and subsidiaries compete on open market

Figure 3.2   Reforms to some of the major institutions in the wool textile industry since the 1980s

Textiles Industry Association. Province-level Textile Industry Bureaus have also become associations or, in some cases, holding companies.

The former Ministry of Commerce underwent a similar demise to become the Bureau of Internal Trade before being abolished as a distinct entity in 2000.[4] In the Central Planning era, the former Ministry of Commerce and its agencies had a dominant role in input procurement and product distribution, including wool marketing. However the liberalization of product markets lessened the roles and reasons for existence of this once all-powerful ministry.

Another specialized economic unit to have undergone reform was the Ministry of Foreign Economic Relations, which became the Ministry of Foreign Trade and Economic Co-operation in 1993. In a move designed to better integrate China's international and domestic economy, the Ministry of Foreign Trade and Economic Co-operation merged with the State Economic and Trade Commission in 2003 to form a new Ministry of Commerce (unrelated to the old domestic market-oriented Ministry of Commerce mentioned above). By mid-2004 this merger had only occurred at the central government level.

State marketing and trade agencies under these specialized economic units have also been stripped of monopoly powers in the wool textile industry. For instance the Supply and Marketing Co-operatives under the former Ministry of Commerce/Bureau of Internal Trade system are no longer the sole, or even main, procurers of domestic wool (see Chapter 7). Chinatex (under the former Ministry of Foreign Trade and Economic Co-operation) and the China Textile Resources Company (under the former Ministry of Textiles Industry), no longer monopolize imports of wool and other textiles into China (see Chapter 6).[5] These agencies remain important in their sectors and are still organized as loosely integrated networks under the umbrella of the new Ministry of Commerce at the central government level. With declining State support however these agencies are being forced to compete on an even footing with other industry actors of varied ownership types.

The relationship between government and enterprises is particularly important in the wool processing sector. Chapter 5 reveals how remnants of the Ministry of Textiles Industry have severed ownership links with State-owned enterprise wool textile mills which have since been transferred to the State Asset Management Commission network at various levels. From this base, many of these former State-owned Enterprises have entered into various non-State ownership structures, or are no longer active in the industry.

3.1.2   Strategic Retention of Interventionist Institutions

Despite the strong tendency for specialized economic departments to be relieved of their interventionist role, the State has strategically chosen to retain some interventionist powers. The State has reserved "macro-control" powers across some sectors of the economy. Because of the lack of relative strategic importance in the wool textile industry, central government interventionist powers are not heavily applied. However at the local level, intervention is still significant in some segments of the wool textile industry.

The agricultural sector is a notable exception to the general trend toward the diminishing role of government in economic and industry activity in China. The Ministry of Agriculture has survived the rounds of government reform intact with an ongoing mandate to implement interventionist agricultural policies and participate directly in industry activity (Waldron 2003). The Animal Husbandry and Veterinary Bureau under the Ministry of Agriculture continues to play a strong role in preproduction and production aspects of the wool industry (see Chapter 8). Compared to the past however, wool production plans are now less rigidly set and adhered to, while pastoral households have greater freedom to determine their activities. The same increased freedom applies to State Farms, which are important players in fine-wool production in China.

The demise of other economic departments such as the former Ministry of Commerce and the Ministry of Textiles Industry also left a gap which has enabled the Ministry of Agriculture and the Animal Husbandry and Veterinary Bureau to play a greater role in wool marketing. In regions like Inner Mongolia, the Animal Husbandry and Veterinary Bureau has been highly proactive and closely involved in wool marketing, while in Xinjiang, an intriguing set of new institutional alliances between government departments, ex-State agencies, companies and associations has been forged (see Chapter 7).

In addition to continued government intervention in agriculture, recent rounds of administrative reforms have also aimed to strengthen the State's macro-control system. An important institutional element has been to replace "specialized economic units" (mainly ministries) with departments (usually termed commissions) charged with "management, monitoring and guidance" functions. These commissions employ a wide range of mechanisms to facilitate the pace of modernization and strategically pursue development.[6]

The structure of these macro-management commissions is in a constant state of flux (see Figure 3.2).[7] Nonetheless their various manifestations have impacted upon industries such as the wool textile industry. For example the State Economic and Trade Commission coordinated the wool spindle cutbacks in 1997 designed to curb overproduction and to modernize the industry. Such measures were also employed in a range of other industries such as crude oil, steel, coal, cement, power and sugar. The cotton textile industry – closely related to the wool textile industry – was also subject to capacity reduction and modernization.[8] As another example of State "management, monitoring and guidance", the State Economic and Trade Commission distributed exemptions on value added tax if textile mills used computer systems for information management systems and product design. In general however, macro-control departments have targeted relatively few interventionist programmes and policies at the wool textiles industry.

Thus the wool textile industry no longer falls under the jurisdiction of any specialized economic departments, and is not deemed strategically important enough to be heavily targeted through agricultural or macro-control programmes. Furthermore the diminishing overall State capacity in the industry has reduced the provision of industry services as outlined in Section 3.2. Nevertheless institutional settings still affect the industry in subtler yet important ways.

3.2 GOVERNMENT SERVICE UNITS

Many of the demoted or abolished specialized economic departments discussed above have become semi- or non-governmental organizations that provide services particularly in the fields of information, research and coordination. Many of these organizations and their new roles are outlined in Section 3.3.

This section is focused on one particular group of "service units" that administer standards and provide testing facilities. In the wool textile industry, these service units have cemented their place in stable macro-control hierarchies. Nevertheless their convoluted institutional structures still exist, and some of these service units have struggled to respond to the new industry environment. One of the reasons is that, unlike government administrative units and State-owned Enterprises, government service units have not yet been subject to reform (see Waldron 2003).

Service units involved with standards and testing are given special attention in this chapter because they reveal crucial issues of institutional transition in China, are important to the future development of the wool textile industry and are not discussed fully in other parts of the book. In meeting the various mega-trends or forces outlined in Chapter 1, mills need access to more tightly specified wool inputs. Standards and testing services are particularly important for raw wool and wool tops where large numbers of producers sell small and heterogeneous lots – through intermediaries – to processors. Most of the discussion below therefore focuses on early stages of the supply chain.[9]

3.2.1   Industry Standards

China has more than 80 sets of standards relating to wool textile products, including raw wool, wool tops, intermediate wool products and garments (see China Textiles Association 2001). The large number of standards reflects the wide range of textile products in China, and the fact that standards are layered on top of each other as the need arises. Thus China now has a detailed set of standards for various types and qualities of wool textile products. Because of the multilayered standards however, compatibility problems arise and many sets of standards are not widely accepted or used.[10] An illustration of the layered nature of these standards appears in Box 3.1, which outlines key developments in the standards for wool and wool tops.

The large number of standards for wool and tops arise for several reasons. First, different standards are required to account for the variability in the quality of wool in China. General standards are sufficient for most of China's wool, but more precise standards are required for higher-quality wool. Marketing companies have an incentive to further differentiate their high-quality wool. Second, different industry actors have developed standards for different uses. For example mills grade according to their own industrial standards that are different to the standards notionally applied for wool assembly and trading. Third, standards have been overseen by different institutions that had jurisdiction over specific industry segments. This institutional dimension requires some explanation with the help of Figure 3.3.

Formally the State Bureau of Quality and Technical Supervision has always had overarching authority for issuing of standards. This body remains in place at province levels and below, but has been merged with other relevant and important institutions to form the State General Bureau of Quality Supervision and Inspection Quarantine at the central government level.

The State Bureau of Quality and Technical Supervision formally issued the National Wool Standards mentioned in Box 3.1. However the development of all wool-related standards was commissioned or delegated to other specialized departments as outlined below:

- Throughout the 1980s and much of the 1990s most standards were developed and issued by the former Ministry of Textiles Industry that had primary responsibility for wool textile mills. Consequently the standards were oriented towards mills.

Box 3.1   *Selected developments in wool and wool top standards in China*

A series of overlapping and changing standards for wool and wool top have emerged in China in response to changing needs and capabilities to monitor and enforce the standards. Longworth and Brown (1995) provide a detailed discussion of some of these standards in Chapter 4 of their book along with an English translation of the standards in a series of appendices. Some of the salient aspects of these standards are:

- Standards for domestic wool were initially developed in the 1950s and in 1978 a National Wool Standard was issued. These standards underwent a major revision in 1993 and revised again between 1995 and 1998. The most recent standard T21004 "Domestic Fine Wool and Improved Wool Tops" was promulgated in 1998.
- An additional standards system more oriented to the requirements of the mills – called the Industrial Woolsorting, Scoured Wool and Top Testing Method Standards – was developed in 1981. Pricing schemes administered around that time by the Price Bureau, the Supply and Marketing Co-operatives and Ministry of Textiles Industry were based around these standards.
- A separate Wool Tops Standard was added in 1993. Wool tops standards for the processing of imported greasy wool were the same as the Industrial Woolsorting, Scoured Wool and Top Standard for domestic raw wool until 1993 when a separate Wool Top Standard was issued.
- A separate Quality Standard for Auction Wool was issued in 1991. This standard involved representation from industry stakeholders at national, provincial and city levels, including Ministry of Textiles Industry, Ministry of Agriculture/Animal Husbandry and Veterinary Bureau, the Fibre Inspection Bureau, various research institutes, and various trading and processing companies including the Nanjing Branch of China Textile Goods and Material Company. Auctions require an accurate and comprehensive description of the products for sale if they are to perform their price discovery role effectively. Furthermore both sellers (to differentiate their products) and buyers (to justify premium bids) require that the wool is specified more tightly than is the case for general standards.
- To differentiate their wool from other premium suppliers, various domestic wool marketing organizations have further developed their own product specifications and standards. These include Sanmu of the Nanjing Wool Market, Sapale of Xinjiang, Saiaosi of Inner Mongolia, and the Merino Company of Xinjiang.
- Imported wool is subject to a separate set of standards (of the exporting country).

- The Fibre Inspection Bureaus also developed standards. Originally the Fibre Inspection Bureaus were established under the Ministry of Textiles Industry. Following the demise of the Ministry of Textiles Industry however, the Fibre Inspection Bureaus have now been integrated into the State General Bureau of Quality Supervision and Inspection Quarantine hierarchy.

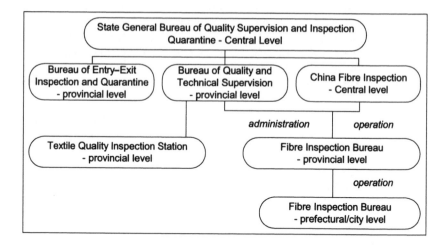

Figure 3.3   Institutions involved in the provision of standards in the Chinese wool and wool textile industry

- The former Ministry of Commerce/Supply and Marketing Co-operatives system was closely involved in the development of standards from the perspective of wool marketing, but is now largely irrelevant to wool standards.
- The Ministry of Agriculture/Animal Husbandry and Veterinary Bureau system was also closely involved in the development of standards from the perspective of wool production.
- For imported wool and wool tops, standards were interpreted by the China Import and Export Commodity Inspection Bureau. Formerly under the Ministry of Foreign Trade and Economic Co-operation, this organization has been moved to come under the Bureau of Entry–Exit Inspection and Quarantine.

Thus wool standards in place in the early 2000s stem from a replicated and fragmented administrative structure of a past era. In the mid-1990s Longworth and Brown (1995) lamented that efforts to improve the industry standards for raw wool and tops had built on the existing, widely understood, but out-of-date systems rather than starting anew. They noted the knock-on effects especially for domestic systems targeting the worsted segment. Institutional changes have occurred since the mid-1990s but the standards remain essentially the same. The need for more tightly specified inputs and other pressures on mill wool procurement make inappropriate standards for domestic wool more of a problem in the mid-2000s than it was in the mid-1990s for producers seeking to access high-value markets.

3.2.2 Inspection and Testing Institutions

Modernizing industry standards in China to promote manufacturing and marketing efficiencies requires that the standards be implemented and enforced. The inadequacies and incompatibilities of the existing standards may partly explain their poor uptake and enforcement. However Longworth and Brown (1995, Chapter 6) showed that testing and enforcement of the prevailing rudimentary standards were problematic. Thus any analysis of modernizing industry standards must take into account the relevant institutional structures. A diagrammatic representation of these testing organizations and their inter-relationships are shown in Figure 3.4.

To enforce national standards effectively, testing must be conducted by an independent and widely accepted authority, be well resourced in terms of testing equipment and skilled personnel, and follow a set of accepted inspection and testing procedures. These conditions do not hold in China primarily because of the convoluted institutional structures that govern inspection and testing procedures. Similar to the case for wool standards, wool inspection and testing comprises a series of multilayered organizations.

In respect of domestic wool, Fibre Inspection Bureaus remain the premier wool products testing institution in China, and perform testing work on behalf of many other organizations (including Supply and Marketing Co-operatives, State Farms, the China Import and Export Commodity Inspection Bureau and auction systems). Even after institutional reforms they retain a vertical hierarchy that extends from central to local levels. However each of the Fibre Inspection Bureaus is a semi-autonomous unit that is also under pressure to generate revenues through testing services and fees. Consequently retesting across administrative boundaries is common.

In the era of centralized wool procurement Supply and Marketing Co-operatives at various levels routinely conducted rudimentary (usually subjective) grading of domestic wool. With the demise of the Supply and Marketing Co-operative system, even this crude form of initial grading collapsed. Instead the vast majority of domestic wool is traded by private dealers who purchase wool on a mixed grade basis outside national standards and testing systems (see Chapter 7).

A range of Textile Research Institutes also tests wool although these are used for research and development rather than for commercial purposes. Various Animal Husbandry and Veterinary Bureau laboratories (especially at breed stations) also offer wool testing services.

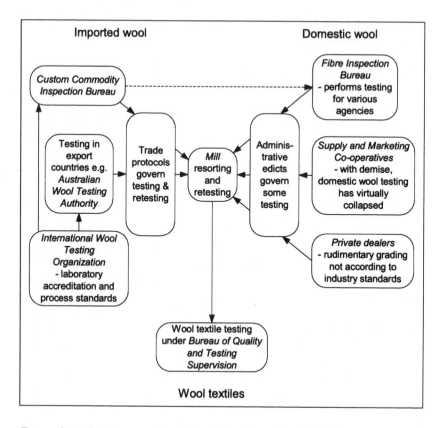

Imported wool

Domestic wool

Custom Commodity Inspection Bureau

Fibre Inspection Bureau - performs testing for various agencies

Testing in export countries e.g. *Australian Wool Testing Authority*

Trade protocols govern testing & retesting

Mill resorting and retesting

Administrative edicts govern some testing

Supply and Marketing Co-operatives - with demise, domestic wool testing has virtually collapsed

International Wool Testing Organization - laboratory accreditation and process standards

Private dealers - rudimentary grading not according to industry standards

Wool textile testing under *Bureau of Quality and Testing Supervision*

Wool textiles

Figure 3.4   Testing agencies in the Chinese wool textile industry

Responsibility for the testing of imported and exported wool (and wool products) lies with a separate organization called the China Import and Export Commodity Inspection Bureau originally established under Ministry of Foreign Trade and Economic Co-operation. The China Import and Export Commodity Inspection Bureau now falls under the Bureau of Entry–Exit Inspection and Quarantine hierarchy, which is separate from Fibre Inspection Bureaus at provincial level and below. Thus testing for domestic and imported wool takes place under two parallel systems.

Another layer of testing agencies occurs in exporting countries (such as the Australian Wool Testing Authority in Australia). The replication of testing across international boundaries continues to be a source of concern in wool trade and is an issue taken up in Chapter 6. International organizations such as the International Wool Testing Organization attempt to facilitate single inspection in the wool trade – through laboratory accreditation and standard procedures – and to make these standards the basis of trade protocols. Despite these efforts, and even when formal protocols are in place, multiple testing and disputes over testing remain a major issue. Apart from these external agencies, most mills have their own testing facilities and test their own inputs and products as part of their internal systems.[11]

3.2.3   Efficacy of Standards and Inspection Systems

Market-oriented reform in China could have been expected to introduce healthy competition, allow more appropriate grade-price differentials, lead to the refinement of standards, and stimulate investment in fibre inspection and testing. In practice, and in terms of the utilization of standards and testing, the system currently functions less well than did the crude practices in the Central Planning and early reform era.

The amount of Chinese domestic wool subject to inspection or testing from an independent authority has fallen steadily throughout the reform era. In 1990, 20 per cent of domestic wool in China was tested, of which 8 per cent was machine (objectively) tested (Zhang et al. 1997). In the mid-2000s the corresponding figures are much lower – less than 5 per cent each. The main reasons for the decline stems from liberalization leading to the collapse of the only network – the Supply and Marketing Co-operatives – with the institutional capacity to inspect domestic wool on a widespread basis. They have been replaced by private dealers who now dominate domestic wool marketing. Dealers purchase wool on a purely subjective basis outside national standards and testing systems. Although this may be appropriate in the coarse and semi-fine wool segment – and much of domestic wool is destined for this segment – the lack of grade-price differentials has decreased incentives to produce and process better-quality domestic wool.

Another indicator of the inadequacies of the domestic wool standards and testing system is that mills regrade and retest all the domestic wool themselves. Resorting of the wool is a labour-intensive task involving significant costs. Furthermore it can impact upon the logistics and planning of wool processing. Despite the extensive costs, mills perceive that the costs of grading and inspecting the wool internally within the mill are justified. Developing a more coordinated, improved and trusted system of grading and testing of domestic wool could change the attitudes of mills to resorting and retesting. Such a system would lower transaction costs for the industry as a whole and may warrant consideration as a government sponsored initiative.

Another significant cost arises as a result of replicated testing both within and across national boundaries. The distinction between the domestic (Fibre Inspection Bureau) and imported (China Import and Export Commodity Inspection Bureau) wool standards and testing systems is a case in point.

Even within the Fibre Inspection Bureau system, replicated testing occurs within China – for example in both the wool production and processing regions.[12] Incompatibilities of the standards and testing procedures can generate disputes, not to mention the added cost and time delays associated with the duplication.

A major impact of government reform has been the reduction in public funding for service units. Wool testing agencies have been placed under enormous pressure to become more commercially oriented, but this has proven difficult given the multitude of agencies that emerged from an earlier era. Not only are diminishing amounts of domestic wool passing through the testing system, but the agencies are still in the process of establishing viable commercial modes of operation. Local governments have also sought to force industry actors to use local testing facilities, even if retesting has or will be done elsewhere, and so have exacerbated the testing replication problems. As a result of the lack of uptake of fee for service arrangements and government underinvestment in testing facilities, most testing laboratories are poorly resourced.[13]

Grading systems established by wool marketing companies and auction systems on a fully commercial basis have also experienced difficulties. The amount of wool that passes through these channels is small in overall terms and has been diminishing in recent years. Producers, mainly State Farms, are choosing to sell direct to mills by utilizing the brands of the wool marketing companies rather than through the auction systems. A major reason for the direct sale to mills is that the additional costs of selling through auctions, which involves specialized grading and testing, does not appear to be offset by any price premiums achieved.

Apart from the issues associated with the testing of domestic wool discussed above, there are separate concerns relate to the testing of imported wool. Because these concerns closely relate to other trade issues, they are taken up in Chapter 6.

3.2.4 Way Forward for Standards and Testing Institutions

The problems outlined above stem from the continued existence of remnants of an outdated system. If there is no conscious attempt to reform these service units, most will just fade away with time. However given the need to improve the precision with which wool is described and traded, another round of reform aimed at creating a modern wool testing system is overdue.

Substantial scope exists to rationalize the number of testing agencies and to consolidate their operations, especially in respect of city-level Fibre Inspection Bureaus. Consolidation may reduce replication and wasteful competition and achieve the economies and throughputs needed to justify

Image 3.1   Wool testing facilities

The testing of domestic wool is rare, not because of the modest infrastructure and skills involved, but because wool growers and dealers have low incentives to use wool standards and testing systems. A range of institutions has the authority and the basic infrastructure to test domestic wool. Replication of testing across national and international borders also increases marketing costs.

better-resourced facilities. Narrowing or even removing the increasingly artificial distinction between the domestic and imported wool testing systems appears to be feasible. Administrative moves to merge the parent organizations of the Fibre Inspection Bureau and China Import and Export Commodity Inspection Bureau at the central level suggest that this process is already under way. As with other administrative reforms, this may be extended to local levels over time.

Such administrative changes would also help testing agencies distance themselves from the specialized economic units from which they originated and move toward becoming more genuine, independent organizations. Issues of governance within the agencies and their funding arrangements are crucial. In particular testing agencies need effective mechanisms to receive or extract fees for the services they perform. The model of a statutory authority attached to – but not controlled by – government and with a mandate to apply levies to industry participants (growers, traders or processors) may be relevant.

Given the fragmented nature of the industry, the collective outcome of individual actions coordinated by market mechanisms is unlikely to provide standards and testing services in the form or at the level desired by the industry or society as a whole. The public good nature of a testing service justifies some public sector involvement. The question is, what should be the scope and form of this involvement? At one extreme there have been suggestions that all domestic wool be mandatorily subject to national standards and testing. Indeed various national and province level regulations promulgated in 1992 made it compulsory to apply national standards and test all wool exchanged.[14] In practice these laws proved impossible to implement in the highly fragmented wool production and marketing systems of the mid-1990s (Longworth and Brown 1995). Given that wool marketing has become more fragmented since the mid-1990s, the task of implementing and enforcing mandatory and comprehensive testing would be even more problematic. Furthermore the costs of implementing these standards in a fragmented production and marketing system dominated by low-quality wool may exceed any benefits that may arise from more accurate pricing. Thus it would seem appropriate that China's coarse and semi-fine wool not be subject to sophisticated standards and testing. That is the current methods of marketing employed by private traders provide a low transaction cost and relatively efficient mechanism of exchange for low-value wool (see Chapter 7).

High-value or premium domestic wool marketed through companies and auction systems is also traded in a way only indirectly related to widely accepted national standards. However producers and processors of fine wool in China appear to have significant economic incentives to differentiate their wool and so resist aligning their product with generic industry standards. The problems of developing generic and widely accepted industry standards are not unique to the wool industry and are evident for example in the protracted efforts to develop a meat grading system for the Chinese beef industry (see Waldron et al. 2003, Chapter 11).

Although national standards and testing systems may only be indirectly relevant to low- and high-value domestic wool segments, they may have much to offer China's substantial mid-value wool market segment. Producers, traders and mills in this segment – and in the industry as a whole – would stand to benefit from access to a well-organized and administered wool standards and testing system. The benefits would include better marketing logistics and more accurate price signals. Such a system could provide considerable incentives among industry participants in this segment to upgrade their product in response to better prices for better grades of wool.

Before such systems can be effectively implemented and benefit a broad group within the Chinese wool industry however, measures to reorganize institutional structures discussed earlier will need to be addressed.

Image 3.2   Resorting of domestic wool in mills

Unlike imported wool, virtually all Chinese domestic wool has to be resorted by mills before processing. This imposes a variety of costs on the mills but is necessary because of the underdevelopment of the Chinese wool marketing system. Wool is classed and graded crudely and standards and testing systems are rarely applied.

3.3   OTHER SERVICE DELIVERY INSTITUTIONS

In addition to government standards and testing bodies, a broad range of other service delivery institutions exists in the wool textile industry. Amorphous categories of these "other" institutions include: associations with a background as specialized economic departments; education and research institutions; associations and companies established by lower level organizations; and peak representative bodies formed by industry actors themselves. With the exception of educational institutions, they all now operate as "civil society" or "third party" organizations that lie somewhere between the government and the commercial sectors.

The institutional position of these organizations can be precarious in any country, but especially in China where the environment for them to operate has only recently developed. Many institutions have yet to establish systems where they can attract or extract sufficient funding to provide quality industry services. Furthermore each organization brings with it an institutional history and set of relationships that continue to exert strong influences. These institutions therefore make an interesting case study in economic transition.

Institutions described in this section mainly deliver services to industry, including information provision, research and development, industry promotion, industry coordination, and lobbying and representation – all services crucial to the development and transition of the industry. However rather than the discussion being based around the type of activity they perform, the following sections focus on their institutional backgrounds.

3.3.1   Associations Derived from Government Departments

Many of the large associations in China had their genesis in government departments with control over particular industries or economic sectors (the "specialized economic departments" referred to above).[15] Despite reforms, strong links still exist with government, with the associations usually staffed by retired or ex-government officials. They have close links to State-owned Enterprises which are association members, although other enterprises also can be members. These associations see their role as bridging the gap between government and industry. They pass on and help government implement laws and programmes such as the case of spindle cutbacks in the textile industry. In turn they inform government of issues and concerns within the industry. Associations provide industry participants with information, produce industry magazines, organize trade shows and industry conferences, and help apply standards and inspection.

The China Textiles Industry Association is an example of this type of ex-government association. From its origins as a fully fledged ministry (Ministry of Textiles Industry) and then bureau, the China Textiles Industry Association was transferred to an organization under the State Economic and Trade Commission before being moved to the State Assets Management Commission. With a staff of about 100, the China Textiles Industry Association receives some government funding, but is under pressure to generate its own funds. One of the sub-associations of the Textile Industry Association is the China Wool Textile Association.[16] The China Wool Textile Association receives membership fees from about 300 association members. Because of their close relationship with textile mills and processing, the China Textiles Industry Association and China Wool Textile Association are discussed in detail in Chapter 5.

3.3.2   Education and Research Institutions

China previously had a large number of universities, colleges and institutes that came under Ministry of Textiles Industry and were specialized in textiles. Their main function was to train and allocate personnel to meet the needs of the industry, especially textile mills. The textile education institutions existed at central, provincial and local levels.[17] With the educational reforms in the 1990s these textiles education institutions become faculties or colleges under broader comprehensive universities under the jurisdiction of the Ministry of Education. Within this structure they have been forced to compete more vigorously for funding and other resources. Many have ceased to exist.

Textile Research Institutes also operated under the Ministry of Textiles Industry hierarchy and existed at national and provincial levels. Textile Research Institutes existed in many wool production and processing areas including Beijing, Shanghai, Jiangsu, Gansu, Xinjiang and Inner Mongolia.[18] Many Textile Research Institutes are now under company structures.[19] They have a mandate to generate revenue through research, trials and testing, and undertaking research and development work for mills developing their products and patents.

In response to the mega-trends (outlined in Chapter 1) and the restructuring occurring in the processing segment (outlined in Chapter 5), wool textile mills have begun to develop and rely more and more on their own product design sections, and less and less on external bodies such as the Textile Research Institutes. However as will be discussed in the following chapter, Chinese wool textile mills have not taken the lead in industry development and product development. Part of this relates to the relative size and resources of the Chinese mills, which suggests that public or industry-wide research and market development agencies may be needed to take on a more active role in this area. However the reforms of service institutions such as Textile Research Institutes which have diminished in size and resources have meant that they have not been in a position to perform this larger role.

3.3.3   Corporatized Institutions

Another form of industry institution involves those established by companies that have identified a commercial opportunity to act as an industry institution. The returns can either come as direct revenue or more indirectly as goodwill from government because they fill a public role.

The Nanjing Wool Market is the earliest established example of this type of organization. It was established in 1988 under the China Textile Resources Nanjing Corporation, one of the independent subsidiaries of the giant China Textile Resources Group that dominates wool imports. The Nanjing Wool

Market collates various types of information, produces and regularly disseminates an industry publication, and arranges conference, training and promotion programmes. Apart from these roles and its connection with wool importation, the Nanjing Wool Market also has a long history in domestic wool marketing. In particular the Nanjing Wool Market was a key player in the initial development of auctions in the late 1980s and early 1990s as well as their attempted revival a decade later.

The demise of the Ministry of Textiles Industry, the Supply and Marketing Co-operatives and the diminishing attention given to the wool sector by the Ministry of Agriculture has heightened the role of the Nanjing Wool Market in guiding and promoting the reform of domestic wool marketing. The diverse role that the Nanjing Wool Market plays in various industry services means that it is a topic of discussion at various points in the remainder of the book.

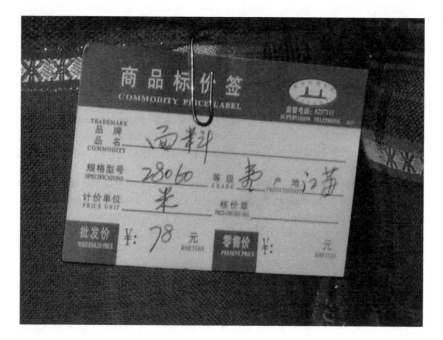

Image 3.3   Commodity information available to final consumers

Standards for raw wool can be extremely precise and exacting but objective information about wool products is shed as it proceeds along the processing stages. The only information that final consumers have to base their garment purchasing decision on is wool percentage and price. This, along with the feel and care instructions for the garment, determine purchasing decisions.

The Xinjiang Fine Wool Association and the Merino Company in Xinjiang Province provide other examples of industry service groups with a strong commercial orientation. Both were formed through interesting and, a priori, unexpected combinations of Animal Husbandry and Veterinary Bureaus and Supply and Marketing Co-operatives at different levels, along with entrepreneurial officials of research institutes. The blurring and forging of new institutional alliances is a fascinating development that is discussed in detail in Chapter 7. These bodies are now in the process of becoming fully fledged companies rather than taking the path of non-profit associations.

3.3.4 Industry Representation Groups

A feature of the industry institutions overviewed above is that they are closely related to government despite their commercial orientation or operation as fully fledged companies. As such they can generally be regarded as corporatized and top-down institutions.

However several types of organizations that could be regarded as bottom-up, industry representation groups also operate in the wool textile industry. These associations tend to be relatively localized and narrowly focused. For instance in the Wenzhou region of southern Zhejiang Province, industry representation groups such as the Wenzhou Fashion Association and the Wenzhou Textile Products Association exist. The latter organization has a membership of more than 40 retailers in one of China's largest worsted fabrics market. These bottom-up organizations in Wenzhou reflect the growth and history of textile industry development in the region as having its base in private households or companies.[20]

3.4 IMPLICATIONS OF INSTITUTIONAL CHANGE

The institutional changes and reforms that have featured so strongly in China since the early 1990s have important implications for the wool textile industry. Specific implications for industry segments are drawn out in Chapters 4 to 8 of the book. This section sets out some common elements of the implications as a precursor to that discussion.

Institutional changes within the wool textile industry have been dramatic, as it was an industry well established in the Central Planning era but is no longer regarded as strategically important.[21] The transition from Central Planning involved a shift towards greater market orientation and the demise of government bodies that exerted direct controls on the industry. The coercive powers of these bodies were limited in the extent to which they could coordinate industry activities across marketing and processing stages, and across regions and activities. Different ministries governed various sections of the industry, and their interests and objectives were not necessarily aligned. The vertical administrative structure of these bodies also worked against an awareness of what was happening in different sectors or industries. Although reforms have changed the nature of these agencies, some of these problems remain.

As these organizations become more removed from direct government control and funding, the delineation between public and private roles becomes blurred and serious conflicts of interest can arise. Furthermore there has been a lag between the demise of centrally planned institutions and the emergence of non-governmental and market institutions to replace them. Relatively few examples arise of strong non-governmental bodies active in important areas of the wool textile industry.

The transition from a centrally planned to a market-based system also requires market support services and structures to facilitate the smooth running of these markets and enable widespread participation. These market support or service institutions however are far from developed, which has an adverse impact on the operation of the market and on other newly formed institutions that rely upon a well-functioning market.

Although coordination problems existed in the Central Planning era, as highlighted by various chapters in Longworth and Brown (1995), it cannot be presumed that these problems dissipated in the post-reform era. The more fragmented nature of the industry, and the removal of sole procurement and distribution powers and market support services provided by government institutions such as the Supply and Marketing Cooperatives, means that many coordination problems have become much more pronounced. That is if the need for cooperation or coordination arose, then under the Central Planning era, organizations had the coercive powers necessary to ensure that coordination occurred. As the governmental influence over individual enterprises becomes more indirect, and as interests become more commercial and more diverse, the possibilities for coordination decline. How to promote coordination and cooperation (where circumstances warrant) among self-interested industry participants without resorting to heavy-handed instruments of the Central Planning era, is an issue that confronts Chinese officials not only in the wool textile industry but in many other industries.

NOTES

1   For a more detailed appreciation of the institutional changes that have occurred within the Chinese wool textile industry since the early 1990s, Figure 3.1 can also be compared with Figure 2.1 in Longworth and Brown (1995).

2   See for example Lieberthal (1995), Niu (1997) and Waldron et al. (2003) for a discussion of vertical and horizontal (*tiao tiao* and *kuai kuai*) institutional management of industries in China.

3   Details on administrative reforms since the 1980s appear in Burns (1997), *People's Daily* (2003) and various notices posted on www.china.gov.cn.

4   Other specialized economic units to have been demoted and then abolished in the same way as the Ministry of Textiles Industry and the Ministry of Commerce include the ministries of Machinery Industry, Metallurgical Industry, Petroleum and Chemical Industry, Light Industry, Building Material Industry, and the Nonferrous Metal Industry. The Bureau of Coal underwent major restructuring to become the Bureau of Work Safety. Conversely the Price Bureau (formerly under the Ministry of Planning) became the Price Department within the State Development and Reform Commission in 2003.

5   These conglomerates were moved from their specialized economic departments to become semi-autonomous activities housed under the State Economic Trade Commission and subsequently the new Ministry of Commerce.

6   Based on government documents and reports of speeches, Unger and Chan (1995) suggest that China's government reform process has been influenced by the Japanese model, where powerful commissions – especially the Ministry of International Trade and Industry – have been able to strategically mould the economy through close business–government relations and within corporatist structures.

7   For example as recently as 2003 the State Economic and Trade Commission merged with the Ministry of Foreign Trade and Economic Cooperation to form a new Ministry of Commerce. The State Development Planning Commission was reorganized into the State Development and Reform Commission. The State Assets Management Commission was also elevated to fall directly under the State Council. While these measures took place at central government level, implementation at lower levels has been very uneven.

8   As a substitute fibre, policy toward the cotton industry affects the wool industry in significant ways. China's huge cotton industry is the beneficiary of many preferential policies and subsidies. Subsidies are applied at the production, marketing and processing stages.

9   Standards and testing also applies at later stages and to products such as fabrics and garments, but involves smaller numbers of sellers and buyers, and exchange is made through contractual arrangements. Testing services for these latter-stage products are performed primarily for dispute resolution purposes and to minimize the incidence of counterfeiting.

10 For an overview of some of the technical problems in the domestic wool standards, see Tian (2001).

11 The sophistication of these testing facilities depends on the size and nature of the mill. However Longworth and Brown (1995, Chapter 6) noted that in some of the wool-producing regions, the large State-owned mills often had much more sophisticated and advanced equipment than the local testing agencies (such as provincial Fibre Inspection Bureaus) and were contracted to do much of the testing in that region.

12 For example both the Xinjiang and Jiangsu provincial Fibre Inspection Bureaus test Sapale wool sold at auction by the Nanjing Wool Market (see Chapter 7).

13 For instance in 2004 there were only 14 Sirolan-Laserscan machines (which are small and relatively inexpensive units used to objectively test wool) in the whole of China, with only six of these in publicly accessible testing agencies.

14 In what was in large part a response to the "wool wars" of 1985 to 1988, the national wool standards and the Standardization Law of the Peoples Republic of China, promulgated in 1992, made it compulsory to buy and sell wool according to standards administered and

inspection by the Fibre Inspection Bureau. Notional severe penalties were set for non-compliance. In 1993 the National Wool Quality Control Regulation was introduced for wool trading.

15   See Waldron et al. (2003) for further discussions of industry associations such as the China Leather Association and China Meat Association

16   Other sub-associations include the China Cotton Textile Association, China Wool Textile Association, China Dyeing and Printing Industry Association, China Bast and Leaf Fibres Textile Association, China Knitting Industry Association, China Coloured Woven Association, China Textile Machinery and Accessories Association, China Chemical Fibre Industry Association, China Non-wovens and Industrial Textiles Association, China Silk Association, China Home Textile Association, China Garment Association, China Textile Employee Political Work Society, China Textile Education Society, China Textile Planning Society, China Textile Exploration and Design Society, China Textile Accounting Society, China Textile Enterprise Management Society, Technical Progress Consulting Centre of National Textile Industry, China Textile International Exchange Centre.

17   Central-level institutions include the East China Textile Engineering Institute (now part of Donghua University) and the Northwest Institute of Textiles Science and Technology (now part of the Xi'an University of Engineering Science and Technology). Some provincial institutions include the Tianjin Institute of Textile Science and Technology (now within Tianjin Polytechnic University), the Wuhan Institute of Textile Science and Technology (now within Wuhan University of Science and Engineering), the former Shandong Textile Engineering Institute, Zhengzhou Institute of Textile Science and Technology (now Zhongyuan Institute of Technology), and the Zhejiang Institute of Silk Textile Technology (now within Zhejiang University of Sciences).

18   An outline and discussion of these textile research institutes as they operated in the early 1990s can be found in Longworth and Brown (1995, Section 6.6).

19   For example the Beijing Wool Textile Science Research Institute is now managed by one of the subsidiary companies (Xuelian) under the Beijing Textiles Holding Company (the reincarnation of the Beijing Textile Industry Bureau). The equivalent in Shanghai was the Shanghai Wool and Hemp Research Institute. It came under Shanghai Wool and Hemp Company which has since become the Sanmao Textiles Co. Ltd. In turn these companies are under the loose management of the State Assets Management Commission.

20   Although the Wenzhou Fashion Association has a large number of both small and large garment makers – all of which are individual family or family-related shareholding companies – the impetus to maintain and develop the Association stems primarily from the larger companies.

21   In this regard the wool textile industry differs markedly from other industries such as beef that emerged only after or as a result of the economic reforms and that were subsequently targeted for development (Waldron et al. 2003).

4. Changing Marketing Channels

Chinese wool textile mills may have hundreds of orders to service in any one year. Nonetheless there are some well-defined marketing channels each representative of a broad class of transaction. Although traditional buyers and channels still predominate, mills are under great pressure to service new customers through new marketing channels. Changes in the way wool textiles are marketed in China are altering the demand for wool textiles, with significant implications for wool textile mills.

To explore this transformation, this chapter describes the users of outputs from worsted mills, and focuses on the complex and changing way that fabric users source their fabric. The two major users, namely institutional buyers (Section 4.2) and garment makers (Section 4.3) source their wool fabric supplies either through fabric markets (Section 4.4), fabric trading companies (Section 4.5), direct from mills (Section 4.6), or through retail or wholesale stores (Section 4.7).

The detailed description and analysis in these sections yield many useful insights on the transformation process. Nevertheless a careful perusal of Sections 4.1 and 4.8 may suffice for readers seeking only an overview of changes in the post-mill-door sector of the wool textile industry and the implications of these changes for overall industry transformation. The complexity, size and dynamics of this part of the wool textile chain are captured concisely in Section 4.1. Key themes and implications for the whole wool textile industry, which emerge from the detailed investigations reported in Sections 4.2 to 4.7, are drawn together in Section 4.8.

4.1 OVERVIEW OF SECTORAL STRUCTURES

Figure 4.1 presents a stylized representation of the structure and diversity of the sector. The left-hand side of the figure lists the stages from textile production to garment retailing and exporting. Products move through the processing stages and marketing chain from the bottom to the top of the figure. The arrowheads provide a guide to the initiator of the product flows. Although the arrow directions are generalizations they reveal a mix of passive

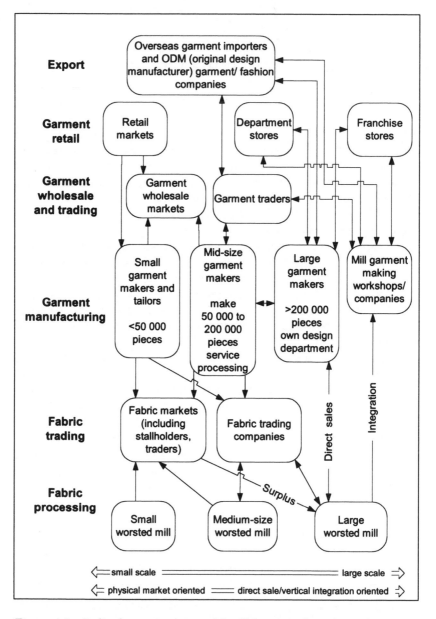

Figure 4.1   Stylized representation of the Chinese wool textile marketing sector

Note: The solid black arrowheads indicate the initiator of the product flows.

orders, active promotion from upstream suppliers and more complex two-way interaction. Exploring the changes in these interactions is a major focus of this chapter.

Various patterns emerge in the structure of the sector. First, small-scale participants (on the left-hand side of the diagram) tend to deal through markets, especially in lower-value products, and this is often an efficient form of exchange for low-value products. Second, larger participants (on the right-hand side of the diagram) deal with each other through more direct channels in higher-value products. Analysis in the chapter reveals that the larger participants depicted to the right-hand side of Figure 4.1 are best equipped to deal with the pressures of modernization and the new marketing environment.

The customers of Chinese wool textile mills are not final consumers but other participants in the wool textile chain such as garment or sweater makers. Final consumers deal with the clothing and fashion industry which uses various fibre and fabric inputs. Wool textiles and textile mills therefore represent an earlier stage in the supply chain and only a small part of the overall clothing and fashion industry.

The dichotomy that exists between the clothing industry and the textile industry determines much of the way wool textile mills and garment makers operate. Wool textile mills belong to the wool and wool textile industries where there is a close connection between the fibre input and the technical processes to produce fabric. Conversely garment makers align with the clothing and fashion industry and have less understanding of fibre inputs. For example when garment makers make and receive orders, there is little detail on the fibre inputs used to make the fabric. Instead garment makers bring samples of the fabric to the textile mills and ask the mills to replicate the style and make the decisions concerning specific fibre input choices and technical processing.

Consumers purchase garments partly on fabric type but more according to price, fashion, style, cut and feel of the garment. In the short term these consumer preferences are reflected in the orders and samples that garment makers pass on to mills. However some final consumer preferences such as the demand for easy-care garments or light weight fabrics are determined by the fibre-inputs that go into making the fabric. In the intermediate and long term therefore mills must respond to changing consumer preferences in relation to these product characteristics.

4.2 INSTITUTIONAL BUYERS

Traditionally institutional buyers such as the People's Liberation Army, Ministry of Telecommunications, tax departments, railway departments, and

Image 4.1   Wenzhou garment maker

From humble beginnings, some of Wenzhou's family-owned enterprises have transformed into large, modern garment makers with sophisticated products and manufacturing systems. The question now is whether they can extend their influence and reputations to match leading international players.

banks have been major customers of State-owned mills, and use the fabric to make staff uniforms.[1] Institutional buyers operate in two ways, either purchasing the fabric directly from wool textile mills and having the fabric made into uniforms by garment makers on a commission basis, or purchasing the uniforms directly from garment makers. The institutional reforms described in Chapter 3 have placed pressure on these organizations to purchase through the most cost-effective channels. Irrespective of whether purchases are for uniforms from garment makers or through direct fabric purchases from mills, fabric ultimately destined for institutional buyers remains a significant outlet for wool textile mills. Furthermore changes in the demand and purchasing patterns of these large organizations will impact upon the industry as a whole, not just wool processing mills.

For State-owned mills in the past, institutional buyers provided a stable customer for generic products. The large repeat orders enabled mills to determine product design and fibre input selection and plan ahead for their wool input purchases. The downside for mills was that prices were determined administratively or that institutional buyers had the power and connections to negotiate lower prices for the fabric and uniforms. In the past the "forced" underpricing of orders for institutional customers was offset by State subsidies for loss-making State-owned Enterprise mills.

The extent to which institutional buyers can pressure State-owned mills depends on their relative purchasing as well as political power. However as State-owned mills now face harder budget constraints in an extremely competitive environment, they cannot afford to incur losses from sales to institutional buyers. In the restructuring of State-owned Enterprise mills, new owners are also unlikely to make the same commitment to institutional buyers. At the same time institutional units are also undergoing their own reform, part of which involves paying full prices for their intermediate inputs. Institutional units have become more discerning buyers requiring higher-quality products but at traditional low prices.

The mills face the conundrum that even if they have no obligation to supply institutional buyers, such buyers will be difficult to replace with alternative customers. Institutional buyers still represent a major customer of many mills. Furthermore the nature of the large repeat orders by institutional units suits the traditional passive managerial, wool purchasing and marketing systems still used by many mills. A move away from this group of customers would involve a lower proportion of repeat orders and the planning and manufacturing of more tailored products.

The nexus between restructured State-owned mills and institutional buyers impacts markedly upon overall modernization of the industry. It highlights the need to coordinate the timing and scope of reforms, so that for example mills and their institutional buyers operate on a level economic and political playing field and respond to the same commercial and political incentives.

4.3   GARMENT MAKERS

Direct sales between mills and garment makers have increased in importance. They offer more lucrative returns to mills than the institutional buyers but also pose their own challenges and risks for wool textile mills. For example some mills complain that garment-maker customers often purchase fabric on credit with a promise of payment after the final garments are sold. Many mills have been paid in kind with garments when garment makers have been unable to sell their garments. If garment makers offer too low a price or seem too risky, mills may still offer to process but on a service fee basis only.

As with other industry sectors in China however the garment-making sector exhibits large diversity. Many garment makers began as household enterprises in the 1980s at the time of a booming wool textile industry. Many have since become large private or shareholder companies operating under their own domestic brand but which also process on commission for overseas customers (see Sections 4.3.2 and 4.3.3). There are also medium-sized garment makers that produce garments for branded companies (see Section 4.3.4), as well as a plethora of small tailors.

Large garment makers tend to produce a range of products rather than specialize in a few. The other distinguishing feature of large garment makers is that they operate integrated process design and are specific in their requirements and timeliness of their orders. Thus they are more exacting customers for mills than smaller garment makers in terms of technical requirements, but at the same time operate under a more standard business code. Large garment makers also integrate more closely into the global wool textile industry and so represent an important link in the modernization and internationalization process.

Wool textile mills usually operate their own garment workshops although typically they use only a proportion of the fabric produced by the mill. To further complicate matters, various garment traders commission garments from medium-sized and small garment makers which they then sell under their own brand. The following section seeks to characterize these different types of garment makers. Examples of specific garment makers are then described to reveal more about how they operate and how they have responded to industry changes.

4.3.1   Industry Concentration – the Case of Wenzhou

Garment makers are concentrated in provinces such as Zhejiang and Guangdong.[2] Zhejiang specializes in men's clothing whereas Guangdong focuses on women's fashions. The warmer climate in Guangdong also means they concentrate more on synthetics and cottons than on wool products. Located in southern Zhejiang, Wenzhou represents one of the largest garment-making areas in China, but it is not an area known for its wool textile mills. Instead garment makers in Wenzhou import fabrics from other parts of China – especially Jiangsu, Hubei and Shandong – and from overseas (primarily Italy and England). The many Wenzhou garment makers that produce high-quality suits use wool textile fabrics as inputs.

The garment industry in Wenzhou originated in the early to mid-1980s primarily through households. Indeed the move of households into garment production and related industries such as shoes in the 1980s transformed Wenzhou into the urban municipality it is now. All enterprises are private, shareholder or foreign-invested companies and so do not have the State-owned Enterprise legacy of many industries and regions.[3] According to industry associations in Wenzhou, in 2002 the city had over 2500 garment makers with a total product value of Rmb30.2 billion which generated Rmb3.72 billion in tax revenue. Although product value increased by about 30 per cent in the second half of the 1990s, it declined by almost 15 per cent between 2000 and 2003. Most products are destined for the domestic market with export sales accounting for only Rmb470 million. Wenzhou lacks port facilities so exports are transhipped through other centres such as Ningbo and Shanghai. Garment makers in Wenzhou also feel that the government has not supported exporting operations in Wenzhou to the extent that it has in the large port cities of China.

In terms of size distribution, over 2000 shareholder companies in Wenzhou employ more than 100 employees each. There are at least 16 companies with sales revenues exceeding Rmb100 million, with a further 800 companies having a sales revenue greater than Rmb5 million. Over 200 companies each produce more than 50 000 garments per year. These large and medium-sized companies sell their products all along the east coast.

Wenzhou garment makers collectively have more than 10 000 franchisee and retail shops throughout China (see Image 1.2 in Chapter 1 – Baoxiniao garment store in Changzhou). Many garment makers market their domestic sales through these franchise outlets. They gather the franchisees and collectively show them the samples so that orders can be placed with garment makers and then sold by the franchisees.

The small-sized garment makers (or tailors) buy fabric through intermediaries or through the larger fabric markets. Fabric markets contain large numbers of stalls that act more as retail than wholesale outlets. Medium- and large-scale garment makers avoid fabric markets, as the prices are relatively high and there is no guarantee of quality. Fabric testing is not mandatory and the "guarantee" of quality by purchasing through a fabric trading company such as Aijian is based on reputation. Very small garment makers typically purchase through wholesale fabric markets or fabric dealers, often in purchases of tens of metres, and supply local low-value markets.

4.3.2 Jodoll Garment Making Company

Jodoll (or Qiaodun in Chinese) is the third-largest garment maker in Wenzhou, the thirteenth-largest in Zhejiang, and the thirty-first in China. This large private company has an interesting history that reflects the transformation that has occurred since the early 1980s in this important wool textile producing centre in China. The company commenced operations in 1983 as an individual family company operated by four siblings. Initially involved in garment sales and distribution, especially in Beijing, it evolved into a worsted fabric trading company in 1992 known as Yuanda. The experience in worsted fabric trading provided the necessary understanding of the garment-making trade and so the Jodoll Garment Company was established in 1996. The company claims the relative profitability of fabric trading or garment making is similar but that there are some important complementarities. That is, as a large garment maker, they need to purchase large volumes of fabric and so can do this through their fabric trading company while also being able to sell any surplus fabric to other garment makers.

In 1997 Jodoll's first phase industrial park complex was established with three product lines reaching international standards. In August 2000 the company was renamed as China Jodoll Garment Company Limited in recognition of its China-wide status and outlook. In 2002 the second phase industrial park complex was established on more than 20 000 m^2 of land. Jodoll now has the capacity to produce 600 000 suits per year. All of the suits with the Jodoll or Qiaodun brand name are for the domestic market (high and mid levels. However the company also does service processing for international companies that are marketing under the foreign brand names (Original Design Manufacturer). Jodoll is one of the few garment makers in China with plans to establish retail outlets overseas selling under their own brand name.

There are 180 franchise outlets in China with the name Qiaodun. However they have established a distribution network of over 300 outlets that sell Qiaodun suits, including department stores. Most of the outlets are located in Northern China (Beijing, Tianjin, Harbin, Urumuqi, Dalian, Shanghai) because of the colder weather and more conservative fashion tastes. All of the outlets, including franchisees, purchase the suits outright from the company.

4.3.3 Baoxiniao Garment Company

Baoxiniao (Spring Bird) is a limited liability group of which the garment company is a subsidiary. It ranks among the ten largest suit companies in China with its main competitors also in Wenzhou and nearby Ningbo. The company started operating in 1996 through a merger of three private companies, designed to build scale and a brand name. Originally known as Zhejiang Baoxiniao, the "Zhejiang" part of the name was subsequently dropped in a strategic growth move to project a China-wide image. The growth in this private company has been substantial. In 1996 it had sales of Rmb60 million and staff of 300 compared with sales of Rmb1 billion and a staff of 3000 in 2003. The company has over 500 retail outlets throughout China (see Image 1.2). Apart from the factory in Wenzhou, another was established in Shanghai in 2001 with a staff of 1000, while new facilities are also planned. The company has also diversified into real estate, investment, import and export activities. In 2003 Baoxiniao was attempting to list on the Chinese stock exchange.

The company primarily makes suits but also contracts with other factories to produce ties, sweaters, socks, shoes, scarves and other accessories under the Baoxiniao name. Another brand, Falansi, is used for the marketing of casual clothes (shirts and other garments using low – 20 to 40 per cent – blend wool). Like many other companies, it manages this brand and contracts out production to other companies. There are around 200 Falansi retail franchises in China.

Being a relatively new company, Baoxiniao has found it easier to concentrate on the domestic market than attempt to compete against established brands on the international market. Like most large garment companies, the company is well known in China but has yet to build a brand identity and reputation overseas.

Image 4.2   Nanjing fabric market

Professor Li Ping examines some wool fabric at a Lanzhou Sanmao mill stall at a Nanjing fabric market. The name of this famous Chinese mill is prominently displayed and the stall is not only on outlet for the mill's products, but also promotes the mill and its product among wholesale and retail customers.

Men's suits are produced for the domestic market and sold under two brands – Baoniao and Baoxiniao. Baoniao is used to target the mid- to low-value segment using 70 per cent wool blends, while Baoxiniao targets the white-collar staff market using pure wool and wool blends of 95 per cent and above). The company buys 1 million metres of worsted fabrics per year to produce around 600 000 suits in their two factories. About half the suits, which are typically a 70 per cent wool blend, are purchased by institutional buyers including banks and the police for uniforms.

Some 80 to 85 per cent of their fabric is sourced domestically with the remainder coming primarily from Italy. Most of the domestic fabric comes directly from a limited number of mills. This is not only for price and quality reasons, but also to maintain secrecy of product design. For fabric sourced domestically, mills are given two months to fill the orders.

4.3.4 Huashan Garment-making Company

Compared with Baoxiniao and Jodoll, Huashan is a small to medium-sized enterprise. Like nearly all Wenzhou enterprises it is a private, family-owned company. The company started making suits in 1988 in Yeqing (in Wenzhou Prefecture) under the name Aotai. Following a move to its current location it established cooperative ventures with other companies. In 1998 it became independent and changed its name to Huashan. The number of workers employed is seasonal, varying from 500 in the busy season (September to mid-December) to 400 in the off-peak season. Huashan has the capacity to produce around 600 suits per day but normally produces around 500. In total Huashan produces about 90 000 to 120 000 suits per year of a mid-range quality.

In 2003 Huashan produced a range of products – worsted, woollens and wool imitation – with pure wool products accounting for 35 per cent of products and synthetics about 65 per cent. Wool use has declined sharply from the year 2000 when the company solely produced pure wool suits. Behind this shift in product mix is the fact that Huashan is now a service processing company only and does not sell products under its own name. The shift from wool blends towards synthetics reflects the demands of their customers which are facing increased competition in a price-sensitive market.

Two types of garment firms may seek service processing contracts. First, the contractors can be garment dealers or brand name owners with no production capacity themselves. Second, other garment makers with production capacity contract service processors such as Huashan when they are too busy to fill their own orders. In the garment industry, a fundamental distinction exists between the brand management or sales companies

(Original Design Manufacturer) and the production companies (Original Equipment Manufacturer).

About one-half of the suits are made on service commission only, where the (usually large) customers supply the fabric. There are many small garment makers in places like Hangzhou that produce 20 000 to 30 000 suits per year but that also operate a brand name. For a company such as Huashan a service processing order for 30 000 suits would be very large, but some orders can be as small as 100 suits. Small customers usually require Huashan to buy the fabric.

After deciding the type of fabric inputs required to produce the garment output, Huashan searches for the best channel to purchase from. Huashan buys fabric from three channels, namely: fabric markets, traders that operate outside of the markets, and direct from the mills. There are several nearby fabric markets such as Hualong and Keqiao comprised of many fabric traders and stalls and these are usually the first-choice purchase channel. Sometimes the required fabric is not available at the markets, in which case other channels must be used. The mills – and also some fabric trading companies – have large sales teams that visit the garment makers. Although garment makers such as Huashan have design departments, they often base their fabric purchase decisions on the type of fabric that the mill or trading company sales representatives show them. Once they have a sample of the fabric, they can make a sample garment and show their Original Design Manufacturer customers. The mills and trading companies have a general idea of the type of fabric in demand, and so can usually supply fabric from existing stock. If it is not available, Huashan – and their customers – have to wait for it to be manufactured.

Huashan is representative of 2000 companies of a similar nature that operate in Wenzhou. In seeking to find a niche within this dynamic and highly competitive segment of the industry, Huashan is seeking to focus on what it does best – namely adding value in a design service for small companies – rather than trying to increase scale. Most service processors have their own product design departments to produce samples and attract customers. Huashan considers that these management systems, products and production techniques could be improved and that service processors should be more proactive in product design.

4.4 FABRIC MARKETS

In the post-reform era fabric markets have formed an integral link in the domestic wool textile marketing chain. However the status and role of these fabric markets is changing rapidly. To highlight the transformation occurring in this important wool marketing link, this section examines three different markets, namely: Qinghe – one of the largest wool fabric markets in North China; Nanjing fabric market – a smaller fabric market typical of markets in many cities throughout China; and Wenzhou Shangmao – traditionally one of the largest markets for worsted fabrics and located in the middle of the intensive wool-worsted garment-making area of Wenzhou.[4]

4.4.1   Qinghe Wool Fabric Market

The Qinghe fabric market is one of the biggest wool fabric markets in North China.[5] The Qinghe fabric market originally operated as a company under the former Ministry of Textile Industries called Maomaosi. Through the process of State Enterprise reform, Maomaosi has become a shareholder company although the State still holds the largest shareholding. The market is located in the Beijing suburb of Qinghe, which is a long-established wool processing centre with many old Beijing mills in the vicinity.

The Qinghe market contains around 100 stalls of which around 25 are mill stalls. The largest stalls sell around Rmb20 million worth of products per year (or around 200 000 metres of fabric), while the smallest have a sales fabric turnover of around Rmb200 000. A seasonal variation occurs in sales, with May to October being a quiet period.

Most stalls operate as wholesalers only. Stallholders pay a rent of about Rmb1100 per month to the market administration. Orders can be as large as 1000 metres of fabric, which equates to about one truckload. The stalls sell wool fabric produced in many parts of China and not just in the Beijing area. However mills with stalls at the market only sell their own product. Examples of a private stallholder and mill-aligned stallholder at the Qinghe markets appear in Boxes 4.1 and 4.2.

Box 4.1   Private stallholder – Qinghe market

One of the private stallholders at the Qinghe markets visited by the authors was an agent for the Yangguang (Sunshine) mill. The value of the fabric in the showroom was Rmb400 000, which placed it as one of the smaller traders at the market. However the nearby warehouse stored fabric for the stallholder with a value of Rmb3 000 000. Despite being an agent for Yangguang, a lot of fabrics were sold from other mills as well. While part of the fabric was sold on a commission – which is usually only about 2 to 3 per cent – most of it was purchased on credit. That is the fabric was purchased from Yangguang (and other mills) but did not have to be paid for until it was sold by the fabric trader. Thus small traders can enter the fabric trade without excessive initial capital requirements, while mills can transfer any price risks to these small traders. Institutional buyers account for 60 per cent of the customers purchasing from this stall, with garment makers and small dealers making up the remainder.

Fabric at this wholesale market is purchased by garment makers, tailors and fabric dealers. Most of the garment makers come from Beijing but many are also based in Hebei (Shijiazhuang, Chengde and Zhangjiakou), Shanxi (Taiyuan) and Tianjin. Many garment makers examine samples at Qinghe fabric market, but then purchase the fabric directly from the mill. Apart from having stalls that also act as showrooms at the market, some of the larger mills operate separate offices in the city (such as Yangguang's office in the World Trade Centre).

Box 4.2   Nijiaxiang stall – Qinghe market

The Nijiaxiang mill established a stall at the Qinghe markets in 1999 which also acts as its Beijing office. At the front of the showroom are racks of fabric samples which are embossed with the mill's brand – Hupao (running tiger). The label has information on sample, composition, weight, yarn (warp and weft) count and width.

The manager of the stall is an employee of Nijiaxiang, while four other staff in the office are paid on a commission basis. Most of their sales occur not through the showroom but by sending agents out to the garment makers.

The annual turnover value of the office is around Rmb20 million and accounts for less than 5 per cent of all Nijiaxiang's sales, with some 70 per cent of Nijiaxiang's sales going through offices in Guangzhou, Wenzhou and export markets. Most garment makers buying from the Nijiaxiang office and showroom purchase in 1000- to 2000-metre lots, compared with purchases from the Guangzhou and Wenzhou offices where individual transactions are around 10 000 metres.

Trends at the market reveal some of the broader changes in consumer preferences within China as a whole. Most of the fabrics sold at the Qinghe market are worsted rather than woollen fabrics. The width of fabrics must meet national standards of 144 cm which is the old normal width. However mills need to be flexible and meet current user demands, which involve fabric widths of 150 cm to 155 cm. Market administrators' perceptions of market developments were that southern mills produce 50 per cent wool fabrics, while customers in North China prefer thicker and heavier fabrics of 70 to 80 per cent wool. At the same time the weight of the fabric is decreasing – from an average of 500 grams per metre in the 1980s down to around 300 grams per metre in the early 2000s. Buyers observe the name of the mill woven into the side of the fabric as an indicator of quality. Many final consumers want comfortable and cheap clothes (including casual wear) and are not too concerned about whether it is pure wool, especially if this means that it is harder to wash and iron. However lightweight fabrics are more in demand now, requiring higher count (namely, lower-micron) wools.

The company operating the market does not provide any price reporting information or accounting services, with market administrators arguing that stallholders preferred to keep their negotiated prices secret for commercial reasons (although tax reporting would also seem to play a part). About Rmb600 000 per annum is spent on television advertising to promote the market and advertisements also appear in the *China Textiles* newspaper.

4.4.2 Nanjing Fabric Market

The Nanjing fabric market is located in a department store like building and is one of a number of similar markets in Nanjing and in other cities throughout China. Although there are over 100 stallholders – a similar number to the Qinghe fabric market – the stalls are much smaller, less well defined and more retail oriented than at Qinghe. Furthermore there is also less variety in the fabrics sold.

The stalls conduct both retail and wholesale sales, with the difference relating to the purchase volume. Most of the customers are retail, but in terms of overall sales volume, wholesale buyers are more important. Small retail stores, small garment makers and tailors act as the wholesale buyers. Stallholders estimated sales at between 20 to 30 metres per day, but wholesale buyers can push sales volume up to 100 to 200 metres per day. To place the size of the market in context, total annual fabric sales through the market equate to around the annual fabric production of one large mill. Like Qinghe, the range of consumer services was limited but it did have tailors to make fabrics into garments and computer-aided garment pattern makers.

Fabric labels are extremely basic with few identifying characteristics – simply the width of cloth and price. Thus both retail and wholesale customers purchase simply on the basis of the look and feel of the fabric plus any other verbal information that the stallholder might provide. Some mills embroider their name and fabric type on the side of the fabric, and this may help mills located in remote areas promote their product among the plethora of small garment makers.

Three different types of stalls operate at the market, namely:

- Mill stalls run by employees from large mills such as Lanzhou Sanmao (Gansu), Nanjing Sanmao, Jiangsu Sanmao, Chifeng Ermao (Inner Mongolia), Yangguang, Shanghai Xinfeng and Shanghai Sanmao. The stalls sell only fabric from their own mill. Quality assurance plaques and advertising for the relevant mill are prominently displayed by these stalls.

- Private stallholders who advertise under the banner of a particular mill (including those above) and sell the fabric of that mill but who also sold a range of fabrics from other sources.

- Private stallholders that sell all types of fabrics from unspecified sources. The prices at these stalls are generally lower than the mill stalls and private stallholders tied up by exclusivity arrangements.

4.4.3 Wenzhou Fabric Market

Wenzhou Shangmao market used to be one of the largest markets for worsted fabrics in China. However its decline in importance relative to other marketing channels has been more dramatic than the fabric markets mentioned above. Activity at the market was extremely strong from the 1980s to the middle of the 1990s. Between 1993 and 1995, 180 worsted wool fabric mills sold at the market, compared with only 40 in 2003. For all fabric types, around 400 fabric trading companies or stalls at the market registered with the Industry and Commerce Administration Bureau in 2003, of which 280 belonged to the Wenzhou Textile Industry Association. Market administrators said that in the peak years of 1993 to 1995, the market traded about Rmb2 billion worth of worsted fabrics per year, but this had decreased to Rmb500 to Rmb600 million by 2003.

Before 1998 about 90 per cent of the fabrics used by Wenzhou garment makers came from this market. But at the end of 2003 this figure was close to 50 per cent with the market in steady decline. Market officials point out that consumer preferences towards more casual clothes and less emphasis on fibre type had also contributed to the decline of the market. There are now more synthetic fabrics on the market with prices around Rmb10 to Rmb20 per metre compared with Rmb60 to Rmb70 per metre for 60s-count worsted fabrics. Thus the emergence of large garment makers as part of industry restructuring has had a profound impact on fabric markets.

Although the shift in domestic preferences has undoubtedly occurred, it does not fully explain the decline of the Wenzhou market. A more telling factor may be that with the increasing size and sophistication of garment makers in and around Wenzhou, a larger proportion of the fabric trade occurs through direct trade with mills, rather than through the market. Only the smaller garment makers (with fewer than 200 workers) and individual tailor operations now buy at the stalls at the market.

Many stalls at the market have changed their focus to becoming agents and acting as intermediaries for fabric importers. In addition the nature of the stalls and shops in the market is changing to that of showrooms and central offices for mobile traders to operate from. As a means of linking fabric and garment makers, fabric markets are becoming less efficient. Given that the absolute volumes of worsted fabrics and garments in China are increasing, fabric markets such as Wenzhou are becoming a much smaller marketing channel for worsted fabrics.

4.5 DOMESTIC WOOL TEXTILE FABRIC COMPANIES

Other key intermediaries in wool textile marketing are wool textile fabric companies. Although numerous small fabric dealers supply localized markets, this section focuses instead on the larger fabric traders that operate on an inter-regional scale and act as intermediaries between mills and garment makers.

There are a number of such companies, especially in large wool textile garment-making and consuming regions such as Shanghai, Wenzhou, Guangzhou and Beijing. Several trading companies including Aijian (one of the largest in China), Yuanda (associated with the Jodoll Company overviewed above) and Wenzhou Yangguang are outlined in this section, while dealers at the Tongxian sweater market are outlined in Section 4.7.4.

4.5.1 Aijian Fabric Company

Aijian's origins stem back to the formation of the People's Republic. Prior to 1949 many textile companies operated in the Shanghai region before being disbanded or nationalized. The reforms of the late 1970s saw the city government return the money to the original owners who in turn established the Aijian Company. The wool textile part of the company commenced in 1985. Aijian was originally administered by the Ministry of Foreign Trade and Economic Co-operation because many of its activities were in import–export and in petrochemicals.

Aijian is involved in a large range of activities and is listed on the Chinese Stock Exchange. The wool fabric company is a subsidiary of the main Aijian Company. At their peak in 1996 the subsidiary handled 3 million metres of fabric but the downturn in the industry since then has reduced its turnover to around 2 million metres or about 1 per cent of all fabric produced in China. Within the fabric part of Aijian, wool textiles is the main business. Company managers claimed more lucrative returns can be made from wool than in lower-value fabrics or in cotton, which both have tight margins.

Aijian managers primarily see themselves as market intermediaries. Their main customers are the small to medium-sized garment makers, but they are involved in a range of activities revolving around the marketing of fabrics. Their 12 retail outlets account for one-third of the 2 million metres of fabrics they handle. The other two-thirds are commission sales. The commission sales now involve filling orders for small to medium-sized garment makers because, as mentioned in Section 4.2, large garment makers deal direct with mills. However Aijian managers would also like to increase the amount of fabric that they sell for mills to garment makers. This channel may take on increasing importance in the new marketing environment where mills need to be more proactive in their marketing and seek out customers, rather than vice versa. Aijian also sells fabric for Hong Kong companies.

On the retail side, the Aijian brand (either "AJ" or the Aijian logo) is embossed on the side of the fabric. Important synergies exist between the retail and the dealing and commission sides of Aijian's business. For instance if Aijian needs to purchase more fabric from a mill than is required to meet an order from a small garment maker, it can sell the surplus fabric through its own retail outlets. Aijian is also partly vertically integrated in terms of producing some of its own garments such as slacks.

Small to medium-sized garment makers that Aijian deals with rarely use physical attributes when ordering fabric. Instead garment makers supply a sample which the mill to whom Aijian sends the order then seeks to replicate. The mill undertakes an experimental or sample run for the customer before a full production run occurs. Mills commonly produce to a particular order but also produce and sell from stocks. Minimum sizes of orders that mills service are around 300 metres for small mills and 1000 metres for large mills. If the size of the order is below the minimum, Aijian simply purchases the minimum and sells any surplus through its retail outlets, meaning it can deal with a wider range of orders than mills or small fabric dealers.

When Aijian places a fabric order on behalf of (garment-maker) customers, the mill usually has 60 days to deliver. As mentioned previously this time constraint virtually precludes mills from sourcing specific types of wool from overseas, and requires them to use commonly available wool inputs in stock in China.

The form of the contract used by Aijian (and other fabric traders) in exchange focus more on timing, dispute resolution and product assurance than they do on product specification. The lack of product specification in contracts is also reflected in the basic labels on the fabric displayed in Aijian's retail and wholesale outlets and distribution showroom which simply indicated wool percentage and width as well as a series of fabric care icons and labels. On an interrelated issue the Shanghai Textile Association conducts fabric testing for Aijian, according to national fabric standards.

Apart from some Hong Kong trade, Aijian does not export fabrics. However it does import and deal in high-quality fabric from European mills for use in the production of high-quality garments. At the end of 2003 its retail store in Shanghai was advertising Louis brand fabric for around Rmb600 per metre and Thomson fabric for in excess of Rmb1000 per metre, which compares with domestic fabric that usually sells for less than Rmb100 per metre. Importing wool fabrics is seen as a growth area for companies like Aijian and increasing globalization will place further pressure on high-quality worsted mills in China.

Image 4.3   Tongxian sweater market

The huge Tongxian market in north-eastern Zhejiang is a labyrinth of sweater dealers and a hive of activity. The sweaters make their way to all parts of China as well as overseas countries. The market has good transport and logistic services to facilitate the distribution.

4.5.2   Yuanda Worsted Fabric Trading Company

Yuanda Worsted Fabric Trading Company is associated with and indeed predates the Jodoll Garment Making Company described in Section 4.3.2. As mentioned, various complementarities exist between the garment company and the fabric trading company. In particular the company sources fabric for its own garment-making operation, and the fabric-trading arm (Yuanda) can sell the fabric to other garment makers as well. Although the Yuanda name does not appear on the edge of the fabric – as is the case with companies such as Aijian – plans were in place to adopt this practice from 2004. The name of the mill that produced the fabric does not appear on the fabric either because, the company managers explained, the garment maker that develops the fabric does not want to convey the source mill of the fabric to other garment makers.

Large garment makers such as Jodoll interpret demand and design fabric, not the mills. This has flow-on effects for associated trading companies like Yuanda.

Because Yuanda deals mainly in mid- to high-value fabrics, it sells primarily to the larger garment makers. Large runs are often made on the basis of the orders from garment makers, but it also has fabric made for speculative trade. It researches the market and develops its own types of fabric, and sometimes have garments made from it as samples to show garment makers. The fabric price varies greatly from Rmb80 to Rmb400 per metre, with institutional buyers at around Rmb110 to Rmb120 per metre. Some fabric (about 20 per cent) is imported, but the remainder is sourced domestically. Orders for worsted fabrics need to be placed 35 to 90 days ahead, with an average of 60 days (which is the industry average). As mentioned in connection with Aijian, this relatively short lead time constrains mills from acquiring special raw material supplies from overseas.

4.5.3 Wenzhou Yangguang Fabric Trading Company

Wenzhou Yangguang is a fabric trader that operates out of the Wenzhou fabric market overviewed in Section 4.4.3. The company has no ownership relations with the large Yangguang (Sunshine) mill group, but is permitted to "hang the plaque" of Yangguang with which it has a close sales relationship. This is a common arrangement between Yangguang (and also other mills) and their sales agents and outlets.

The sales divisions of fabric traders such as Wenzhou Yangguang place their orders with the mills up to six months in advance, pay a deposit (about 20 to 30 per cent), pay the balance on delivery, and then try to sell the fabric. If the fabric cannot be sold, attempts are made to return the fabric to the mill at a negotiated price. Three categories of buyers deal with Wenzhou Yangguang, namely: garment makers in Wenzhou; garment makers and tailors from throughout China; and garment traders from Guangzhou who buy the fabric and have it made into garments on a commission basis.

Intermediary companies such as Wenzhou Yangguang take all the risk in interpreting the demand from the three types of customers mentioned above. In the past mills would send fabric samples to the trader who would have it made into sample garments for display in the company's showroom at the Wenzhou Fabric Market. Garment makers would then reject or accept that product. This still happens but now the trading company has to be more proactive in requesting samples from the mills. Most ordering decisions still rely on subjective judgement rather than on any objective assessment of demand. Credit relationships are negotiable but traders are often wary as many garment makers go bankrupt and no insurance system operates for traders in this case.

4.6 SOURCING FABRIC DIRECT FROM MILLS

As pointed out earlier, many of the larger garment makers now source their fabric direct from mills. In this case garment makers place the fabric order with mills no more than 60 days ahead, although this can sometimes be longer for fabric sourced from overseas. The large garment makers have departments that design the fabric patterns on computer and then discuss the design with the production department at the mill. The mill can usually produce a sample of the fabric within 20 days. Mills are often forced to redesign the product, with most problems arising from colour matching. Responsibility for decisions about which raw wool (or wool top) materials and which milling processes to use reside with the mills rather than with the garment company.

Direct orders with mills can be as little as 500 metres, but standard orders between large garment makers and mills usually fall in the 5000 to 20 000 metre range. Each fabric order is specified on a separate order form, even if the difference between orders is small. The order form contains specifications including external appearance and lustre, width, source of wool and weight.

The factors behind the decision by garment makers to place their orders with particular mills are price,[6] quality, and the ability to retain confidentiality of the fabric order so they can differentiate their product from other garment makers. The latter factor also explains why large garment makers only deal with a limited number of reputable mills.

4.7 RETAIL CHANNELS

4.7.1 Brands

The plethora of garment makers and the highly dispersed nature of the garment sector make it difficult for them to differentiate their products and to attract premiums for higher-quality products. One approach has been to develop and promote branded products. Establishing a brand is essential for companies to move out of service processing, as garment makers cannot sell their own product to final consumers – even to institutional buyers – without a brand name. A brand name can also help develop the sophistication of their marketing and distribution channels and facilitate exchange within an even more fragmented retail sector. It can also make it easier to expand and modernize, as a brand is important in applying for bank loans, seeking investors or listing on the stock market.

The advantages for garment makers to develop a brand name are reflected in the massive proliferation of branded garment products over recent years. The larger and well-established companies and brands are well known by the public in China. These companies maintain brand recognition through extensive promotion and advertising campaigns, quality control programmes and retail franchise stores.

Most of the growth in branded garment products however has been by small and medium-sized garment makers. These companies cannot sustain the high costs and risks associated with building and maintaining a well-known brand name. Instead they simply undertake the straightforward process of registering a brand (with the local Industry and Commerce Administration Bureau) and attaching labels to their products. In such cases it is difficult to see how branding attracts premiums and achieves product differentiation. Furthermore the proliferation of brands has crowded out medium-sized enterprises that might have otherwise been able to establish niche brands.

Because of the proliferation of brands and the high costs of developing and maintaining a brand, many of the small and medium-sized garments makers have been forced to limit their role to that of a service processor. In this regard the gap between large garment makers and other garment makers appears to be widening.

One means of differentiating brands – while also maintaining the position of pre-eminent brands – is reflected in administrative status. As is common throughout China for all products, brands are given an administrative status based on their size. In Wenzhou for example, 44 brand names have received an "excellent level product" certification through the National Quality and Inspection Bureau. Two brands – Baoxiniao and Judger – are classed as "internationally renowned", two others – Meters Bonwe and Fapai – are "nationally renowned", while another 16 brands have (Zhejiang) provincial-level status.

The problem of branding is even more pronounced for the export market. Chinese garment makers export a significant proportion of their product overseas, often use English-language brand labels and have well-known domestic brand names. Nevertheless very few Chinese garments makers have established any form of international brand familiarity. In contrast with much of the domestic marketing, virtually all of the garments exported from China are produced under license for the overseas garment companies. In some cases this takes the form of joint venture arrangements. Some garment makers in Wenzhou are developing their facilities with the hope of outright purchase by a foreign joint venture partner in the post-WTO era.

Consequently one of the major challenges for Chinese garment makers will be to establish a more independent foothold in international markets. This will take the form of not only establishing international brand names but also developing overseas marketing expertise. If the experience of the large Japanese and South Korean conglomerates can be replicated by the Chinese garment industry, it will represent a massive transformation for the Chinese textiles industry.

4.7.2   Wool Fabric Retailing

Wool and wool blend fabric is sold through a variety of retail outlets including individual fabric shops, large retail outlets and department stores, and mill retail outlets.

The first type of retailer – small fabric shops – exists in large numbers in towns and cities throughout China. The fabric is sourced in a variety of ways but typically from fabric markets or from the smaller fabric dealers. Retailers are unlikely to purchase fabric directly from mills because of the relatively small size of particular product lines held in the stores. Fabric sold through these outlets is typically unbranded, mixed-fibre cloth at the lower value end of the market.

A second type of fabric retailer is the large retail outlets or department stores that either specialize in or have large fabric departments. Many of these outlets were originally State-owned stores, but have since been restructured. One such example is the Lao Jiefu store in Shanghai. In contrast with the smaller stores, most of the fabric sold has the supplier's name on the fabric edging, reflecting that much of the fabric sold in the store comes from some of the larger local mills in the region such as the large mills of Yangguang (Sunshine) and Shanghai Sanmao in the case of Lao Jiefu. However fabric was also sourced from large wholesalers such as Aijian described in Section 4.5.1. Product information appears on the fabric label but is limited, and so buyers purchase again on look and feel rather than on any objectively measured characteristics of the fabric.

Some of the larger mills have their own retail outlets. For example the large Yangguang (Sunshine) Group had its own stores in Nanjing Road, Xizang Road South and other stores throughout Shanghai – and indeed throughout China. In another example the Nanshan Group, which has some modern textile mills in north-eastern Shandong, has more than 150 retail outlets throughout China. Thus large mills that need to sell large volumes through the domestic market and who have an established brand name or reputation with everyday consumers may well integrate into retailing. The branding of worsted fabrics and the operation of their own retail outlets for fabric is an important development for mills.

4.7.3 Wool Suits

The distribution and marketing of final consumer goods such as wool suits, sweaters and other apparel is an enormous area beyond the scope of this book. However some comments are made about the marketing of suits from the garment makers mentioned in Section 4.3.

Large garment makers such as Baoxiniao have over 500 retail outlets throughout China. Others such as Jodoll (Qiaodun) have 180 franchise outlets in China and over 300 outlets in China sell Qiaodun suits, including department stores. Unlike arrangements for company-managed outlets, franchisees purchase the suits outright. The Louis Long Garment Company operates a chain of around 160 stores in China. The Dandinghe Garment Making Company is associated with 70 franchise stores as well as three of its own stores.

4.7.4 Wool Sweaters

Wool sweaters retail in a similar manner to other wool textiles. This section describes the Tongxian sweater market which provides an integral link between wool sweater manufacturers and final consumers.

The Tongxian sweater market in the north-east of Zhejiang Province is divided into nine sections and has over 4500 stalls. Each of these basic stalls covers an area of about 50 square metres containing samples at the front of the stall, some of their stock, while remaining inventory is warehoused nearby. Despite the small and basic nature of the stalls, they have a substantial turnover, each stall selling around 500 000 sweaters per annum.

The market is primarily a wholesale market although the sweater stalls do have some retail customers. The stalls are primarily to showcase samples of the trader's (or mill's) produce, which they then sell to retailers throughout China as well as to export traders who sell into the Middle East, Russia, Korea and other countries. The stallholders make use of market storage and loading facilities for delivery by their own trucks and by those of contractors, or organize garment makers to pick up the products. Although orders can be placed over the phone, many remote buyers still prefer to have face-to-face negotiations with traders, at least in the case of sweaters.

Although some of the sweater stalls are wholesale stalls of garment makers, most of the stalls are run by garment traders who operate their own brands. That is they commission small garment makers (with about 100 workers and 100 machines) to produce standard products, to which they then attach their own trading brand.[7]

4.8   EMERGING THEMES AND IMPLICATIONS

A number of themes have emerged from this investigation of the wool textile marketing sector, all of which have major implications for wool processing mills (discussed in the next chapter) and indeed for the whole wool textile industry.

First, as the sector closest to end consumers, garment makers are in the best position to assess consumer preferences for final products and to relay price signals down the marketing chain. One clear signal is that competition from synthetic fibres is rapidly increasing, especially on the highly price-sensitive domestic market for lower-grade generic textiles. Wool products are unlikely to be able to sustain acceptable margins in this low-value market over the long term.

Conversely, in the high-value domestic and overseas markets, consumers are becoming increasingly discerning about attributes such as weight, drape, easy care, colour, fashion and style. As wool is a major input into the fashion, suit and "white-collar" garment markets, this places enormous pressure on the wool textile mills. The pressure emerges not only in terms of technical and production practices, but also in terms of developing closer relationships between industry participants at this end of the industry.

Another crucial theme to emerge is that there seems to be scope for large garment makers, mills and trading companies to coordinate more closely. One important area of cooperation is required to more proactively develop markets and promote products. If such alliances could impact upon orders for, say, next season's fashion, this would allow the companies more time to prepare particular products, rather than being forced to rush orders through. The issue of timeliness is paramount. More proactive companies would have time to develop products, manufacturing and technical processes, rather than trying to replicate product from samples on very tight deadlines. Mills would also have more time to order the specific type of wool inputs required to produce the particular fabric in the most cost-effective way, rather than having to rely on readily available inputs that may be suboptimal. Such a process would also improve exchange of information across the top end of the marketing chain. For example mills would know more about consumer demands while garment makers would know more about the fibre inputs and processing techniques used in the manufacturing of the fabrics they buy. It would also increase the use of objective measurement and specifications on attributes throughout the chain, rather than objectively measured specifications being lost as they pass through the hands of trading companies.

Such a process would facilitate more direct exchange between the larger mills and the larger garment markers. Larger trading companies would still play a valuable role, but traditional channels such as fabric markets and smaller traders are unlikely to be key players in the more sophisticated, higher-value wool textiles chain. It may however facilitate the activities of medium-sized companies with their product differentiation and branding.

The view among many garment makers – large and small – in China is that processing mills should take a more proactive role in leading the whole industry. This requires mills to become more involved in the fashion market, producing commercially oriented fabrics based on extensive consumer market research, and then marketing this fabric to garment makers. This view is based on garment makers' perceptions of what happens in other countries, especially key European countries such as Italy.

Although only to a limited extent, large Chinese mills do observe changes in final demand informally through dealings and contacts or by attending trade fairs and fashion or fabric shows held by various textile industry organizations in China or overseas. In addition many mills develop their own samples that are used for marketing at the trade shows or directly with garment makers. Many of the larger mills also have their own design departments and research new products and weaving techniques. Much of this is based on what is technically feasible rather than on rigorous consumer research.

Nevertheless Chinese mills have not pushed the industry in the way that their European counterparts have, and are unlikely to do so. In essence mills have neither the experience nor skill to play a major role within the fashion industry. Their ability to take on risks is limited given the low profitability of the sector in recent years. Because mills only produce big runs on order from the garment makers, the latter take the risk in consumer acceptance of the fabric.

A more coordinated joint approach or alliance therefore is needed between the larger mills and garment makers. The scope for such alliances would seem feasible given the close relationship between larger garment makers and a relatively select group of larger mills. As mentioned earlier, large garment makers deal with a limited number of reputable mills to secure confidentiality over the type and specifications of the fabrics used to make their garments. This source of differentiation by garment makers would become much less important if mills were to take the lead in promoting particular fabrics.

Fashion Industry Associations and Wool Textile Associations could pursue some more generic promotion of fabrics but, as discussed in Chapters 3

Table 4.1   Features of passive versus proactive systems

Area of business	Passive system	Proactive system
Orders	Textile mills wait to receive orders (based on sample)	Textile mills and fabric traders proactively market to fashion houses and garment makers, based on a range of high-quality samples and technical specifications
Time	Rush to fill orders	Sufficient time to employ best practices and procure best inputs
Inputs	Use readily available inputs	Order specific inputs that can most cost-effectively make the best product
Coordination between sectors	Mainly to fill specific orders	Long term market and product development
Specifications	Based on subjective appraisal to look or feel like sample	More objective with specified attributes
Relationships between participants	Through intermediaries	More direct between major participants with close interaction in areas such as product design
Markets	More generic products	More differentiated products
Product identification	Locally known branding/labelling, with little product specification	International/national level branding. Company and/or alliance names as quality assurance

and 4, these institutions do not have the resources or structures to lead the industry in more specific ways.

A more coordinated approach would have broader beneficial consequences in terms of wool procurement. In the European case, because mills lead the research and development of fabrics for the following season, they have sufficient time to purchase specific wool inputs to produce the fabrics they feel will lead the market. In China however the passive response (as described in Table 4.1) means that mills have little time to procure wool inputs and produce fabrics to order. The industry "average" is for garment makers to give mills 60 days.

Although this period is considered sufficient from the garment makers' perspective, as explained in Chapters 5 and 6 the logistics for mills of sourcing specific wool from overseas make it virtually impossible for mills to purchase, ship and manufacture the fabric within 60 days under current arrangements. Thus garment makers exert an indirect pressure on mills to source the wool from available stocks of raw wool or wool top in China. Those stocks are usually of more generic types of wools. This may conflict with efforts by mills to buy more specific lots of wool or wool top to manufacture particular fabrics to an efficient product design and in a cost-effective manner.

The ongoing transition processes therefore centre on the move toward becoming more proactive, precision oriented, flexible and coordinated. Some aspects of a modern proactive system compared with the traditional passive system are outlined in Table 4.1. The three key industry segments that need to work more closely to create a more proactive system for marketing wool textiles are the mills, the garment makers and the textile trading companies.

NOTES

1   Wool textile mills and garment makers also supply uniforms to large non-governmental companies in China and to institutions in other countries.
2   There are other intensive areas of garment manufacture in other localities in China such as sweater production in Haiyang County in eastern Shandong.
3   Many shareholder companies are, in essence, individual private companies with a dominant shareholder or group of closely related shareholders. As these individual companies become larger, it is ideologically more acceptable for them to be referred to as shareholder companies even if ownership or management structures change little.
4   Apart from these three fabric markets, Section 4.7.4 provides a description and discussion of another (wholesale) wool textile market, namely the Tongxian sweater market in northern Zhejiang.
5   The Muxiyuan market in the south of Beijing is also a large market but deals in many other fabrics as well as wool. Another big market called Muyushi operates out of Liaoyang City in Liaoning Province.
6   In general, prices are considerably higher through the markets than directly from the mills. This is one reason why large garment makers bypass the markets and deal directly with mills, and also why small garment makers may suffer a competitive disadvantage in sourcing supplies.
7   Although the Tongxian market handles a vast number of sweaters, there are concentrations of sweater makers in other parts of China as well. One of the largest wool sweater production areas in China is Haiyang County in eastern Shandong Province. There are over 360 wool enterprises in the county (mainly wool sweater producers) that employ 100 000 people. In 2002 county officials had plans to establish a large sweater trading market (in competition with markets such as that in Tongxian).

5. Restructuring the Processing Sector

Processing mills occupy a central position in the wool textile supply chain. The economic health of the entire wool and wool textile industry depends on the mills. Potentially the mills could play a pivotal role in completing the economic transition of the industry. They are in the position to interpret the changes in the demand for finished products and translate this into demand for raw and semi-processed wool. [1] They can lead the adoption of new technology with the potential to maintain and expand the international competitiveness of the Chinese wool textile industry.

Domestically, especially in parts of eastern China and in the poorer, remote areas of western China, the mills represent large centres of technology, capital, employment and a source of government revenue. Furthermore they have a strong connection with wool growing and marketing, and have been used to promote regional development in some pastoral areas. Even excluding this mass of households and companies up- and down-stream of the wool processing sector, wool processing mills in China employed some 600 000 workers in 2003, although this figure was well down on the 1 million workers employed before 1989.

Outside the wool textile industry however wool processing has struggled to build a status as an economically important or strategic industrial activity. [2] Wool textile mills have faced the brunt of economic and enterprise reform measures and have had to come to terms with new market realities with few industry specific measures to soften the blow.

Changes in the structure of the wool processing sector and the forces behind these changes are the focus of this chapter. The wool processing sector comprises mills of many and varied types. Thus much of the chapter explores similarities and differences in the adjustment paths of the different types of mills.

The central issue for mills is how to adapt from an environment where all mills could survive by producing generic products, often with State support in some form or another. The commercial realities in a new political and agribusiness environment require more differentiated products and manufacturing processes. Not all mills have or can make the transition. Key factors analysed in this section include the ability of mills to withstand macro-reform and policy measures while at the same time making changes to internal structures, including specialization, technological and management changes. The type of mill influences the way these transformation challenges are met.

Sections 5.1 and 5.2 give an overview of the stages of reform in the wool textile processing sector, and the connections between policies and institutions designed to facilitate industry restructuring with the actual changes in ownership, governance and management practices. The remaining part of the chapter uses this framework to discuss these components in detail.

5.1 OVERVIEW OF RESTRUCTURING IN WOOL TEXTILE MILLS

Although wool textile mills have been undergoing transition for many years, the restructuring process began in earnest in the mid- to late-1990s. In this section, official statistics from the Statistics Centre within the National Textile Industry Bureau are used to reveal the broad nature of the restructuring process that has occurred since the mid-1990s. This big picture serves as a prelude to the detailed discussion of policies, institutions and reforms at the enterprise level that have impacted upon wool textile mills.

Figure 5.1 highlights the proportion of loss-making wool textile mills by three broad groups of mills, namely State-owned or controlled mills, collective enterprises, and foreign-invested enterprises.[3] The proportion of wool textile mills incurring losses over the 1997 to 2002 period was extremely high, with almost half of State-owned or controlled enterprises incurring losses. Although the proportion of loss-making mills declined over the period, they remained very high in 2002 suggesting that restructuring is still very much in progress. Foreign-invested enterprises (around 35 per cent) and collective enterprises (around 20 per cent) had a much lower proportion of loss-making mills, but again the proportions suggest that further changes are likely.

The restructuring manifested itself in various ways including a change in the number of wool textile mills by type, as illustrated in Figure 5.2. The numbers of State-owned or controlled enterprises as well as the number of collective enterprises fell by around 40 per cent between 1999 and 2002. In contrast the number of foreign-invested enterprises was much more stable.

However the decline in numbers of wool textile mills has not been matched by a corresponding decline in the value of wool textile production, as illustrated in Figure 5.3. Thus the restructuring especially among State mills and collective enterprises has involved a move to fewer but larger mills,

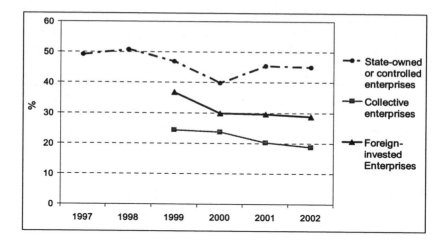

Figure 5.1   Proportion of loss-making wool textile mills by type

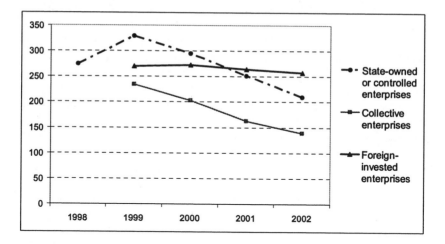

Figure 5.2   Number of wool textile mills by type

and is associated with for example mergers of loss-making mills or sections of mills into broader groups or company structures.

Indeed as shown in Figure 5.4, the level of annual investment in the wool textile industry increased substantially from around Rmb0.5 billion in 1998 to Rmb2.5 billion in 2002. Thus the restructuring process that took on a renewed vigour and emphasis with some of the measures outlined in Sections 5.2 and 5.3 has required significant investment capital. Figure 5.4 reveals that

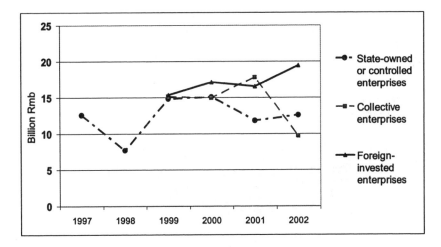

Figure 5.3   Value of output of wool textile mills by type

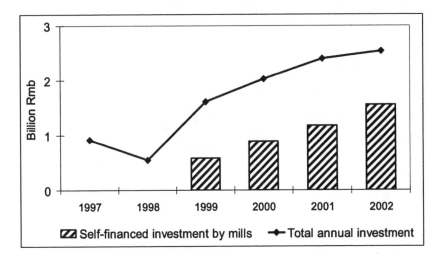

Figure 5.4   Annual investment in wool textile mills: 1997 to 2002

much of the investment has been self-generated by the mills themselves, rather than coming from external sources of capital. Figure 5.5 breaks down the sources of investment in more detail for 2002. Around two-thirds of the investment came from self-generated capital with the remainder relatively evenly split between foreign capital and domestic loans. Investments sourced from the government or share markets were insignificant. Overlooking the definitional weaknesses of the data and some of the more innovative efforts at raising capital in very recent times, the figures highlight the need for enterprises to generate their own sources of capital in the restructuring process.

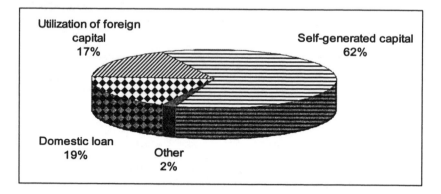

Figure 5.5   Source of investment capital for wool textile mills: 2002

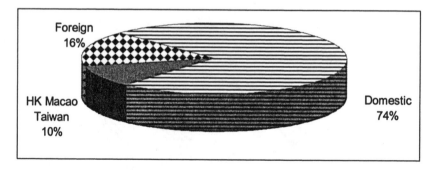

Figure 5.6   Source of investment capital in wool textile mills by region: 2002

The need for mills to raise their own capital creates problems however when viewed in the light of the proportion of mills making losses as shown in Figure 5.1. Thus mills have had to restructure to generate equity in a situation where retained earnings or past savings may be minimal given the chronic losses being incurred. Thus enterprises have had to move to a diverse array of ownership and governance structures to generate funds, including employee and management equity and other means facilitated by the Asset Management Commissions as outlined in Section 5.4.3.

Figure 5.6 reveals the source of this investment capital by region of registration, which is channelled predominantly to mainland Chinese (domestic) enterprises. Figures 5.7 and 5.8 provide a further breakdown of the registration statistics of the wool textile mills that were recipients of investment capital in 2002. For domestic enterprises, over one-third of capital in 2002 was directed to State-owned or controlled enterprises. However shareholder and various other limited liability companies received almost half of the capital invested in 2002, which is an indicator of their growth and likely importance in the future. It also indicates that these ownership types are favoured over State-owned Enterprises and Township and Village Enterprises (which account for just 8 per cent of new investment) as vehicles for future development in the industry. About half of the investment by foreign-invested companies took place though wholly owned foreign enterprises.

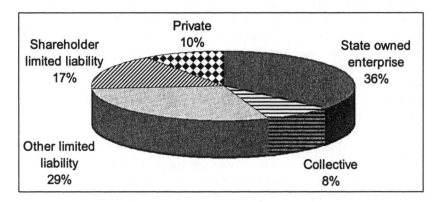

Figure 5.7   Proportion of capital invested in domestic wool textile mills by registration status: 2002

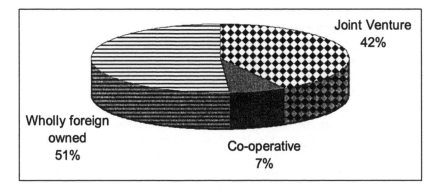

Figure 5.8   Proportion of capital invested in foreign-invested wool textile mills by registration status: 2002

The following section outlines some of the strengths and weaknesses of the traditional ownership structures that were brought into the new structures, along with an overview of the link between the new structures and the institutions and policies implemented to facilitate the restructuring.

5.2   STAGES OF REFORM IN THE PROCESSING SECTOR

The overview of restructuring in Section 5.1 revealed a challenging and dynamic path of reform that has gathered pace in recent years. Figure 5.9 captures some elements of this path. The top of the figure highlights the sequential nature of reforms involved in the transition process. Substantial progress has been made in macro-level reforms that have shaken up ownership and governance structures. Within this broader environment, mills must now address more micro-level reforms related to mill management, information, accounting, research and development, logistics and marketing, mill infrastructure, input/output selection and analytic skills. Most mills currently lie on the dotted line that distinguishes between these macro- and micro-level reforms.

Institutional reform has taken place in parallel with the broader economic and industry reforms. As discussed in Chapter 3, institutional constructs of the Central Planning era have been abolished and specific functions transferred to newly established institutions. These measures have been effective in forcing change in ownership and governance structures of the mills. As with mills, industry institutions – associations in particular – must now address the challenges of micro-level industry reform within the industry. This involves playing a facilitating rather than coercive role, especially in the delivery of services. To be effective in these roles requires an upgrading of their institutional capacity.

There are several dimensions to the reform of the mills themselves. Mills have embarked on the reform process from different ownership structures, simplified in the diagram to include State-owned Enterprises, Township and Village Enterprises, private mills and foreign-invested mills. Regardless of ownership and governance structures, mills must make the transition to become progressive and efficient mills with the characteristics shown in the right-hand side of Figure 5.9. If not, they face closure because of their unviability, because they do not comply with environment regulations, or because they become entangled in periodic government programmes to cut surplus and outdated capacity (bottom of Figure 5.9).

With regard to ownership and governance reform, different types of mills take different paths to becoming more progressive and efficient. One feature of the process is that both State-owned Enterprises and Township and Village

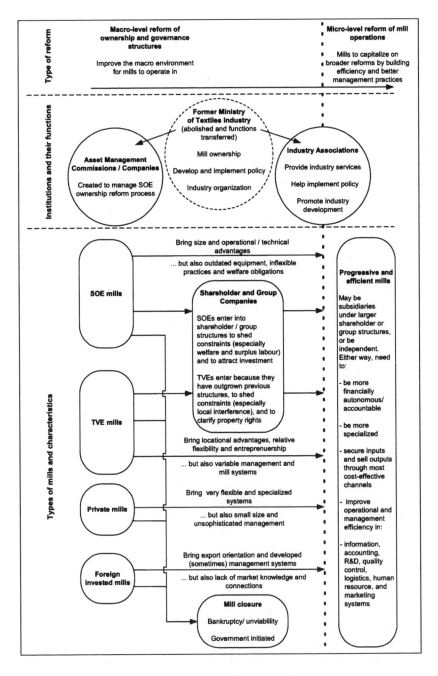

Figure 5.9   Elements of reform in the Chinese wool processing sector

Enterprises have, in a process of convergence, tended to use group company structures as a vehicle for reform. Both State-owned Enterprises and Township and Village Enterprises enter into these structures to shed constraints, but the specific reasons vary. State-owned Enterprises form into shareholder or group companies as a means of reforming governance structures, raising capital from both within and outside the State-owned Enterprise, and shedding surplus labour and welfare obligations. Most Township and Village Enterprises entering into shareholder or group structures have outgrown previous structures and need to shed the confines of collective and localized governance. Private companies, many of which can also be classed as Township and Village Enterprises, and foreign-invested companies do not have the same ownership and governance constraints and so can approach the transition process from their existing structures.

The arrows spanning the left and right sides of Figure 5.9 illustrate the characteristics that different types of mills carry into the reform process. The top sides of the arrows list advantages while the bottom sides list disadvantages. Distinguishing the advantages and disadvantages of mill ownership types is problematic because of the variability within each type. Nevertheless some interesting patterns or features emerge that often conflict with popular belief. State-owned Enterprises have relatively well-established mill systems (in areas such as information, accounting and inventory) as well as substantive infrastructure and technical skills that can be an advantage in facing the operational challenges of the modern wool textile industry. These characteristics can be lacking in Township and Village Enterprises and private mills. However Township and Village Enterprises and private mills flourished, particularly in the first decade of the post-reform era, mainly because they did not have the administratively imposed high cost structures, the employee welfare obligations and inflexibility of the State-owned Enterprises. However as these constraints are removed for all enterprise types, and with the influx of new entrants, Township and Village Enterprises will need to find new sources of competitive advantage.

Regardless of their backgrounds and structures, mills in the modern era of the wool textile processing need to be progressive and efficient if they are to survive and flourish. These mills will tend to be more financially autonomous and specialized in particular activities. This holds even for companies that are subsidiaries of large group structures. These companies will come under pressure to source cost-effective inputs and identify profitable market outlets, which may lie outside the group structure. Hence progressive companies need to be highly skilled and well equipped to integrate with other industry actors. Well-developed mill systems in information, accounting, research and development, quality control, logistics and marketing will be essential, along with strong infrastructure and highly skilled technicians and managers.

Few mills in China fit such a description and so sit on the dotted line on the right-hand side of Figure 5.9. As such, despite the years of successful reform of institutional, economic, industry, ownership and governance structures, the overall reform process is far from over and is entering a new phase centred around micro- and mill-level reform. For many mills this part of the reform process is extremely challenging and so will usher in further industry rationalization.

5.3   SPECIFIC POLICY INSTRUMENTS

Enterprise reforms relating to ownership transition have been implemented in earnest in the wool processing sector. Furthermore the adjustments have not been significantly softened by other compensatory measures.[4] That wool textile mills have borne the full brunt of reform measures is a result of their relative unimportance in terms of economic size and strategic role in the economy as a whole. Nonetheless there are various policy measures that have impacted upon the wool processing sector and warrant mention. Collectively the measures are oriented towards structural adjustment through consolidation, modernization and streamlining of the industry.

5.3.1   Spindle Cutback

China has implemented a series of programmes since the mid-1990s to cut back capacity in a number of industries including textiles, oil, fertilizer, cement, power, steel, coal, sugar and pharmaceuticals. The primary aim has been to rein in rampant overproduction (ChinaOnline 2000). However the opportunity has also been taken to restructure, increase value and modernize industries in a so-called "adjustment of industry structures". Specifically capacity is curbed by: removing old or dated manufacturing equipment; restricting purchases to new equipment; limiting output but encouraging exports and the development of high-value markets; laying off and aiding redundant workers; and targeting small and polluting companies. With regard to the latter, small companies have been pressured or coerced to merge with larger groups (as outlined in Section 5.6). The State Economic and Trade Commission and the Central Economic Work Commission implemented the capacity-cutting measures through incentives and by decree.

A highly visible part of this programme in the textiles industry has been the spindle cutback programme. The main target was the cotton processing sector where spindle numbers fell from approximately 40 million in 1997 to 30 million in 2000 with a government outlay of Rmb1 billion under multi-faceted terms (China Textiles Industry Association, personal communication).[5] The measures were targeted at ameliorating the impacts of laying off 1.2 million workers. Together with the assistance provided to domestic cotton production and marketing, the cotton processing sector is heavily subsidized. Wool processing mills and representative bodies have complained about the high and distorting level of subsidies provided to the cotton sector, but with little impact in key decision-making circles.

For the wool textile sector in particular, the spindle cutback programme involved the setting of a target in 1998 to cut the number of spindles in the wool processing sector by 1 million, 300 000 of which were to be cut in 1999. Subsidies were available to State-owned or controlled mills. For every 10 000 spindles cut, subsidies of Rmb14 million were to be provided to woollen mills and Rmb7 million for worsted mills. For mills in western China, the capital came solely from the central government. Mills in central China received government payments on a central to provincial government ratio of 7:3, while the ratio for eastern mills was 1:1. The stated aims of the programme in the wool textiles industry were to "cut output, improve the remaining capacity, improve quality, develop new products, overtake well known international manufacturers, improve market competitiveness, and build new economic levels".[6]

In reality the plan was not executed until 1999 and did not take effect until 2000 when a total of only 300 000 spindles were cut. Since 1997 the programme has only been partly responsible for cutting spindles from 4.08 million to 3.58 million.[7] Wool industry insiders complained this stemmed from capital being tied up in the cotton spindle cutback programme, with few subsidies actually provided to wool mills. The Chinese Premier, Zhu Rongji, also directed that only small mills that produce poor products or those in western areas be targeted.

Thus the spindle cutback programme has not been highly influential in the wool textile sector. However it does highlight the way that the Chinese government would like to go about the process of industry restructuring and the challenges it faces in some industries. The spindle cutback programme is also closely related to some other policies discussed below.

5.3.2   Other Policy Measures

The spindle cutback programme has been implemented in concert with a range of other policy measures, such as environmental regulations. These measures have exerted an impact similar to the spindle cutback programme in terms of consolidating industry structures.

Environmental issues feature prominently in the wool textiles industry, especially in relation to the management of scouring effluent, residual dyestuffs and chemical additives. In 1995 the textile industry discharged up to 900 million cubic metres of wastewater, a large proportion of which caused pollution in some form. China has implemented a series of national industrial and discharge standards and international standards such as ISO14000. A market for "green" textile products has also developed, especially in other countries.[8]

The environmental standards have proved difficult to attain, particularly for small mills. Since October 1996 about 10 000 small to medium-sized enterprises in the textile industry have closed because they could not meet national wastewater discharge standards. However it is not only the small mills that have experienced problems. Large mills under financial pressure have also found it difficult to install environmentally sound equipment, use better inputs, and employ better practices.

The closure of small mills, or their merger into larger mills or groups for environmental reasons, coincides with the broader programme toward consolidation described elsewhere in the chapter. Furthermore it coincides with tangible outcomes of the "Develop the West" programme which have facilitated contact between eastern and western mills. In several cases this has led to some high-profile mergers into larger groups. The concordance of policy outcomes has contributed to the dynamic and rapid restructuring of the industry.

5.4 INSTITUTIONAL SUPPORT FOR RESTRUCTURING

The scope and ongoing nature of enterprise reform and policy changes require institutional support. The broad institutional background upon which the reforms have been implemented was outlined in Chapter 3. Two institutions most closely related to wool processing mills – the Textile Industry Association and the State Assets Management Commission – are discussed in more detail below.

5.4.1 Textile Industry Association

The China Textile Industry Association and its local equivalents descend directly from the former Ministry of Textile Industry which held jurisdiction over all State-owned Enterprise mills and exercised strong planning and interventionist powers. As a specialized economic unit, the Ministry of Textiles Industry was subject to a series of administrative reforms that led to the severing of its ownership links with mills and its demotion to a non- or semi-governmental association.

The key elements of the reform process commenced in 1993. At the time the Ministry of Textiles Industry had a staff in excess of 500. The reform led to the Ministry of Textiles Industry being replaced by a Textile Industry Assembly with a staff of 200. In 1998 this body was further downgraded to the Textile Industry Bureau under the newly founded State Economic and Trade Commission, with a staff of 70. In another round of key administrative reforms in 2000 the bureau was disbanded. In its place a Textiles Industry Association was established with a staff of 100 people. Staff numbers are no longer subject to administrative decree but rather determined by the fees it can generate to employ staff.

Formally the Textile Industry Association is a non-governmental, non-profit organization charged with providing services for its members. On a vertical level, it comprises units at least down to provincial level. The horizontal organization of the association consists of a management hierarchy and a large number of member associations. [9] The organizations divide according to textile type (such as cotton, wool and silk), processes (such as dyeing and printing, machining, garment making) and other categorizations (such as textiles accounting and education).

Box 5.1   *The China Textile Industry Association*

The China National Textile Industry Association (also known as Council) acts as a peak body for all textile related industries and is a non-profit organization. According to the association's website, its aim is to provide services in the modernization of China's textile industry. The scope of services is as follows:
- Work out the guidelines and rules to supervise the performance of the industry; set up and improve the self-discipline working system; and protect the interests of the industry.
- Study and research the development and trends in the domestic and international textile industries.
- Participate in or provide consulting services for developing strategy, industrial policy, technological upgrading, market promotion and research, reform and opening up of the industry.
- Bridge the link between enterprises and the government, make recommendations and reports to the government, and undertake the various tasks entrusted by government.
- Coordinate the economic and technical relations between various sectors of the textile industry to promote the industrial rationalization and consolidation and strengthen value-chain integration and cooperation.
- Carry out international technical and economic cooperation and interchanges, conduct international visits, in-service education and training; organize trade meetings, international conferences, seminars and domestic and international exhibitions to expand markets.
- Participate in developing and amending the industrial standards; organize the relevant resources to implement these standards.
- Carry out promotion activities in trade, science and technology, investments, human resources and management for textile industry.
- Edit, publish and distribute textile industry publications.

The Textile Industry Association – like other associations derived from a government background – provides a link between government and enterprises and provides highly important industry services. The activities of the association are summarized in Box 5.1. Much of the activity of the Textile Industry Association occurs at the provincial level. The cases of the associations in Jiangsu and Shandong, outlined in Boxes 5.2 and 5.3, reveal how these associations operate.

Box 5.2   *Jiangsu Provincial Textile Industry Association*

The Jiangsu Provincial Textile Industries Association operated as a provincial Textile Industry Bureau under the former Ministry of Textiles Industry. In the reforms of 2000 when the central-level Textile Bureau was abolished, the provincial level Jiangsu bureau split in two ways. Some staff (and several enterprises) went to the Jiangsu Economic Trade Commission which manages small and medium-sized enterprises and has a role in exports and technical innovation. The remaining staff formed the Jiangsu Textile Industry Association. The association deals with various administrative aspects of the textile industry in Jiangsu, including services, macro-planning, and coordination between enterprises. It is structured into two main departments, namely planning and development (where plans are set for technology, projects, technical development and quality issues) and enterprise management (involving trade fairs and marketing).

Through the reform process, the bureau also formed a company called the Jiangsu Province Textile Group Corporation which is involved in many aspects of the textiles industry including machinery trade. In 2000 the corporation had an annual sales value of Rmb1.4 billion, export value of US$50 million and import value of US$10 million. It has a design department with ISO 9002 accreditation along with a research institute mainly concerned with chemical fibres. The corporation also has a wool quota and import rights.

5.4.2   China Wool Textile Industry Association

One of the member associations or sub-associations of the Textile Industry Association at the central level is the China Wool Textile Industry Association. A main office with seven staff operates out of Beijing while sub-branches can be found in provinces like Shanghai and Zhejiang.

The wool textile industry association receives levies from about 300 association members. Members include mills, traders, Supply and Marketing Co-operatives, the National Livestock Association, standards and testing authorities, Australian Wool Innovation, the Veterinary Station of the Animal Husbandry and Veterinary Bureau and other broader economic and trade groups. The association plays a major role in organizing conference and training activities. It also acts as the Chinese member of the International Wool Testing Organisation, and so is an integral link with the global wool

---

Box 5.3   Shandong Textile Industry Association

The Shandong Textile Industry Bureau had an office in each of the 17 prefectures and cities in the province. With the move to the Economic and Trade Commission at the end of 2000, the newly formed Textile Industry Association mainly provided services rather than administration or government control. At the prefectural city level, some of the former Textile Industry Bureaus became companies while others became associations. Prior to the reforms in 2000 the forerunner of the Textile Industry Association had ten departments and 70 staff. By mid-2002 it had downsized to two departments and 30 people, and was in the process of changing from what is essentially a government agency to an industry association. The association recognizes the importance of providing more specific information and services of direct use to the mills if they are to attract mill members once they lose their government financial backing.

One of the departments in the association analyses industry and trade production, exports, sales and "economic efficiency" information each month. This type of information is not used by mills themselves but by government units that feed information up to the central-level Textile Industry Association. Other duties include guiding mill planning and development, guiding technology development, and passing on government regulations such as the spindle reduction policy mentioned in Section 5.4.1. Mills do their own technology development work but the association can help them make contact with the Science and Technology Commission and other bodies for assistance to access subsidies or soft loans. The association conducts market research but only at a broad market level and not for specific types of products. The Shandong Textile Research Institute is under its administration but operates independently.

---

textile industry and its organizations. The International Wool Testing Organisation provides an important forum for the global wool textile industry in development of industry standards, laboratory accreditation, and the transfer of information and promotion of research and development through regular conferences. Thus the International Wool Testing Organisation, through the China Wool Textile Industry Association, provides the Chinese industry with a window on, or gateway to, the global wool textile industry.

The demise of specialized economic departments such as the Ministry of Textiles Industry has drastically reduced coercive powers over industry participants, including mills. However the reform also reduced China's institutional capacity to facilitate industry coordination, either within specific segments (such as processing mills) or between segments (for example upstream suppliers and downstream customers of mills). The institutional vacuum is one reason behind the lack of integration in the wool textile industry highlighted throughout this book.

In the absence of the development of an equivalent alternative organization, the Wool Textile Industry Association potentially has a key role to play in the future of the industry. Despite the "public good" or industry-wide nature of the services the association provides, government funding for its activities has declined to negligible levels in recent years. Thus the association relies on fees from members and charges for services it provides that, at present, allow it to perform only a small proportion of the services it could provide and which would be of benefit to the industry as a whole. To play a more proactive and expansive role, the association must become more oriented toward the needs of a modernizing industry, and provide services that industry actors are prepared to pay for in terms of fees, enthusiasm, effort and time. In other words the development of a more coordinated industry approach requires input from the industry actors themselves (especially mills). There are signs that this is occurring, both within and outside the Wool Textile Industry Association and where mills are organizing groups outside it.

5.4.3 State Asset Management Commission

After the disbanding of the Bureau of Textile Industry, the State Asset Management Commission was phased in to take jurisdiction over textile State-owned Enterprises at various levels. The commission is a powerful body directly under the State Council. However it is designed to be a temporary administrative home for State-owned Enterprises, especially at the local level. Its primary aim is to facilitate the transition of State-owned Enterprises to other ownership types and to ensure that the transition occurs properly without issues arising such as asset stripping and undervaluation. As mentioned in Section 5.1, new investment to facilitate enterprise restructuring primarily has to come from the enterprises themselves. A key role for the commissions involves finding or facilitating innovative ways this own equity can be generated in an environment where retained profits are low or negative.

The State Asset Management Commission has a vertical hierarchy at least down to the provincial level. Its reach at lower levels of government varies by region. In most prefectural-level cities, the functions of the commission are carried out by more proactive State Asset Management Companies, and these companies can be extended to county levels if and when the need arises.[10] To understand how these companies operate at local levels, consider the case of the Changzhou State Textiles Management Asset Company located in the heart of the wool-processing area of southern Jiangsu.

The Changzhou State Textiles Management Asset Company is one of three such companies in Changzhou City – the others relate to machinery, as well as chemicals and light industry – all of which fall under the broad umbrella of the Changzhou Industry Investment Company which ultimately answers to the Changzhou Economic and Trade Commission. The Changzhou State Textiles Management Asset Company has a board of seven directors, a supervisory committee and five departments, namely an Administrative

Department, an Investment Development Department, a Political Work Department, a Personnel Department, a Finance Department and a General Office. When the Changzhou Textile Industry Bureau was abolished, about half of the 40 staff came to work for the Changzhou State Textiles Management Asset Company. So the demise of the Textile Industry Bureau system and the establishment of the State Asset Management system (along with the establishment of Textile Industry Associations) are closely related.[11]

The Changzhou Textiles State Assets Management Company held jurisdiction over 25 textile State-owned Enterprises in 1998. As these mills underwent transition to other – primarily shareholder – ownership types, the number of companies fell to only six by the end of 2003. Ultimately the company expects to have longer-term jurisdiction over only one or two companies that have difficulties in attracting investors.

The main purpose of the Changzhou Textiles State Assets Management Company is to facilitate the ownership reform of State-owned Enterprise mills and to choose the most feasible and appropriate form of reform. Several specific roles are involved. First, the asset management company acts as an intermediary between the mills and various government departments for the flow of information on financial reporting (including tax and asset valuations), so as to help implement government policy and to coordinate on issues such as wool import quota allocation. It also makes personnel decisions for the mills under their jurisdiction, often involving the appointment of managers to oversee reform at the mills. The company monitors the way that the mills (and other textile enterprises) deal with retired workers during the transition process. It is also highly proactive in seeking and attracting outside investment to facilitate reform. However the company is not involved in specific mill operational and managerial decisions such as production, purchases and sales decisions.

The Changzhou Textiles State Assets Management Company does not receive government funding. In the early years it received a levy from the companies under its jurisdiction, but in recent years it has generated revenue from shares held in the companies it has invested in.

Besides attracting shareholders to the mills, and investing in mills itself, the company operates several other business ventures. For example the company administers the Textiles Industry Park in Changzhou which involves attracting companies to establish textile operations in the park and charging the associated fees and taxes. The park opened in 1991 and by 2003 had attracted 150 textile companies in areas including spinning, dyeing and finishing. The size and functions of such State Asset Management Commissions and companies clearly make them pivotal players in the economic transition process, which may continue for many years to come.

5.5 MILL REFORM MEASURES

China has witnessed dramatic changes in ownership structures of wool processing mills in the early 2000s. The changes have been prompted by a series of government and enterprise reforms some of which were outlined in Chapter 3. In general there has been a consolidation of mills, and especially in various stages of processing within the same region. However the effect of the reforms has varied depending on the original type of mill and region concerned.

The discussion below highlights some convergence in the ownership transition of mills in the worsted sector. Both State-owned Enterprises and Township and Village Enterprises are tending toward shareholder and group structures – or leaving the sector. The differences between these shareholder companies and other ownership types such as private and joint ventures[12] are becoming less significant in terms of competitive advantage. Furthermore the remaining disadvantages of being of a mill of a particular ownership type (especially State-owned Enterprises) can be offset by other advantages such as experience and infrastructure. Thus the ability of mills to make a transition is based less on ownership than on the ability to adopt new technology and management practices.

5.5.1 State-owned Enterprises

The history of the Chinese wool processing sector extends deep into the Central Planning era. State-owned Enterprises under the various administrative levels of the Ministry of Textiles Industry were the base on which the sector entered the reform era. Features of this era for State-owned Enterprises were directives of what and for whom to produce at what price, and where to source raw materials at what price. State-owned Enterprises still face obligations with regard to surplus labour and welfare payments,[13] pay higher effective tax rates than non-State-owned Enterprises, and face some administrative interference (especially with regard to personnel). The obligations still apply in a period when debt forgiveness, subsidies and preferential policies are becoming increasingly scarce.

The obligations and pressures made State-owned Enterprises highly vulnerable to the entry of the less constrained Township and Village Enterprises in the early reform period of the 1980s. Consequently they have struggled to adapt to the ongoing series of market changes and reform measures. Numerous large mills that operated in Beijing, Tianjin, Shanghai and other centres have closed or become technically insolvent. In 2002, of the 224 State-owned or State-controlled worsted (weaving) mills in China, 94 (or 42 per cent) incurred total losses of Rmb503 million (CNTIC, 2003, p. 38).[14]

Despite these competitive disadvantages, State-owned Enterprise mills have several distinct advantages over mills of other ownership types that are often overlooked. Detailed investigation of many mills of different ownership types revealed that State-owned Enterprises have consistently better technology, skilled and trained staff,[15] testing facilities, information systems and accounting systems. These features figure prominently in the modern wool processing environment for higher-value markets and explain why the largest and most advanced mills in China are State-owned Enterprises. Thus the issue for government and enterprise reforms is how to restructure State-owned Enterprises in a way that these favourable traits are not lost in ownership changes.

China's approach to the State-owned Enterprise reform process notionally follows the maxim of "retain the large and release the small; allow unprofitable enterprise to go bankrupt and sell profitable enterprises".[16] Supporting regulatory measures implemented include tax reform, bankruptcy regulations, and mergers and acquisitions embedded in the 1994 Company Law. The urgency of enterprise reform increased in 1998 when Zhu Rongji issued an edict that State-owned Enterprises were to be viable within three years.

Another influential edict came from the then President Jiang Zemin in 1996 to promote the formation of group or conglomerate structures into which many State-owned Enterprises have been absorbed. As will be discussed in Section 5.7, almost all large "comprehensive" mills have split into smaller subsidiary companies that perform specific functions and which, in turn, have been structured to come under the umbrella of a larger group company.[17] In other cases, the mills have been absorbed into very large group structures with other fully fledged, independent, subsidiary companies. Subsidiaries essentially run independently for the purposes of tax, profit retention and bankruptcy, but the group structure provides scope for transfer pricing and absorbing losses. In addition to filling the higher-level edicts, the creation of group structures provides a vehicle for mobilizing finance (such as through stock exchange listing) and other resources.

Fundamental to State-owned Enterprise developments has been the directive for government departments to divest themselves of State-owned Enterprises (see Chapter 3), a process that has occurred in several ways. Large central-level enterprises deemed strategically important to the State were transferred to relevant commissions. Bodies discussed elsewhere in this book such as the Supply and Marketing Co-operatives (Chapter 7); Chinatex and the China Textile Resources Company (Chapter 6) have been transferred to the central (Large-scale) Enterprise Work Commission. Several large group enterprises discussed in this section such as Huayuan that have bought local-level mills also fall under the loose jurisdiction of this commission.

Although these groups still have significant autonomy to make their own decisions, State involvement persists in terms of personnel and strategic decisions.

At the local level, the means of separating State-owned Enterprises from their specialized economic bureaus (government departments) has been to divest them to local government. A multilayered network of local government bodies are charged with overseeing State-owned Enterprises, including Economic and Trade Commissions, Planning Commissions, Supervisory Committees, State Asset Management Commissions, and State Asset Operating Companies. This has been the case for the vast majority of wool processing mills in China, and the base from which the wool textile processing sector has entered into the further reform measures discussed below. However ownership reform is always a messy business, and the reform process varies for different mills and regions as illustrated by the five examples below.

The first example concerns the Changzhou Spinning and Weaving Mill which lies in the heart of Chinese wool processing in southern Jiangsu. In 2003 the Changzhou mill fell under the jurisdiction of the Changzhou State Assets Management Company. Shares in the company have been purchased by a relatively small number of "insiders" (senior managers in the previous State-owned Enterprise), with only a small percentage being purchased by workers.[18] The mill has paid off workers to leave the company in order to reduce the workforce. Although this model has spread over most parts of Jiangsu and the industrialized east coast, some problems associated with it have been voiced by officials closely involved in the process. Some of the concerns inevitably relate to the welfare of workers, either with the company or laid off. Others involve the valuation of assets, especially where problems of information asymmetry arise in terms of managers (share purchasers) of the mill being in a superior position to know the real value of the mill. Assets of the State are effectively transferred to a small number of individuals who take out loans for the purchase using the valuation of the mill as collateral. The valuation of the company can be significantly increased after restructuring and then sold without net gains for the state or workers. Such a process does not necessarily conform to the notion that privatization will improve efficiency. However as elaborated below, management structures, technology and information systems may well be more important determinants of the long term viability of a mill than ownership structures.

A second example of ownership transition – common in the key wool textile province of Shandong – is illustrated in the case of the Ruyi Worsted mill. From 2002 the mill became one of 20 subsidiaries companies under the larger Ruyi Group. However all of the subsidiaries and the group itself are located in Jining City, and were closely associated State-owned Enterprises prior to the restructuring. The reform had two components. One component was the creation of the local Ruyi Group Company (which by late 2003 was applying but yet to be listed on the stock exchange). The second component involved reform to the ownership structure of the mill itself, under the administration of the local State Asset Management Company. The State Asset Management Company retained 10 per cent of the shares. The other shares were distributed more widely than in the case of Changzhou. The largest investor had 15 per cent of the shares, while other shareholders included 15 managers of the mill, and a series of institutional investors (including overseas investors), with a small distribution to employees.

A third example – common for large former State-owned Enterprises in western areas of China such as Chifeng Ermao and Lanzhou Sanmao – is where mills have been absorbed into larger, inter-regional group structures. These are among the better and more renowned mills in western China, and so have been able to attract outside investment to facilitate transition. The investors include the State-owned Enterprise Holding Company Huayuan Group (under the Central Enterprise Work Commission) based in Shanghai which has investments in a plethora of companies in the textile sector (including the newly acquired Wenzhou Lanbao garment maker). Huayuan invested around Rmb6.3 million in Chifeng No. 2 mill in eastern Inner Mongolia in 1998 – which then became a subsidiary of the Huayuan Group.[19] Another group called Kaikai has also incorporated the Lanzhou Sanmao mill.[20] Industry analysts surmised that these companies were encouraged to invest in the mills as part of the Develop the West programme.[21]

The fourth case involves numerous examples of mills being requested to merge with other mills in the vicinity to form group structures. For instance the Xiyu mill in Changji in Xinjiang combined with two other mills (Xinjiang No. 2 Worsted Mill and Xinjiang No. 3 Worsted Mill) at the end of 1999 to fall under a common group structure. However the mills claim that they still run independently for the purposes of tax, profit retention, bankruptcy and other key matters. Another example is the Bayi mill at Shihezi in Xinjiang which was established in 1958. This mill has recently merged with several other companies to form a group known as the Xinjiang Bayi Worsted Textile Company. Part of the initial reason for the formation of the group was the unsuccessful attempt to list the company on the stock exchange. Three other mills operate under the group structure namely the Shihezi Woollen Mill (blankets), the Shihezi Wool Production mill and the Yili Xibu Textile Mill (cashmere sweaters). The benefits from integration of disparate mills are not always obvious however and the group structures in some instances may have more to do with absorbing loss-making companies. The Xinjiang Production and Construction Corps has sunk considerable investment into the Bayi mill including Rmb20 million in 2000 and another Rmb25 million in 2001 to update equipment and product development.

A fifth form of restructuring for State-owned Enterprise mills has been to leave the wool textile sector altogether. That is they may have gone bankrupt or temporarily closed, or alternatively moved into completely separate activities (such as pure synthetics). These mills have not been able to attract the investment for a transition of ownership from either within the company (notably managers) or from outside investors. They have struggled to move up market segments or meet environmental standards, or have outdated equipment, and so have been eligible for the spindle cutback programme which essentially acts as a form of redundancy payout for the mills. These mills are most common in northern and western China. For example of the 12 sizable mills formerly in Xinjiang, only a few remain. In other major western cities, only one of the three mills in Lanzhou remains; none of the three mills in Hohehote (the capital of Inner Mongolia) remains and only one of the three in Chifeng City (in eastern Inner Mongolia) remains, while all the worsted mills in Beijing are effectively closed.

5.5.2 Township and Village Enterprises

The other major ownership type in the wool processing sector – Township and Village Enterprises – transformed the whole structure of the industry in the 1980s and 1990s. Township and Village Enterprises were originally developed not only as collectives, but also as private and foreign-invested companies. Township and Village Enterprises have undergone several waves of reform through privatization, contracting out to individuals, or through the development of group structures. The largest mill in the wool processing sector in China – the Sunshine Group – is a township and village enterprise. There are vast clusters of wool textile Township and Village Enterprises of all sizes in areas such as southern Jiangsu (Sunan), northern Zhejiang and eastern Shandong (Haiyang). For details on Township and Village Enterprises in the sector, see Lyons (2000).

At the time Township and Village Enterprises entered the sector, they had several advantages over the existing State-owned Enterprises including fewer welfare obligations, lower tax commitments and greater management flexibility. At the same time however, Township and Village Enterprises usually began as low-cost, unsophisticated operations. They did not have the technology, management systems, information infrastructure or technical expertise of the large State-owned Enterprises. Some companies such as Sunshine and Nanshan have developed these capacities. However the majority remain competitive in low-cost markets and struggle in more differentiated and higher-value markets. The vastly differing capabilities explain why some Township and Village Enterprises went bankrupt and left the industry during the major downturn in domestic wool textile demand in the late 1980s while, at the same time, more advanced and better managed Township and Village Enterprises surged ahead.

There are several similarities and differences between the reform processes of State-owned Enterprises and Township and Village Enterprises. Both are adopting shareholder or group company structures. In the case of Township and Village Enterprises, individuals are buying shares from the local collectives, and there are fewer restrictions on shareholder concentrations for Township and Village Enterprises than for State-owned Enterprises. Furthermore as Township and Village Enterprises were established later and had more freedom in their hiring and firing decisions, they had many fewer surplus workers compared with State-owned Enterprises. Consequently the lay-off of surplus workers and welfare payments for retired workers have been less of an issue for Township and Village Enterprises.

Numerous examples exist of Township and Village Enterprises undergoing a restructuring process. The Jiangyin Woollen Textile factory (Deimei) was set up in southern Jiangsu in 1981, and started undergoing reform to a shareholder company in 2002. The Nijiaxiang Worsted Mill, established in 1985 under a contract management system became one of the largest mills in China with around 50 000 spindles and 20 top combing machines and a production of 10 million metres of worsted fabric. The mill is undergoing reform to a shareholder company within a larger Nijiaxiang Group that is involved in everything from topmaking to dyeing, chemical products, building materials and textile machinery. The Nanshan Group amalgamated a large number of Township and Village Enterprises that operated independently within Nanshan Township in north-eastern Shandong. New wool processing mills were established in 1995 with modern equipment, and one large mill with 40 000 to 50 000 spindles is now one of the most capital intensive in China. The Nanshan Group is a publicly listed conglomerate of Township and Village Enterprises with activities ranging from power generation to an international tourist resort.

5.6   GROUP STRUCTURES AND SPECIALIZATION

As highlighted in Section 2.2, wool processing covers a range of processes, from raw wool sorting, scouring, topmaking, dyeing and recombing, spinning, weaving and finishing. State-owned Enterprise mills in the past performed all or many of these processes within workshops within a single comprehensive mill. However most worsted mills now concentrate on a few core processes (especially dyeing and recombing, spinning, weaving and finishing), or even a single process (such as spinning). In the process of reform, some workshops or processes have been split off to form completely independent companies. However often they still fall under the umbrella of the group company – which involves close buyer–seller relationships, utilization of common overheads, and transfer pricing between the subsidiary companies.

One of the many prominent examples that exist is the Xiexin Mill at Wuxi. Originally Xiexin was established as a State-owned Enterprise in 1935. It is one of the largest textile companies in China. The Xiexin Group comprises ten companies all associated with wool including a topmaking company, a spinning and weaving company, a sales and marketing company and a joint venture garment company.

Irrespective of the degree of independence of the subsidiary companies within the group, the issue is that subsidiaries are becoming increasingly specialized. Inefficient or unprofitable activities or workshops find it harder to survive in the new company or group structures as intermediate inputs and outputs can be sourced or serviced elsewhere. The trend to increasing specialization partly works against vertical integration and requires closer integration between the different wool processing and marketing stages throughout the industry as a whole. The group structure appears to be the reform driven or administrative answer to these seemingly opposing forces. Yet it is not clear that the transaction costs of linking specialized processing units is minimized under the group-type structure, or that the benefits from agglomeration or group overhead economies are realized. Notionally ownership may even be closer under the current group structures than when departments operated as separate State-owned Enterprise mills. However political ties to coerce product flows between different departments or mills in the Central Planning era may have been stronger than the economic or management ties within the current group structures.

5.7 RESTRUCTURING IN EARLY STAGE PROCESSING

Although in value terms a relatively small part of the wool textile chain, there are large numbers of early stage wool processing companies in China,[22] and it has been one of the most dynamic segments of the industry. As shown in Figure 2.1 in Chapter 2, early-stage processing can involve the stages of assembly and sorting of greasy wool, scouring, carbonizing, carding and combing depending on whether the wool is destined for worsted or woollen processing. Some early-stage processors specialize in specific tasks, while others – such as topmakers – assemble, scour and comb the wool. The early-stage processing sector has undergone a dramatic restructuring that differs in several respects from that described in the previous sections. Several features or developments within the early-stage processing sector are worthy of mention.

First, many local county-level scours and topmakers were established in inland wool producing areas such as Inner Mongolia and Xinjiang during the 1980s. The rush to develop scours was in response to fiscal reforms which encouraged regions to develop their own sources of fiscal revenue which for the more remote, industrially backward pastoral areas meant a shift into livestock product processing. Brown and Longworth (1992) however showed that the proliferation of up-country scours in the late 1980s and early 1990s resulted in excess capacity and destructive competition. Combined with a lack of technical expertise in scouring, many county scours experienced severe financial problems within a short period of time. A decade and a half later in the mid-2000s, few of these county scours or topmakers in pastoral areas remain.

Partly offsetting the demise of the up-county scours has been the proliferation of scours that have emerged on the east coast in areas such as Li County in Hebei Province. Developments in the overall wool processing sector of Li County are profiled in Box 5.4. On outdated, low-cost equipment, these scours process large volumes of wool and collectively account for a significant proportion of the scouring of domestic wool in China.

One difference with the aforementioned scours in the pastoral areas was that the east coast scours process wool for the woollens system. The quality of the scouring for the woollens system is less important than for the worsted system for which a lot of the up-country scours were seeking to process.

For the worsted sector, much of the wool imported into China is in greasy wool form that is subsequently processed by Chinese early-stage mills. Traditionally the tops have been produced by topmaking departments within large integrated mills, or by specialized topmaker mills associated with State-owned, later-stage processing mills. This structure continued throughout the 1990s and even into the early 2000s. That is tops destined for worsted processing were produced by a large number of medium-sized topmakers (processing around 1500 tonnes of wool per annum). Apart from these standard topmakers, a few larger, modern and more specialized topmakers such as Nanhai Pindar (Guangdong), Ningbo (Zhejiang) and Mingfeng (Shandong) emerged in the 1990s.

Since 2002 however there have been considerable developments in the specialized scouring/topmaking sector, and the entry of a number of large modern facilities. Many of these facilities are joint ventures or alliances with overseas wool exporters (such as Tianyu and Lihua), while there has also been a wave of entry of wholly owned foreign enterprises (such as BWK and Michells).

Box 5.4   Restructuring of wool processing in Li County, Hebei Province

Li County has a concentration of wool processing enterprises and is a microcosm for observing change in the industry, especially the non-worsted side of the industry. Wool processing in Li County is somewhat unique in that it primarily centres on small private companies. Originally a large cotton-growing area, Li County had a base in textiles that commenced in 1978. Enterprises started by importing waste fibres (noil) from the big wool State-owned Enterprise mills in Beijing to make blends, before buying more specialized equipment. These factories began as private companies, and so have not gone through the ownership transition process. In general they conform to the perception that private companies are small and unsophisticated. The limits of their technical, management and other capacities have become increasingly apparent, and they have struggled to enter the more discerning market even for woollens, yarn for hand-knitting, and carpet yarn.

At the end of 2003 the county had 210 wool textile mills with 150 000 spindles and producing 100 000 tonnes of wool yarn of which 70 per cent was polyester blends and 30 per cent was pure wool. There are no collectives or State-owned Enterprises – all enterprises are privately owned or shareholder companies. With an average of only 750 spindles, they are also very small. From a peak of 279 companies in Li County in 1996, the number fell to 210 by 2003, and these changes are only precursors to more closures and mergers.

Companies of various sizes have felt the mounting economic and financial pressures. For instance despite various support and modernization programmes, the Qifa mill has not been immune from the mounting pressures despite at one stage being the third-largest mill in China with a production value in excess of Rmb300 million. Several private companies have sought a complete change in direction to reverse declining fortunes. One of the more successful examples involves a former woollen mill that had struggled to compete and make profits. In 2000 the owners decided to look for more lucrative opportunities elsewhere in the wool processing sector and settled upon the manufacture of carpet wool yarn. With relatively few large-scale mills that manufacture carpet wool yarn in China, they are now the largest. The decision to switch from making yarn for sweaters to making yarn for carpets, at least for this company, proved a profitable switch.

Furthermore low-cost yet outmoded scours appear to be very active in Li County, supplying the woollen yarn and carpet yarn processors. The success of any individual company therefore depends crucially on its ability to foresee growth areas, along with the capability and flexibility to move into these areas.

The entry of these large modern facilities may have a profound impact not only on the early-stage processing sector but also on the entire wool textile industry. With regard to the impact upon early-stage processing, new entrants have added 100 000 tonnes capacity in the southern Jiangsu region alone, representing a significant proportion of the existing early-stage processing capacity. The extra capacity exerted immediate pressure on existing large processors such as Nanhai Pindar which saw its throughput of tops fall from about 4000 tonnes in 1997 to 1000 tonnes in 2003. Medium- to small-sized traditional topmakers were not immune from the pressure of additional industry capacity and have also undergone rationalization in recent years. Nonetheless the new entrants are highly capitalized and require significant utilization of their capacity to remain viable and compete with the older, but lower fixed cost, traditional topmakers. Spinning mills now have a much wider choice of sources for their tops, and all topmakers are under increasing pressure to supply tops at a competitive price and in a form spinning mills require.

The entry of the new large topmakers partly reflects overseas operations moving offshore into China in response to shifting comparative advantage in early-stage wool processing at an international level. For instance companies like BWK and Michells are seeking to move their Australian early-stage processing operations into China to supply not only their top orders in China but also for re-export to spinning mills in other countries.

The impacts of the new early stage processors however extend beyond questions of capacity and capacity utilization. The new entrants have large modern plants and a global customer base. Of major consequence, the entry of "global" topmakers may change product specification. One key theme raised in this book is that broad Chinese types have been used to exchange wool tops which are not well suited to the manufacture of specific or tailored products. Few Chinese topmakers have used the more precise specifications common to the trade of wool tops in other countries.[23] One reason developed at various parts in this book is that the need to sell tops from stocks in order to meet customer deadlines restricts the number and variety of wool top lines produced by topmakers. However the global topmakers that have recently established in China already have to specify their tops more precisely for overseas customers. These more precise specifications would also be available for Chinese customers (mills) enabling them to specify their top requirements in more detail. Thus developments in the early-stage processing sector in China will have an important impact on input choice, manufacturing systems and the timeliness by which inputs can be delivered to other segments of the industry.

5.8   MODERNIZING MILL SYSTEMS AND PRACTICES

In recent years the wool processing sector has undergone a turbulent period, with the reform of ownership, governance, institutional and policy structures and the injection of new technology. The broader macro-level changes have not often translated into internal reform of systems and practices within the mills themselves. That is macro-level reforms will not necessarily by themselves create more progressive actors at the micro level.

Similarly much of the emphasis on improving mill operations in China has involved introducing new equipment and, to a lesser extent, technical processes without much thought as to how best to utilize these innovations. Technological change is a necessary and important aspect of mill modernization, but is not an end in itself. New technology and equipment must be targeted at areas where it can generate the most profitable returns – such as to produce particular types of products, to allow diversification into a new area, or to overcome bottlenecks in the manufacturing process. Decisions about equipment and technology however often are not made on a whole-of-mill basis. Furthermore the introduction of new equipment must be matched by skilled managers and technicians. In the past divergences have arisen between companies that are well financed to purchase advanced equipment but that had relatively unskilled staff (such as some Township and Village Enterprises), and companies without the capital to upgrade equipment but that had more highly skilled staff (such as some State-owned Enterprises).

Information systems have been particularly slow to change. As a legacy of the transition from a planning era, State-owned Enterprise mills collect enormous amounts of information, that since the late 1990s are often kept in electronic form.[24] Much of the information is used to track inventories and throughputs (particularly important under the command economy), for tax purposes, or for *ex post* review of mill performance. Although all of these remain important, the information needs to be used in a more proactive, *ex ante* analysis of options or choices, and also for managerial accounting rather than just tax accounting purposes. Considerable scope exists to improve the way mills utilize existing sources of information so as to raise overall performance within their existing ownership structure, technology and equipment (Brown et al. 2005).

A more proactive approach to information management feeds into all aspects of mill operations. One of the most important areas concerns the assessment of which market segments, market channels, customer types, product types and specific orders are likely to deliver the highest returns. Estimating the returns from particular product types also requires an understanding of the costs associated with filling that order. Many managers currently make these key decisions based on intuition and experience. Various management, accounting and information tools can supplement this intuitive experience and provide a more scientific grounding to the decisions. These tools are rarely used in China at present, but pressure for their development and adoption will increase in a more competitive environment. Box 5.5 outlines the CAEGWOOL model the authors have been involved with, which is designed to generate mill- and product-specific information to enable managers to make more rigorous decisions.

Box 5.5   CAEGWOOL

CAEGWOOL is a *Visual Basic* model embedded in a Microsoft *Excel* Spreadsheet that is designed to assist managers and technicians at Chinese wool textile mills in their managerial accounting and economic evaluation of a wide range of mill decisions. The model has been developed by researchers from the China Agricultural Economics Group at the University of Queensland and the Chinese Research Centre for Rural Economy in close association with mill managers and technicians from various Chinese wool textile mills and organisations. CAEGWOOL was the subject of a 3-day Chinese-language workshop held in Wuxi in June 2004 attended by managers from 15 mills. Subsequently, a paper on the model was presented to the over 300 mill representatives attending the 2004 Annual Conference of the Chinese Wool Textile Association. The main intent of CAEGWOOL is to trace out in detail the costs, revenues and physical flows associated with a particular product order. Specifically, the model enables managers to input details about the amount and type of the product order and interactively specify the design of the product through all of the processing stages. Based on the product design, CAEGWOOL endogenously estimates a range of parameters such as prices and cost and yield coefficients, and then evaluates the full financial and physical implications of the product order. The model generates a series of outputs that disaggregate costs and revenues by type and mill workshop. A profit statement in the format Chinese mill managers are familiar with is generated along with other items including intermediate prices, opportunity costs and net value added by each workshop that are useful in making managerial decisions such as the worthwhileness of a particular product order, how it should be produced, and what prices or fees should be charged for it. A feature of the CAEGWOOL model is that it has been tailored to suit individual mills and to draw upon their existing sources of information. The Chinese version of the model and manual can be found in Zhao et al. (2005) while Brown et al. (2005) present an English version of the model and manual.

The ability to make decisions on a more proactive basis has other implications. Mills can engage more in product development prior to orders being placed, including product research, design and the conducting of trial runs. The ability to develop new, technically feasible products most profitable for the mill and that help differentiate the mill's products prior to orders being placed, is potentially more lucrative then passively waiting to receive an order or filling common repeat orders. The risks may also be higher. However it is the mills that have the capacity to enter into and manage these risks that will prosper in the new environment and become industry leaders. In addition more complete information about the technical processes and costs associated with the product can reduce the risks of entering into the manufacture of new products.

As well as the processing aspect of the modernization of mill systems, proactive mill management also applies to output marketing and input sourcing. The development of new textile products may help mills develop new customer bases and enter new markets, possibly using new marketing channels. Closer contact with participants further up the marketing chain, including garment makers, textile traders, retailers and fashion houses, enables mills to better understand and anticipate customer requirements and consumer preferences. As discussed in Chapter 4, the notion that mills should be more involved in product development and play a greater role in leading the industry is often raised but rarely acted upon in the Chinese industry.

The development of products in anticipation of demand and the establishment of longer-term supply contracts with customers should also give mills more flexibility in their raw material input choices. As elaborated in Chapters 4 and 6, to fill immediate short-term orders, mills are forced to source their inputs of wool and wool tops from readily available stocks of common types. This wool may not be the optimal input choice, especially if the order is a custom or niche order and not a generic or repeat type of order. Thus if mills are able to secure more time to purchase and import more specific types of wool, better matched to the processes and product involved, this could reduce input or processing costs or increase the quality and value of the product. Better input–output selection and more precision in manufacturing processes are key aspects of mill modernization, but are yet to be seriously tackled by the vast majority of mills.

The failure to address the upgrading of management and management processes in mills is an example of the, as yet, incomplete third phase of the economic transition in China. This issue, as highlighted in Chapter 9, arises not only in other segments of the wool and wool textile industry but also in many other Chinese industries.

NOTES

1   As mentioned in Chapter 4, textile mills lead the entire garment industry in many European countries. Similar expectations also surface in China – the difference being that Chinese mills presently lack the wherewithal (capital, skills, coordination) to play such a role.

2   The exception has been in the context of western development where ongoing support for some inland mills in the 1980s and 1990s centred on the notion that they could lead wool industry development and so improve herder incomes in the strategically important pastoral areas. The failure of early-stage wool processors, the ongoing losses of some inland mills, their difficulty in adapting to the changing textile industry, and the general unprofitability for small herders to raise fine-wool sheep, has seen attention turn to other areas to promote western development since the mid-1990s.

3   Information from the Statistics Centre within the National Textile Industry Bureau include other groups of mills which overlap some of these categories. Furthermore several definitional issues associated with these statistics arise that are too complicated to explain in a concise manner in this section. Thus the graphs and discussion in this section serve only to paint the big picture as the precursor to the more detailed discussion in Sections 5.3 to 5.8.

4   State-owned Enterprises in general have been eligible for some government funds to help in the process of reform, particularly to aid laid-off workers. However State-owned Enterprises in the wool processing segment have not received the same support as those in some other economic sectors.

5   The Textiles Industry Association website stated that 9 million spindles were cut between 1999 and 2001. Terms of assistance to facilitate the spindle cuts included: (1) for cutting 10 000 spindles, Rmb3 million was to be paid to the mill in equal portions by the Central and local government with the local government taking the responsibility for banks providing interest subsidies of Rmb2 million to update equipment and pay out workers; (2) the encouragement of banks to be lenient on the debts and repayments of mills that have closed or merged; (3) other funds to be provided for re-employment services as well as housing and medical services to laid-off workers; (4) after cutting spindles, mills could use the revenues from land and other assets to compensate laid-off workers; (5) export rebates were increased to 11 per cent for 1998 and 13 per cent for 1999; (6) strict limits and registration applied to the purchase and import of machinery, especially for worsted yarn; and (7) mills exporting cotton fabrics that used cotton from Xinjiang as a raw material to replace imported cotton paid no tax from 1998.

6   In the same vein the Science and Technology Commission provides some capital or preferential treatment to wool textile mills for certain purposes. For example in Shandong, tax exemptions on value added tax are available if mills install computer systems for the purposes of information management systems and product design.

7   In Shandong for example, only 12 000 spindles (out of close to 400 000 spindles in the province) were closed through the spindle cutback programme. In Changzhou City in Jiangsu Province, only 3336 wool spindles were cut. Most of these spindles were in the small, poor-quality mills which were experiencing severe and increasing economic stress.

8   The ultimate aim is for mills to have biological effluent treatment facilities (aerobic or anaerobic–aerobic dual systems) rather than just primary or settling treatment facilities with additional chemical treatment. In addition mills ideally will use new chemicals (dyestuffs, additives), upgrade equipment (including scours, boiler and boiler water feed systems) and employ practices such the recycling of air conditioner cooling water. Requirements for the "green" textile products extend further down the supply chain in terms of sustainable sheep stocking rates and utilization of China's grasslands.

9   There are 33 associations listed on the Chinese version of the Textile Industry Association website (www.cntic.org.cn), but only 19 are on the English site. Further details about the structure and the role of the Textiles Industry Association can also be found at this website.

10   State Asset Management Companies often report to Economic and Trade Commissions at the local level. However the Economic and Trade Commission has been reformed at central level (through a merger with the Systems Reform Commission) and in time this process will extend down to local levels. At the same time State Asset Management Commissions are becoming more common at city levels. The institutional support for State-owned Enterprise reform described in the case of the Changzhou Textiles State Assets Management Company has been widely adopted across China, but regional differences do arise in the model used and the industries involved.

11   At the Jiangsu Province level half of the staff of the former Jiangsu Textile Industry Bureau went to work for the Jiangsu Economic and Trade Commission (which incorporates the State Assets Management Commission system) and the other half were employed within the Jiangsu Textile Industry Association.

12   Because of the international nature of the industry, there are many joint ventures including; Minfeng (NZ), Sanfeng, Haiyang Dongtai Dyeing and Textiles Company (Macao), Haiyang Haida Hengjia Fabrics Dyeing Co. Ltd. (Japan), and Reward (Taiwan). However compared with the garment sector described in Chapter 4, there are few private companies in the wool processing sector, with some exceptions in pockets like Li County in Hebei Province.

13   For example one State-owned Enterprise mill in Shandong in 2002 had 1934 workers but 5200 people on its payroll. Most on the payroll are retired and must be supported at wage levels that can be higher than working employees (Rmb800 to Rmb1000/month compared

with Rmb700 to 800 for ordinary mill employees). Thus the labour costs of these State-owned Enterprise mills can be around 30 per cent higher than other mills, even though the other mills often offer higher wages. Furthermore the exodus of mill technicians and managers to the higher wages of non-State-owned Enterprise mills has severely disrupted the nature and impact of their staff training programmes.

14   The equivalent figures for the 48 State-owned Enterprise woollens (knitting) mills were that 11 were losing money to a total of around Rmb15 million. However the problems are not confined to State-owned Enterprises. Of the total of 1166 worsted (weaving) mills in China, 258 (or 24 per cent) were losing money, to total Rmb910 million in losses. Total losses in the woollens (knitting) sector amounted to Rmb184 million.

15   Although State-owned Enterprise mills have been the breeding ground for good wool processing technicians and managers, many of these managers and technicians are subsequently lured to the other mills where conditions and wages may be better. This training role of State-owned Enterprises is a benefit often overlooked. Management skills in Township and Village Enterprise mills vary widely.

16   The general goal revolves around the State shedding itself of assets and liabilities through a process of ownership transition. However the process also enables the shedding of jobs and welfare obligations in a politically feasible way, namely in a situation where State-owned Enterprises can not do this, but non-State companies can.

17   As described in Section 2.2, wool processing covers a range of processes, from raw wool sorting, scouring, topmaking, dyeing and recombing, spinning, weaving, and finishing. State-owned Enterprise mills in the past have performed all or many of these processes within workshops within the single mill. However most worsted mills now concentrate on a few core processes, or even a single process. In the process of reform, some workshops have been split off to form their own companies. Although seemingly independent, most of the companies still come under the umbrella of the group company. Among the numerous examples is Changzhou Spinning and Weaving Mill in southern Jiangsu which is part of a group that includes a number of subsidiary companies including a topmaking mill, a cotton processor and a synthetic fibre operation. One of the largest wool State-owned Enterprises of Xiexin at Wuxi (established in 1935) is also part of a group of ten companies all associated with wool processing including a topmaking company, a spinning and weaving company, a sales and marketing company and a joint venture garment company.

18   One manager controls 30 per cent of the shares, with seven managers controlling another 60 per cent, and the remaining 10 per cent of shares in the hands of employees.

19   The Chifeng Worsted Company is one of 25 subsidiaries of the Huayuan Group involved in the textile sector. Otherwise known as "China Worldbest", the group was established in 1992 with a mission to "to revitalize China's textile industry and to explore a pathway for the reform of China's State-owned enterprises". The group has now branched out into life sciences and logistics and claims to be the largest textiles and pharmaceuticals company in China and the fourth-largest industrial group in Shanghai.

20   The Shanghai Kaikai Industrial Co. Ltd. is a group company whose principal activities are the manufacture and distribution of shirts, suits and wool sweaters, department stores operations, retail and wholesale outlets for fabrics, and distribution of pharmaceutical products. Textiles accounted for 47 per cent of its revenues in 2001, pharmaceuticals 35 per cent and department stores 18 per cent. The company is headquartered in Shanghai and is listed on the Shanghai Stock Exchange.

21   As another example of this the Jiangyin Diemei Group in Jiangsu was encouraged to develop trade and investment relations with Western enterprises.

22   An industry official, for example, said that China has nearly 300 wool scours and 1000 topmakers, although these include stand-alone companies and those integrated with other processors.

23   The specifications are based on attributes such as micron rather than the broader Chinese type system based on "count" as the main unit. One Chinese topmaker, Ningbo, has been an exception, selling at least part of its wool tops according to more detailed specifications.

24   With some exceptions, Township and Village Enterprise mills collect relatively little information and it is rarely well organized or accessible.

6. Reforming Trading Arrangements[1]

The Chinese wool textile industry has long been heavily reliant on imported wool supplies and exports of wool textiles. Given the mega-trends impacting upon the industry this reliance can only increase, especially given the developments in domestic wool production and marketing analysed in Chapters 7 and 8. Thus the Chinese wool textile industry needs a trading system that can facilitate the flow of specific types of wool inputs and wool textile outputs in an accurate, timely and cost-effective manner. The analysis below however indicates that the current trading system does not meet these needs – especially in regard to raw material inputs – and has been unable to do so for more than a decade.[2] The demands of a more precision-oriented industry mean that it is even less likely to be able to service the emerging needs of the mills in the future.

Much of the attention on the trade sector has focused on formal trading arrangements. Indeed in this respect the sector has undergone significant changes in response to World Trade Organization accession and other bilateral agreements with supplying and consuming countries.

Although more transparent, open and clearly defined trading arrangements are welcome, they do not address the systematic or underlying problems that afflict the trade. The systematic problems have the potential to derail or adversely impact on the processing sector's transformation outlined in the previous chapter. This chapter explores some of these underlying problems and identifies what further changes may be needed to facilitate future trade in wool imports and wool textile outputs.

Ideally mills should be directly involved in purchasing their greasy wool or wool top supplies as they are most aware of their own specific fibre input needs. The transaction costs of doing so however are too high for many mills because of factors such as their inability to access credit, unfamiliarity with overseas wool supply marketing systems and the small size of the lots they need to purchase. Consequently many mills – including those currently with the right to import directly – still purchase most of their requirements through market intermediaries or traders.

Despite the reliance of mills on trading intermediaries, the latter do not always operate in the best interest of the mills in terms of meeting their

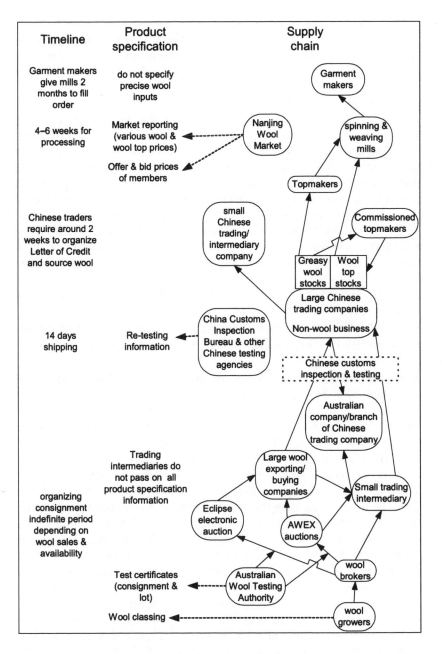

Figure 6.1   Imported (Australian) wool supply chain

specific needs. Agent or commission sales of specific lines of wool are not favoured by traders because of the low margins. Instead, traders prefer to speculate and buy and sell opportunistically with little use of formal risk management tools. Combined with the fact that wool forms only a minor part of their overall trading activities, traders often focus on major lines, and so are less inclined to service very specific orders.

The developments occurring in other parts of the wool textile chain will exert pressure on traders to specialize and differentiate their activities. However the concentrated nature of the trading sector means that change in this direction will be slow, and is likely to hold back developments in other parts of the wool textile industry.

Figure 6.1 provides a diagrammatic representation of the imported wool supply chain (assuming that the wool is sourced from Australia) and some of the issues it confronts such as product specification and timeliness of deliveries. Although a gross simplification of the actual supply chain, it highlights some of the key relationships taken up in the remainder of this chapter.

6.1 TRANSITION ARRANGEMENTS ASSOCIATED WITH WORLD TRADE ORGANIZATION ACCESSION

Wool import arrangements that have operated in the early 2000s were negotiated in a protracted series of bilateral meetings with major wool exporting countries such as Australia and New Zealand before World Trade Organization accession.[3] The arrangements sought to address some of the more overt concerns and distortions that had arisen in the Sino-Australian wool trade, and to subject the trade to a more clearly defined set of rules. Most of the arrangements were formalized with China's accession to the World Trade Organization including a transition phase between 2001 and 2005. However some complications arise because arrangements for greasy wool, scoured wool and carbonized wool come under World Trade Organization Agricultural Negotiations while the World Trade Organization Textile and Clothing Agreement governs the arrangements for wool tops. Given that the reform agenda and timing of reforms varies between the agricultural and textile negotiations, distortions can arise between raw wool and wool tops in areas such as the abolition of import quotas. Furthermore, various issues and ongoing negotiations on wool import arrangements are occurring as part of the discussions concerning the China–Australia Free Trade Agreement.[4]

An examination of changing wool trade arrangements since the late 1990s reveals the key distortions the new arrangements have sought to address. Furthermore the discussion below uncovers the way some aspects of the transition may impact upon industry participants and exacerbate the distortions. The discussion also highlights the application of these trading arrangements as China enters the post-World Trade Organization accession era.

One key aspect of the transition phase has been an attempt to remove distortions associated with the operation of wool import quotas.[5] A feature of the rapid development of the wool textile industry during the 1980s and 1990s was the application of wool import quotas. Notionally, quotas were in place, but the aggregate quota was not systematically or regularly reported – nor applied – in periods of strong domestic demand. At other times, and especially when domestic wool stocks increased, import quotas were strictly enforced.[6] The uncertainty associated with the administration of the wool quota arrangements created problems for mills that were seeking secure, reliable supplies of imported wool.

Wool import quotas created a series of other distortions. Quota allocations normally occurred twice per year. But the rush to access quotas in high-demand periods led to seasonal price variations and left traders unable to purchase wool for specific or anticipated orders. Thus quota allocations attracted significant value under particular market conditions which on many occasions exceeded Rmb3000 per tonne.

Another element of the import arrangements involved the strict licensing of importers. The licensing arrangements have been gradually relaxed from a few State-owned trading companies initially, to a larger group of trading companies and even some mills, and with the intention to move eventually to automatic licensing.[7] As will be discussed in Section 6.2, State trading companies also underwent restructuring to comply with World Trade Organization guidelines in the lead-up to accession. The issue of licences and quotas created secondary markets for imported wool, whereby large provincial trade corporations that had access to quotas as well as foreign exchange could sell surplus wool to those traders and enterprises that did not.[8]

The traditional wool import arrangements involved the State Development and Planning Commission allocating import quotas to the Provincial Planning Commissions who subsequently allocated them to traders and large mills in their province. The transition arrangements removed provinces from the quota allocation process in an attempt to base allocation more on mill demand rather than equity across regions or political connections. Thus the new arrangements may alter regional import patterns and be one step in the process of aligning allocations and imports with regional comparative advantage. Importers now lobby Central rather than provincial officials for quota allocations. Larger trading companies and mills with the resources and connections to lobby higher-level officials may have been given an advantage by the reforms.

Image 6.1   Fine-wool merino rams in Xinjiang

Professor John Longworth inspects merino rams at the former Chabuchaer Ram Breeding Station in Xinjiang located in Yili Prefecture near the border with Kazakhstan. This breeding station or stud has now become part of the Merino Company discussed in Chapter 8. Despite the lengthy efforts to develop Chinese fine-wool production (Chapter 8), the Chinese wool textile industry still relies heavily on imported wool

The transition in quota arrangements was intended to shift away from the old system of allocating quotas based on experience, performance or political connections to a system based on a "first-come-first-served" means of allocating quotas. The success by which the allocation process will be implemented and sustained remains to be seen (AWI 2004), while it may have generated its own set of distortions. For example if overall quotas are perceived to be limiting, trading companies or mills may seek quotas on a first-come-first-served basis even if they do not subsequently use the quotas or are not in the position to make the best use of them. Combined with the shift from a twice-yearly allocation of quotas to an annual allocation, the first-come-first-served system may exacerbate the problems as mills rush in to buy imported wool just to ensure that they receive some quota wool. Thus a single allocation could lead to a disorderly wool import market and purchasing behaviour not necessarily compatible with developments in other parts of the wool textile processing and marketing systems. In particular, mills may have specific – and not necessarily repeat – orders that arise throughout the year for which they are unable to obtain the necessary import quota. Furthermore they may not have the capital with which to purchase large quota allocations at the beginning of the year.

The new wool import arrangements also sought to address a chronic source of concern in the Chinese wool import trade, namely contract enforcement and dispute resolution. Memorandums of Understanding have been developed on inspection procedures and wool contract arbitration arrangements, along with the introduction of a standard wool contract. However as indicated in AWI (2004), disputes still arise about mandatory Chinese inspection and different sampling procedures. The so-called "standard" contract is rarely, if ever, used.

Impacts on the wool import sector can be expected as the transitional phases of the new arrangements proceed and as further changes are made. Nonetheless the broad intent or direction of the reforms is to bring about a more open trading regime along with more transparent and clearly defined rules and procedures. Operating within a more formal set of protocols determined in a multilateral forum is an important aspect of the overall modernization of the industry. Yet the new arrangements do little to address the longer-term, more systematic problems that have beset the wool import sector. These problems and the industry transformation needed to overcome them are discussed in the following sections. Unless these systematic problems can be resolved, the World Trade Organization-initiated reforms – although well intentioned – may have little impact.

6.2 STRUCTURAL CHANGES TO STATE TRADING COMPANIES

Traditionally, large State-owned national trading corporations such as the China Textile Resources Company and the provincial Foreign Trade Corporations had the right to import a wide range of commodities (passed down from the Central Planning Commission and the former Ministry of Foreign Trade and Economic Co-operation), and to engage in actual trade through various agencies under their control. These large foreign trade corporations however underwent significant changes in the late 1990s and early 2000s, primarily in response to World Trade Organization accession.

In the case of the main wool textile-producing and wool importing province, namely Jiangsu, the provincial Foreign Trade Corporation became the Tongyuan Jiangsu Import–Export Company. Tongyuan operates as a large import–export company involved in the trade of many commodities and products such as automobiles, wool, steel products, rubber, vegetable tallow and machinery. The company receives import rights directly from the Ministry of Foreign Trade and Economic Co-operation. Various subsidiary companies and enterprises are associated with Tongyuan. For example Huawei Enterprises Co. Ltd engages in wool trading. However Tongyuan has very little direct investment in the subsidiary companies. Subsidiary companies like Huawei rely on the parent Tongyuan for the import license or quota and little else. The easing of important quota and licensing arrangements as part of World Trade Organization accession will diminish the relevance of the parent holding company, and some of Tongyuan's subsidiary companies may split with the parent company. In any case, the subsidiary companies have taken on a more commercial and private role, even if staffed by many former officials of the Foreign Trade Corporation.

In neighbouring Shanghai, the Shanghai Foreign Trade Corporation – a large trading conglomerate which handles the import and export of many products – restructured as Orient International Holdings in 1998. Like Tongyuan, Orient is essentially a holding company with a number of subsidiary companies involved in trading. For instance one of the orient subsidiaries, the Dong Song International Trading Company, is a trading conglomerate in its own right dealing in many commodities and products including wool. In 2002, Orient had only an 8 per cent share in Dong Song, which is similar to its share in other companies under the Orient umbrella. Once again, Orient acted primarily to provide the licenses to import and export for the subsidiary companies.

Only three companies had rights to import wool in Shandong Province in 2003, namely Shandong Oriental International Trading Corporation, Shandong Foreign Trade Corporation and the Jintel Company. All three companies operated under the former Ministry of Foreign Trade and Economic Co-operation. With a staff of around 4000, the Shandong Oriental International Trading Corporation runs several branch companies, factories and warehouses and operates under the Shandong Animal By-products Import–Export Corporation. The Jintel Company was established as a subsidiary under Shandong Textiles Import and Export Corporation as part of the enterprise reform process in 1999, and has primary responsibility for wool imports.

The move from large provincial foreign trade corporations to smaller, commercially oriented, subsidiary companies was prompted by domestic enterprise reforms and the need to align State trading with the World Trade

Organization principles, namely away from designated or State trading to a "market economy" arrangement. Some advantages may arise for a relatively smaller commodity trade such as wool as the subsidiary companies are more knowledgeable and devote proportionately more of their time to wool trading than the monolithic parent foreign trade corporations from which they were spawned. However this depends heavily on the management and staff of these semi-privatized subsidiaries, especially since in many cases wool remains a relatively minor part of the activities of these subsidiary companies.

6.3 MODES OF OPERATION

A detailed understanding of the imported wool supply chain is a necessary part of developing strategies and measures to overcome the systematic problems that the formal measures discussed in Section 6.1 are unable to address. What is required is not only an appreciation of the detailed structure as outlined in Figure 6.1, but also an awareness of how industry participants behave and operate, especially Chinese trading companies.

6.3.1 Agents or Traders

Wool textile mills depend on traders for a variety of reasons. First, mills without import quotas have used traders to access quotas granted to the large State trading companies such as China Textile Resources Company and Chinatex. The phased reform of import quotas and licensing under World Trade Organization accession will remove this particular dependence. However other reasons exist for mills to rely on traders, that reforms to import arrangements will not alter. In particular, mills use traders to obtain Letters of Credit to purchase the wool. Many mills do not have the foreign currency, working capital or international bank accounts needed to open an acceptable Letter of Credit essential for the import of wool. Trading companies can open a Letter of Credit in the trading company's name for the import of the wool for which they will charge the mill a service fee. Even if mills have authority to import and sufficient capital, the constraints imposed by language and unfamiliarity with overseas wool marketing channels mean that they may still avoid dealing directly with overseas exporters and so use traders instead.

Trading companies operate in two main ways. First, they act as agents purchasing wool for mills and other customers for a service fee (usually around 0.8 per cent).[9] For most traders, this mode of operation represents a secure, but minor, part of their activities and source of revenue. For the larger traders – such as the major provincial China Textile Resources Companies – commission sales account for less than 10 per cent of volumes traded. For smaller traders – such as Shandong Jintel – the proportion tends to be much higher and can be around 50 per cent. Many trading companies act as commission agents to build up relationships with particular mills.

The second mode of operation – accounting for the vast bulk of trading company activities – is the purchase of wool for speculative trading. That is traders purchase and store wool with the expectation of a future price rise. This mode takes on two forms, namely the purchase of greasy wool for speculative trade with Chinese topmakers, or the purchase of greasy wool which is then processed by a commission topmaker for the speculative sale of the tops to Chinese spinners.

Thus it is the trading companies and not Chinese mills that primarily make wool import purchase decisions. Although the demand by traders derives from the demand by their mill customers, characteristics of the way traders operate can break this linkage with mill demand.

Foremost among these characteristics is the tendency for traders to speculate on price movements. For practical reasons, given that wool often forms only a small part of their overall commodity trading activities, the speculative behaviour means that traders tend to purchase only a limited number of common lines of wool or tops. The common lines have a much broader spectrum of potential buyers than the smaller, more specific lots that have fewer potential buyers. As Chinese trading companies have limited, if any, use of risk management tools to reduce price or currency risks (Section 6.6.1), a strong incentive arises for them to focus their risk-bearing trading activities on commonly traded wool lines. In turn, mills gravitate to the purchase of common lines to fulfil the strict timelines of their customer orders because traders have them in stock rather than having to wait for more specific lines to arrive from overseas.

Part of the price speculation activities by the major trading companies has also been based on the import quota arrangements. That is large traders often purchased in the quiet season – away from January and July when quotas were allocated and all companies were buying – and released stocks as the quota allocations and purchases were used up. The reform of import quotas will reduce this form of speculation, but not fundamentally change their preference to trade in more common lines of wool or tops.

6.3.2   Direct Purchase or Through Intermediaries

Relative to other fibre markets such as cotton, there are few wool importers or traders in China. Moreover wool tends to be only a minor part of their business. Thus marketing channels and risk management tools are

Image 6.2   Modern wool textile processing equipment

The use of modern imported equipment and precision processing systems requires smooth and timely access to particular types of high-quality, imported wool. Traditional trading channels are not well suited to providing mills with access to precisely specified raw materials in a timely fashion. Modernizing mill equipment without reforming wool trading illustrates the barriers to China's economic transition created by uneven progress in strongly interdependent segments of an industry.

unsophisticated in the wool trade and wool traders are unwilling to make the investment that would allow them to purchase direct from overseas suppliers or to access better market information. This filters through all aspects of the trade. For instance traders often accept inferior service from overseas wool agents simply because wool is a minor part of their overall trading portfolio, and efforts to identify better wool supply channels would be at the expense of more lucrative parts of their trading portfolios. This augers poorly for a more specified wool supply chain that would require an increasing number of more specialized wool traders.

Few Chinese trading companies or mills purchase wool direct from Australian wool auctions (organized by the Australian statutory authority known as the Australian Wool Exchange or AWEX). Despite their size, large traders such as Jiangsu Foreign Trade Corporation – which uses Jiangsu Overseas Group as their wool purchasing contract name – do not buy wool at the Australian Wool Exchange auctions. Instead they buy from one of the larger wool-buying companies listed as members of the Australian Wool Exchange.[10] The wool buyer offers to sell certain wool to Jiangsu Overseas Group at a negotiated price. A contract is signed with the wool buyer which may have the necessary wool in stock or which is prepared to take the risk that it can fulfil the contract before the shipment date (which can be up to two months into the future).

Furthermore even the larger Chinese traders will often approach smaller agents in Australia to negotiate with the Australian Wool Exchange member offering the best deal. The wool is then bought directly by the trader, with the agents receiving a small commission for linking the trader with the overseas supplier. Thus a long wool supply chain – consisting of one or more Chinese Trading Companies, independent Australian agent, Australian Wool Exchange wool buyer, and Australian wool broker selling on behalf of the growers – arises between Chinese mills and Australian wool producers. Among other disjunctures, this causes distinct breaks in the flow of information about wool specifications along the chain.

Problems are exacerbated by traders of all sizes being poorly informed about developments in overseas markets and sources of information on these markets. Local agents are known more for their skills in trading than in wool per se and furthermore have a vested interest in keeping traders uninformed.[11] Even if they were better informed it may still be worthwhile for Chinese traders to purchase through local agents because the transaction costs of them operating directly in overseas markets are too high. Nevertheless a Chinese wool trading sector that was better informed about overseas marketing and purchase options would force the local agents to provide a better marketing service.

6.4 DELIVERING ORDERS TO SPECIFICATION

Traditionally import channels focused on the cost of the raw material rather than on product specification. Mills could only specify requirements in the broad grades represented in the Chinese wool type system as compared with the much more tightly specified Australian-type system. The centralized importing agencies under Chinatex sought to minimize purchase costs by buying at the very bottom of these broad purchase grades. The length of both the administrative channel (to secure an imported wool allocation) and marketing channels for an agency such as Chinatex to source the wool, also worked against mills receiving the specific type of product they required in a timely manner.

Although problems of this nature have always impacted upon the operation and profitability of mills, the impact was lessened in the past because most of the orders were for generic wool textile products and often comprised repeat orders. These types of orders now generate low or negative margins in the more competitive wool textile environment. With fibre inputs accounting for more than half of total costs, there is also a need to identify and acquire least-cost fibre inputs. That is specialized products potentially offer more lucrative, though riskier, returns but also require more tailored fibre input selection.

Various efforts have been made to improve the precision of fibre input and textile product selection as discussed in Chapter 5. The application of spinning prediction models and associated research to Chinese mills is part of these efforts.[12] For mills to take advantage of these tools and be more precise in their input specification also calls for wool supply channels that can deliver the specified wool in a manner suitable to the mills in terms of timeliness, lot size, specification accuracy and batch homogeneity.

The post-World Trade Organization wool import arrangements notionally improve the access of mills to all types of wool. Whether the imported wool supply channels that operate under the new import arrangements will lead to the more precise use of specifications and trade that mills need to sustain their competitiveness is an open question. The discussion which follows in Sections 6.4.1 and 6.4.2 identifies a number of breaks between user preferences and information to suppliers. The second column in Figure 6.1 highlights some of the linkages between product specification, information flows and the imported wool supply chain.

6.4.1　Import Channels and Product Specification

Marketing channels for imported wool remain long, with many points of exchange. Each of these points contains the potential for marketing information and signals to break down, especially given the nature of the participants that interact at these points of exchange. As a result of these factors, current marketing channels work against a differentiation of imported wool lines.

Consider a typical situation. To meet particular orders, mill production departments determine their wool input requirements. Because various fibre input combinations can produce a particular wool textile output, production departments may provide alternative purchase options. However most mills cannot or do not determine the relative profitability of fibre input choices as well as the relative prices they could afford to pay in order to be indifferent between the selection of particular wool inputs. The requisition orders pass to the purchasing division of the mill, introducing the first break in the system. Purchasing divisions of mills have their own set of budgetary constraints, pressures and incentives and may well try to purchase slightly lower-quality wool at reduced prices.

Although some mills now have the authority to import directly, for the reasons outlined in Section 6.1, purchase orders usually go through large Chinese wool traders. Rather than purchasing wool directly from overseas auctions, as mentioned earlier these Chinese traders purchase through agents. A large number of overseas Chinese have set themselves up as wool dealers or agents in Australia. However again many of these agents do not buy direct through the auctions but through other auction buyers who are members of Australian Wool Exchange.[13] As mentioned in Section 6.1, the skills and experience of staff in these wool agents draw from a trading rather than a wool-buying background. More importantly, their remuneration depends on their trading ability rather than their ability to purchase wool true to specification.

That traders do not buy direct from auction adds a further link in the imported wool supply chain. Given that Chinese wool importers generate most of their returns from trading rather than acting as agents (Section 6.3.1), it is even less likely the premiums and discounts that mill production departments are willing to pay for alternative wool types will be relayed back to wool suppliers.

Efforts to promote more tailored textile processing systems, and fibre input and textile product selection, must also take into account changes in the Chinese early-stage wool processing sector as outlined in Section 5.7. Chinese topmakers have become increasingly competitive with imported topmakers partly because they can meet mill orders for wool tops more quickly. Thus the ability of topmakers in China to produce differentiated and accurately specified tops in a timely manner is crucial to more tailored wool textile processing systems. The relocation of a number of overseas topmakers to China as outlined in Section 5.7 may overcome some of the problems raised in this chapter of having detailed and accurately specified tops available to Chinese mills in a timely manner.

Apart from the new overseas or joint venture entrants, most Chinese topmakers are small to medium-sized mills that confront the same problems as other textile mills, including a lack of working capital and the inability to take on high levels of risk. Consequently product ranges are limited, at least for products not sold to order. Thus spinning mills may have few options other than to purchase popular, standard lines of tops. This may force mills to either pull back from specialized orders or to use standard tops most closely aligned to – but which still differ substantially from – the specific tops required by the tailored production systems. Similarly, topmakers have an incentive to steer spinners away from specific lines and encourage the continued use of the standard lines.

More specific fibre input selection may increase transport and other assembly costs.[14] These extra costs arise from the handling and logistics systems being built around the generic or standard wool import lines, and that the potentially smaller individual orders may have higher unit costs generated by the diseconomies of small orders. Although relative costs of these specialized, smaller consignment imports could be expected to decline as they become more significant in overall imports, there appear to be other more compelling reasons for the slow pace of transition to importing the more specific lines.

6.4.2 Product True to Specification

One chronic problem besetting the import of wool into China has been disputes over the accuracy of product specification. That is, results of mills' or traders' own testing of the wool often vary from the specifications certified on consignment. This has been one of the most contentious issues confronting the imported wool trade. As specifications tighten, these problems can be expected to become even more pronounced.

To date, the problem has been tackled from a legal and institutional perspective with efforts to introduce a standard wool contract, authorized (pre-import) test certification, and improved dispute resolution procedures. Although these measures are necessary and desirable, in isolation they are insufficient to overcome problems that are more systematic in nature.

Overseas test certificates are normally provided only for the average of the wool consignment as a whole. Consignments are made up of various lots which in turn comprise various bales. While the average test results for the whole consignment may be correct, there can be significant variation between lots and between bales, and so large variation within the whole consignment. The average test results for the whole consignment may be of little benefit and a source of contention for mills looking to use wool imports with precise specifications to satisfy specific orders. The problem is exacerbated when objectively matched lots are used within the consignment rather than the more homogenous farm lots.[15]

The variation becomes a problem when it creates major differences between the prices of consignments and their value to mills. For instance a consignment may have an average vegetable matter percentage that is within a mill's capability to process. However the overseas supplier may combine lots with low vegetable matter with lots of high vegetable matter to achieve an average across the consignment that is within contract specifications and reduces the price of the consignment. If the high vegetable matter is unable to be processed by the mill or unable to be used in a way intended to complete specific orders, it becomes a major problem for the mill and a source of contention. In essence, mills need to know specifications of individual lots, and in some cases bales, within the consignment if they are to use the raw material to maximum advantage in the manufacture of more precisely specified fabrics.

Image 6.3   Workers checking and packing garments for export

Producing finished garments to meet exacting requirements of export markets or premium domestic markets demands control and coordination of the entire wool textile supply chain, including that for imported wool.

Notionally, overseas test certificates are available on each lot within the consignment and testing can even be organized for individual bales. However intermediate traders often "neglect" to pass on these lot certificates to the mills. The loss of this certification does not relate to the cost of testing, which is small relative to the value of wool and, more importantly, to the value of more accurate knowledge of the wool. Mills can request certificates for individual lots within a consignment, but traders will normally demand a premium for such consignments – a premium that markedly exceeds the cost of the testing. Thus there is a reluctance on the part of mills to force traders to supply lot certificates.

The provision of accurate, disaggregated product specification and certification may be perceived as a commercial issue between mills and traders, with traders viewing the passing on of individual lot certificates as a value-adding service. However if imperfect and asymmetric information means that mills, unaware of the precise specifications and true value, are only prepared to pay a minimum amount for the wool, providing the additional information may adversely impact upon the returns to traders. If reconciling consignment specification with processing systems becomes a widespread and ongoing problem for mills, it may be in the interest of overseas suppliers, traders and Chinese mills to establish publicly accessed information on lot specifications for specific consignments.[16]

Central to the debate about obtaining product true to specification is the testing or retesting of the wool in China. Chapter 3 highlighted issues that arise in relation to the accuracy of equipment and testing procedures, as well as the coordination of testing across agencies and centres. Mills that are dissatisfied with consignments they have purchased can retest the wool themselves or use one of the Chinese testing facilities to check the specification of the wool. As might be expected, there is considerable scope for retesting in China to yield results significantly different to the specifications for the consignment claimed by the trader contracted to supply the wool. Disputes over specifications and contractual details have therefore plagued wool trading for decades.

Upgrading testing equipment and procedures in China to match those used elsewhere in the world, the development of a "standard wool trading contract", and the establishment of an agreed dispute resolution procedure are all steps towards reducing the likelihood of costly disputes. However a fundamental problem is that a guarantee of specification only occurs up to the port of entry where it is inspected and certified as correct by one or other agency. Ownership or control of the wool at this point is then taken up by the domestic (Chinese) wool importing company that may not necessarily be the end-using mill. Opportunities exist for the imported wool to be repacked and resorted prior to leaving the port or at any subsequent stage. Thus, Chinese mills not organizing their own purchase and transport from the point of customs or purchasing through lesser-known intermediaries still face a specification risk even if the wool arrives at the port true to specification.

The design of institutional arrangements to ensure the accuracy of consignment and lot specification must account for the entire imported wool supply chain (supplier to final purchaser) rather than just part of the chain (supplier to point of entry in China). Traceback systems of varying levels of sophistication operate in livestock and meat markets primarily for disease prevention and food safety reasons. Given the importance of accurate wool input specification for wool textile mills, some form of reliable but cost effective traceback system warrants consideration.

6.5 DELIVERING ORDERS ON TIME

To source greasy wool, scoured wool or wool tops from overseas, wool traders take an absolute minimum of about 15 days to process an order and organize a Letter of Credit. There are then five to eight days' shipping from a major Australian port to a Chinese port such as Shanghai, another 20 days in China to clear customs and arrive at the mill door in an east-coast province such as Jiangsu. Consequently an order takes a minimum of 40 days to arrive, but more often up to two months. The left-hand column in Figure 6.1 highlights some of the timelines associated with the imported wool supply chain.

To minimize time delays, importers specify that the order has to be filled and shipped by the overseas supplier within a certain period. Ideally, suppliers have around two weeks to secure the wool. However at certain times of the year when there is little wool available for purchase – such as in May or June – the time to shipment can be as long as six weeks.

Most Chinese wool traders purchase on a cost–insurance–freight (CIF) basis and have the overseas agent organize the freight to the port. When purchasing on a CIF basis, overseas agents naturally seek the cheapest shipping route possible which may involve lengthy delays. Thus buyers lose control of the shipping and supply time. Partly in response to these problems, a limited number of the larger traders have begun to organize their own shipments and identify suitable vessels and routes.

This time lag creates major problems for mills trying to use specific wool inputs to meet a particular order. In essence, mills simply cannot afford the 40 to 80 days it takes to source wool from overseas. As highlighted in Chapter 4, garment makers give mills a maximum of two months or less to process orders, which involves both securing wool supplies and manufacturing the fabric. To meet the deadlines imposed by their customers, mills normally have to start processing within a week of receiving the order. Consequently mills are forced to purchase wool that the trader has in stock closest to the specifications of the wool they require. That is the timelines and logistics force mills to purchase common wool types in stock. Facilitating more specific orders and tailored production systems requires either the holding of a much wider range of wool (tops) in China, or new alliances between garment makers, mills and traders to enable sufficient time to procure specific wool inputs from overseas. Implementing either option has proved problematic and presents a critical obstacle in the transformation of the entire industry.[17]

6.6 NEED FOR BETTER RISK MANAGEMENT AND INFORMATION SYSTEMS

Central to an efficient trading system is the smooth and complete flow of information between industry participants, as well as the management of risks associated with changing product prices, exchange rates and interest rates. Most firms engaged in international trade consider this a core part of their business practice. However this is one area where China lags behind its overseas counterparts. For a commodity such as wool where product attributes determine processing possibilities and costs, and where prices vary significantly over time, this can create serious problems.

6.6.1 Price Risk

Section 2.8 highlighted the volatility in wool prices that arises from supply factors affecting overseas greasy wool prices, exchange rates that impact upon imported wool prices as expressed in Renminbi, and the demand for wool textile outputs. During the era of the Australian wool reserve price scheme (1970s and 1980s) the Australian government absorbed much of the price risk related to overseas greasy wool prices. The collapse of the reserve price scheme and the sale of the stockpile built up by the scheme transferred much of the price risk to traders and other industry participants.

As specifications tighten, there will be fewer sources of supply and so greater competition for specific lines of wool. Price volatility will increase with increased smaller market segmentation. Furthermore if stocks of the more specific lines of wool held in China do not turn over as quick as the more generic lines, the price risks for traders associated with the holding of these stocks for any significant length of time will also increase.

Section 6.2 highlighted that most of the large traders buy wool on a speculative basis. Although there are various dimensions to their activities (obtaining credit, facilitating exchange, negotiating, transport logistics), traders view their ability to foresee market and price developments as a key part of their business. Rarely, if ever, do traders or mills have price risk management strategies in place. To purchase wool on a speculative basis in anticipation of sales at a future point in time, firms need to review their purchases, prices, currency and warehouse stocks on a regular basis. Despite being crucial to operating in this manner, rigorous market or price analysis is not conducted.

As mentioned previously, wool trading forms only part of the activities of Chinese importers. Consequently, one form of risk management among traders involves their focus on a limited number of more popular lines, rather than risking trying to understand and be abreast of developments in a large number of low-volume, specific lines. Besides this strategy, risk management rarely extends beyond loosely defined forward contracts.[18]

At least some of this price risk could be managed through futures trading. In exporting countries such as Australia, wool financial instruments have increased and these can be accessed by Chinese traders or mills. For instance the Sydney Futures Exchange offers a number of (greasy) wool contracts, while Macquarie Wool Futures once offered an even larger range and greater volume of trade for a short period of time.[19] Furthermore the Australian Stock Exchange recently commenced a wool top futures market where, importantly, the tops are specified according to the broad Chinese types. Chinese traders and mills choose not to use these instruments of exchange for several reasons, including that many of the instruments deal in tops rather than greasy wool and that there is no wool futures markets in China. Although the viability of a greasy wool futures market in China may be questionable, a wool top market with a large number of buyers and sellers (to hedge their price risk) and speculators (to take on the price risk) may be a different matter.

Chinese companies are likely to pay more attention to risk management in the future. The pressure to change these practices is already under way, prompted by greater international competition. In the medium term, a greater focus on risk management will come from the increasing cohort of business graduates and managers in the trading companies and wool textile enterprises trained in these practices. For trading companies, risk management involves managing both the inherent commodity price risk as well as the exchange and interest rate risks. As more traders engage in these practices, the range of forward contracts available to mills (hedged fully or partially by the trader on futures markets) will increase. Traders not involved in these developments therefore risk losing a competitive edge. Nonetheless, widespread use of risk management instruments in wool importing in China appears to be some time off.

6.6.2   Improving Information Flows

Although trading systems and imported wool supply pathways have been effective in securing large volumes of overseas wool, they have fallen short in meeting the needs of a more tailored and modernized Chinese wool textile industry. The trading systems to date have focused on price and cost at the expense of providing the precise inputs required by end users. Although this reflects more general problems of using traders in cases where specific inputs are required, there is also the need for more information for both Chinese traders and end users (to know what types of wool are available) and overseas suppliers (to know the type of wool in demand). To date, the sources of information have been unsuitable or underutilized.

Efforts to improve information flows have occurred both within China, such as through the Nanjing Wool Market, and in overseas supplier countries, such as through the Australian Wool Exchange.

The Nanjing Wool Market operates under a major State trader – China Textiles Resources Nanjing Corporation – but has a broader role in disseminating price information and, indeed, tries to maintain a "non-aligned" presence within the industry. The Nanjing Wool Market has a network of members that include most of the major mills and traders in China. From this network, "bid" and "offer" price information is collected and reported for greasy wool, wool tops, yarn, noil, chemical fibre and other products. Apart from prices, the information includes some detail on product specification as well as the amount being offered. The information is collated and published in a weekly magazine along with other wool price indicators derived from various sources.

Image 6.4   Transport and distribution centre at Tongxiang wool sweater markets

Efficient transport and logistics are a vital element of a successful transition of the wool textile industry whether it be for the export of finished garments or the import of raw wool.

The Nanjing Wool Market also has visions of establishing a virtual wool exchange. Some of the information is available in electronic form, including a searchable database listing the available stocks of wool and wool tops in China.[20] Member traders or mills can list the type, amount, location and price of wool or top they have for sale. This segment of the site potentially could serve an extremely useful role as mills can search for particular types of fibres to satisfy particular fabric orders and traders can enter their stocks for sale directly into the database. In practice, the site has served more as a source of information and a forum for members to showcase their products and prices than as a platform for exchange. The wool types used in this database are the Chinese types developed from and closely related to the now superseded Australian Wool Corporation Wool Types that dominated market reports in Australia for decades. As mentioned previously, Chinese trade is still heavily dependent on this typing system and this fact explains their use by the Nanjing Wool Market.

The Australian Wool Exchange, which has statutory responsibilities over wool marketing in Australia, operates various electronic trading services through its ECLIPSE system. The ECLIPSE electronic trading system commenced in July 2000. The system allows buyers and sellers to transact sales on a real-time, online basis, and an "offer board" allows for sellers to list a selling price and for buyers to match the asking price or lodge a counter bid. In addition, ECLIPSE provides close to real-time access to the open outcry auction results. In its first year of operation, ECLIPSE had 45 trading companies and 1900 wool growers registered and offered 75 000 bales or around 4 per cent of the Australian wool clip offered for sale.

Although developments within the Nanjing Wool Market and organizations such as the Australian Wool Exchange are encouraging with respect to improving information flows, they have yet to bridge the information gap between overseas wool suppliers and Chinese wool textile mills and traders. Given the transaction costs and reluctance by Chinese mills and traders to participate in the physical auctions, the ECLIPSE system would seem to provide an attractive alternative to traders and mills contemplating direct exchange. However unfamiliarity with the system, language issues and a different wool description system[21] are among reasons for a lack of use by Chinese participants. Even if they do not use the auctions or virtual exchange mechanisms of the Australian Wool Exchange outlined above, Chinese traders and mills could become associate members of the Australian Wool Exchange, which would provide them with access to much greater information which they could use to improve the efficiency of transactions through other channels.

In summary, both the Nanjing Wool Market and the Australian Wool Exchange have well developed information sources as well as existing

(ECLIPSE) or potential sale by description and electronic exchange services. Yet both systems appear focused on only one side of the wool supply chain. The need for the Australian Wool Exchange and the ECLIPSE system to access Nanjing Wool Market's long-established, extensive and strong network of Chinese traders and mills is paramount, as is the need for the Nanjing Wool Market to link more with Australian wool growers, brokers and exporters (a linkage that the Australian Wool Exchange and ECLIPSE offer).

Unless the gap is bridged, the benefits of these systems in terms of information flow across the entire wool supply chain will not be realized. Although these systems have developed independently and somewhat in competition, the existence of strong complementarities warrants closer consideration of increased cooperation in the future.

Evidence that there may be moves to address these problems is reflected in the recent trial "auction" of Australian wool in China held in November 2004.[22] The trial involved the sale of a limited quantity of Australian greasy wool (943 bales from 12 growers) along similar lines to the standard Australian wool auction system, although the wool remained in Australia at the time of the auction. An important aspect of the design of the trial in the context of the discussion above is that it involves one of Australia's leading agribusiness firms (Elders Ltd and its BWK Elders subsidiary in China) and the key Chinese wool industry organizations of the Nanjing Wool Market and the China Wool Textile Association. If the trial is successful and the system expanded, it has the potential to bring the Chinese wool textile industry and overseas wool growers and exporters closer together and to improve efficiency and overcome many of the problems raised in this chapter associated with importing wool.

Apart from the Nanjing Wool Market and the Australian Wool Exchange, there are a variety of other information providers that Chinese mills and traders could draw upon. For instance Australian Wool Innovation has a "Pricemaker" online program which determines the price for a particular wool line or type based on user-specific wool attributes. Furthermore Elders – a large Australian pastoral and wool-broking company – has a readily accessible, public and freely available site that provides detailed market reports and price statistics for Australian greasy wool.[23] Few Chinese textile industry participants are aware of or use this publicly available information that may be of substantial benefit even if only as background information.

NOTES

1   The authors would like to acknowledge the many useful and specific comments from, and discussion with, Ben Lyons who is currently investigating issues associated with Sino-Australian wool trade as part of his PhD at the University of Queensland. For some preliminary findings from his study, see Lyons (2003).

2   Problems associated with importing wool to China have long been subject to investigation (see for example IWS 1995), but without effective prescriptions as to how to overcome them. It is to be hoped that longer-term, more rigorous investigations such as those being carried out by Lyons (2005) can eventually resolve some of the chronic problems besetting the trade.

3   Details of the various elements of the new wool import arrangements – including their staged implementation as well as a discussion of some of their impacts – appear in various reports such as Quirk (2002) and Holloway (2002).

4   For details of some of the ongoing debate about the Free Trade Agreement from an Australian industry perspective, see AWI (2004).

5   There were several elements in the reform of wool import quotas associated with the new arrangements, including a move to tariff rate quotas where wool could be imported beyond a certain quota level but at (prohibitively) high rates of tariff. For a broader discussion of tariff rate quotas, import licenses and related matters associated with China's World Trade Organization accession, see Colby et al. (2001).

6   However as noted earlier in Chapter 2, the import restrictions had little impact on domestic wool stocks as the mills replaced the imported wool with synthetic fibres rather than domestic wool.

7   In June 2004, there were 300 designated traders that could import wool and wool top.

8   Licensing impacts upon many other industries as well. Longworth et al. (2001, Chapter 16) demonstrate the profound impact of licensing on cattle imports in China.

9   Agent fees are competitive and do vary but are usually around 0.8 per cent. Fees for some traders can be as low as 0.5 per cent but can be at the expense of the quality of the service provided, particularly with regard to fibre specification.

10 For example the Jiangsu Overseas Group has purchased a significant proportion of the more than 14 kt that it imports from Kathaytex Australia Pty Ltd, a Chinese wool-buying company that is an Australian Wool Exchange trading member. However it also uses other wool-buying companies including China Textile Resources Company Australia, H Dawson and Sons, Kreglinger, Lempriere, Louis Dreyfus, Startoy and Michells.

11 Trading companies also have a tradition of recruiting staff from a trading or business background rather than from a wool textile background. Thus, deficiencies in technical knowledge can be a large impediment for Chinese mills trying to order more precisely their desired raw material needs.

12 See for example research conducted as part of an Australian Centre for International Agricultural Research funded project on the development of specification and processing prediction techniques for the Chinese and Indian wool industries as described at http://www.aciar.gov.au/web.nsf/doc/ARIG-62F8EZ.

13 Dealers can buy direct through the auctions if they become Australian Wool Exchange members for a relatively modest annual fee and if they register for Australian tax purposes.

14 For greasy and carbonized wool, the minimum order size is typically around 50 tonnes, while for tops it is less. However customers can book shipments of 25 tonnes or even down to 13 tonnes which equates to about one container. Certificates are normally issued with these lots of greasy wool.

15 Objectively matched lots comprise wool from different farms that are too small to make an individual lot on their own. The different wool is organized into lots by specialized brokers based on key characteristics of the wool. Objectively matched lots sell at a discount to more homogeneous farm lots, which is precisely what makes the objectively matched lots attractive to Chinese traders. However many Chinese mills have difficulties handling the variation implicit in objectively matched lots and it would be more cost effective for them

to purchase more homogeneous lots. (The problems can be even more pronounced for bulk classed and interlotted wool.) Objectively matched lots are clearly indicated on auction sales catalogues. However the breaks in the marketing channels and information flows described above mean that many mills do not receive this information.

16   Mills could access information on the Australian Wool Exchange system by cross-referencing with the Australian Wool Exchange Lot Price Buyer guide. The fact that mills are unaware of the possibilities of, or averse to the costs of, sourcing information from overseas, even as minimal as the Lot Price Buyer guide, highlights the information gaps between Chinese mills and overseas wool marketing systems.

17   Nonetheless some alliances have begun to emerge in recent years especially between topmakers in southern Jiangsu and large Australian wool buyers and exporters.

18   Lyons (2003) argued that loose contractual arrangements are also a form of price risk management in terms of Chinese wool importers being able to pull out of contracts if prices move adversely against them. However as highlighted in Section 6.4, loose contractual arrangements can create even more serious risks for Chinese importers and their mill clients in terms of wool specification and heterogeneity. Thus more direct and formal methods of managing the price risk other than through misuse of contractual arrangements would seem desirable.

19   Macquarie Wool Futures stopped operation in July 2004 and has since sold its interests in wool trading.

20   Members of the Nanjing Wool Market pay an annual fee of Rmb1000 for the membership number or code and password to access the internet site.

21   The Australian Wool Exchange wool reporting system is based on a new (improved) Australian Wool Exchange wool description system. However this system is unlikely to readily replace the Chinese type system for the reasons outlined previously.

22   For details of this trial see the news item from November at www.woolmark.com

23   See http://wool.elders.com.au/marketreport.asp

7. Redesigning Domestic Raw Material Supply Chains

Although China has a large sheep flock and wool clip, much less than half of the clip is fine wool and only a small proportion of the fine wool is suitable for processing in worsted textile mills. As will be discussed in Chapter 8, much of China's pastoral region and many of its sheep herders are not well suited to fine-wool production. In addition, the traditional methods used to prepare, assemble and market raw wool in China were not conducive to sourcing domestic wool in a form suitable for worsted mills. This chapter examines how wool marketing has changed since the early 1990s,[1] and whether these changes have created marketing systems better suited to the needs of wool textile mills.

7.1 STRUCTURE AND CHANGE IN DOMESTIC WOOL MARKETING

Transition within the domestic wool marketing segment has been complex, extensive and, superficially at least, unpredictable. As a prelude to describing and analysing the intricacies of these changes, this section overviews the elaborate institutional and organizational changes that occurred throughout the 1990s as well as the current structure of domestic wool marketing in 2004.

7.1.1 Institutional Labyrinth of Domestic Wool Marketing

The institutions and organizations involved in domestic wool marketing involve a labyrinth of complex relationships. In part this reflects the transition from a centrally planned to a market economy, but also the transition to a more consumer-oriented and sophisticated marketing environment. The process has not been as straightforward as replacing sole procurement powers with private interests. Instead both State and non-State industry participants restructured to jostle for position within the new marketing environment.

In the process, many of the traditional institutional lines of responsibility have become blurred as alliances are formed to advance interests in this new marketing environment.

Figure 7.1 attempts to capture and simplify some of the dynamics of these changed institutional relationships. Subsequent parts of the chapter provide a detailed discussion of these relationships. To simplify the figure, only organizational changes that occurred within the largest wool (and especially fine-wool) producing province of Xinjiang appear in Figure 7.1. Changes that have occurred in other provinces are also described elsewhere in the text.

The columns in Figure 7.1 represent the main vertical hierarchies relevant to wool marketing. As described in Chapter 3, the Ministry of Textile Industry and the Ministry of Commerce no longer exist. Nonetheless the origins of the emerging institutions can be traced back to these vertical hierarchies. For instance while the Ministry of Commerce underwent several reincarnations before being abolished in 2000, the Supply and Marketing Co-operatives and Animal By-products Companies once governed by the Ministry of Commerce remain. Similarly although the Ministry of Textile Industry was abolished, organizations previously under this ministry such as Nanjing Wool Market continue to operate more or less on an independent basis.

The horizontal division in Figure 7.1 relates to two time periods, namely 1992 and 2002. The 1992 period represents the state of domestic wool marketing just prior to key government reforms in 1993. The 2002 period represents the situation a decade later and includes some of the relationships that have only recently emerged.

At the start of the 1990s, domestic wool was marketed through the sole procurement agency of the Supply and Marketing Co-operatives (or Animal By-product companies). Even at this time however the government sought to heighten competition by allowing new participants in wool marketing, notably agencies from other departments or ministries. The Ministry of Agriculture and Ministry of Textile Industry viewed the Supply and Marketing Co-operative system as stifling wool marketing – the Ministry of Agriculture was concerned about returns from their State-owned farms while the Ministry of Textile Industry was seeking better-quality wool for its textile mills. Consequently an alliance between the Ministry of Agriculture and the Ministry of Textile Industry introduced some wool marketing reforms such as the introduction of wool auctions. The Ministry of Commerce and Supply and Marketing Co-operatives vehemently opposed the auctions as a threat to their control over wool procurement.

Longworth and Brown (1995) and Brown (1997) highlighted the poor design of many of the marketing reforms and foreshadowed their subsequent demise. Wool auctions became defunct from 1993 through to the end of the

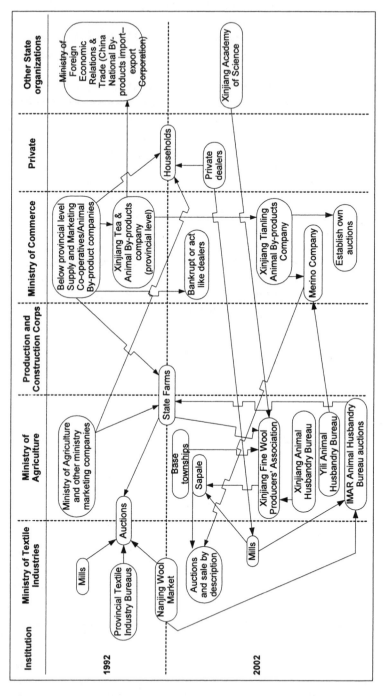

Figure 7.1 Overview of institutional relationships in domestic wool marketing: 1992 and 2002

1990s. Efforts to revive them have been made by one of the original key players in the auctions, the Nanjing Wool Market. With less government emphasis on fine wool and consequent downgrading of fine-wool activities in the Ministry of Agriculture and other ministries, along with the demise of Ministry of Textile Industry, much of the responsibility for promoting fine-wool production and marketing reforms has fallen on organizations like the Nanjing Wool Market. However although aligned with a large State import export agency (the China National Textiles Resources Nanjing Corporation), the Nanjing Wool Market has limited staff, resources or direct incentive to pursue domestic reform. More details about the Nanjing Wool Market and its involvement in other domestic marketing activities can be found in Box 7.1.

As will be discussed in Chapter 8, there has also been a reduction in fine-wool production as mutton production and other agricultural activities have become more lucrative for a broad group of pastoral households. Alarmed at the decline in genuine fine-wool production, agencies within various organizations began to develop companies and associations to promote and market fine wool. Some of these efforts appear in Figure 7.1 in the "2002" section. For example the Xinjiang Academy of Science, with support from the Xinjiang Animal Husbandry Bureau (part of the Ministry of Agriculture) has formed alliances with various State Farms and fine-wool producing areas

---

Box 7.1   Nanjing Wool Market

The Nanjing Wool Market was originally founded in 1988 as the Wool Trade Centre of Nanjing by the China Textile Resources Nanjing Corporation which came under the Ministry of Textile Industry system. It is still very closely linked to this corporation, even though the corporation was – and still is – focused on wool imports and textile exports. As highlighted in Section 3.3.3 and Section 6.6.2, the Nanjing Wool Market has been involved in various activities within the wool textile sector. When the company turned some attention to domestic wool marketing, it received funding from the Poverty Alleviation Office of the State Council, Ministry of Textile Industry and the Ministry of Agriculture. It is now registered as a civil organization that provides services by the Industry and Commerce Administration Bureau and is essentially a non-profit organization, with a staff of about eight.

The Wool Trade Centre of Nanjing began auctioning fine domestic wool in 1989, and the organization and development of a viable auction system continues to be a major interest of the Nanjing Wool Market. However it is also active in other aspects of the domestic wool industry, including promoting the use of domestic wool standards, training and organization of shearing, grading and wool assembly at local levels, and the provision of price and other information for producers and mills. As emphasized in Section 6.6.2 in Chapter 6, Nanjing Wool Market also publishes a magazine called *Nanjing Wool Market Information*, runs a website (http://www.woolmarket.com.cn) containing price information for imported wool and wool products, and operates a bulletin board for trade of various intermediate products.

to create the Xinjiang Fine Wool Producer's Association which markets their fine wool under the "Sapale" brand. Institutions left out of these arrangements – the Xinjiang Animal By-products Company/Supply and Marketing Co-operative and the Animal Husbandry Bureau of Yili Prefecture (the major fine-wool producing prefecture of Xinjiang) – developed another integrated production marketing organization known as the Merino Company. A more detailed description and discussion of these organizations may be found in Section 7.3.1.

Thus in the new agribusiness and policy environment, old institutional alliances have been redefined. The alliances that have emerged are complex and in flux, although the detailed discussions in the sections that follow reveal that there is often a logical explanation for why such alliances have emerged.

Domestic wool marketing in 2002 differs fundamentally from 1992 because of the emergence of private dealers. The Supply and Marketing Co-operative dramatically lost its market share once it lost its sole procurement status. The private dealers operate in very different ways to the traditional State procurement agency.

7.1.2   Current Structures in Domestic Wool Marketing

Largely as a result of the institutional reforms and changing alliances that have occurred, current structures take a form represented in Figure 7.2. The horizontal axis of the figure represents a continuum from low-value wool used by woollens mills (on the left-hand side of the diagram) to higher-value wool used by worsted mills (right-hand side). The vertical axis highlights the regional dimension to wool marketing in being organized from local production areas (top of the diagram) to higher administrative levels often involving inter-regional flows (bottom of the diagram). The various wool marketing channels and actors fall into this matrix.

The vast majority of China's wool – which is mainly low value – flows down the left-hand side of the diagram. The wool takes two main forms, namely fleece wool and wool shorn or removed (fellmongered) from skins. In both cases there are various stages of transactions and transformation. Except on State Farms, fleece wool is shorn by independent households and sold through a hierarchy of private dealers to eventually reach the woollen mills that are usually located outside of the production regions. In some cases, the dealers contract early-stage processors in scouring and topmaking to transform the wool before delivering it to more distant woollen mills. Wool from skins follows a slightly different path. Independent households sell their sheep to local slaughter units which then sell on the skins through a range of channels including skin dealers, skin markets, or to specialized skin

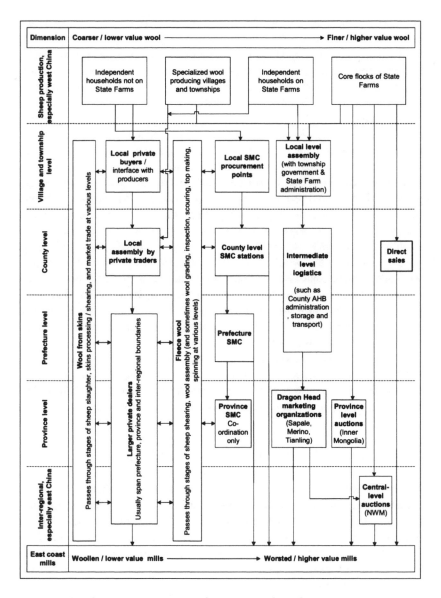

Figure 7.2   Current structures in domestic wool marketing

processing companies. The wool from the skins passes through various levels of intermediaries to reach the woollen mills.

Much of China's mid-value fleece wool also passes through private dealer channels and is sourced from independent households and from households on State Farms. In some provinces such as Xinjiang, Supply and Marketing Co-operatives (or ex-Supply and Marketing Co-operatives) still play some role in mid-value markets. The Supply and Marketing Co-operative system is organized in a hierarchy stemming from local purchase points, through the administrative hierarchy, and on to woollen or, in some cases, worsted mills.

In some rare cases, private dealers purchase higher-value wool from individual household wool growers (such as in the case of the famous premium Erdos wool from Wushen County in Inner Mongolia). However because of the lack of grading or price-grade differentials in the above marketing channels, separate and shorter marketing channels have been established for high-value wool, as represented in the right-hand side of the diagram. Much of this wool derives from State Farms – especially core fine-wool sheep flocks, but also the households that run their flocks on the State Farms. In addition some townships that have specialized in fine wool production operate in a way similar to State Farms. These State Farms and specialized areas sell either to large wool marketing organizations, through auctions, or direct to worsted mills.

The diverse wool marketing channels shown in Figure 7.2 and described above are subject to ongoing changes. The remaining discussion in this chapter therefore analyses why the changes have occurred in the way they have as a guide to understand where future changes may be heading.

7.2   PLIGHT OF THE DOMINANT PLAYERS

A major feature of the transformation of domestic wool marketing systems in the post-reform era has been the demise of the State wool marketing agencies and the emergence of private dealers. These changes could be expected in a transitional economy. However the process by which it has happened and the outcomes for the wool textile industry are not obvious. Indeed the changes have adversely impacted upon the ability of some mills to source the raw wool inputs they need.

7.2.1   Demise of Supply and Marketing Co-operatives

The Supply and Marketing Co-operative network acted as the sole procurement agency for wool throughout China until the early reform era in the 1980s. When the wool market was first liberalized, the Supply and

Marketing Co-operative share of wool trading declined from over 90 per cent in 1984 to less than 50 per cent in 1992 (for more detail see Longworth and Brown 1995, Figure 7.1). Initially the loss in market share went to other competing government buyers or agencies such as the Animal Husbandry Industry and Commerce Company (under the Ministry of Agriculture) and the China National Animal By-products Import–Export Corporation (under the former Ministry of Foreign Economic Relations and Trade).[2] These government agencies are no longer actively trading in the domestic wool marketing sector.

In addition to these government agencies, other marketing channels emerged in the early 1990s, including auctions, direct sales between State Farms and mills, wool markets and private dealers. Indeed by 1992 the market was liberalized to the extent that producers could sell to any buyer and mills could purchase their wool through any channel. The Price Bureau no longer set wool prices from 1991, although other administrative means such as guidance prices continued to be used within the State-controlled marketing channels.

The period from the early 1990s also saw subsidies and preferential policies incrementally withdrawn. For example Supply and Marketing Co-operatives no longer receive low-interest loans for working capital (from banks and special national loans) to buy wool or for storage and stockpiling.[3] Supply and Marketing Co-operatives buckled under the weight of an enormous debt (said to be around Rmb10 billion nationally) and at a time when they were being forced to make loan applications to banks on a commercial basis. The Supply and Marketing Co-operative system also underwent internal reform. Individual wool purchase sales points gained independence and started competing with each other, while practices such as transfer pricing diminished. In addition, as Supply and Marketing Co-operatives lost their role as the main supplier of inputs and services to farmers, their relationships with farmers broke down.[4]

As a result of these forces external and internal to the Supply and Marketing Co-operative system, the market share of Supply and Marketing Co-operatives in domestic wool marketing has further eroded since 1992, although some regional differences arise. In Gansu in 2001, Supply and Marketing Co-operatives claimed to trade about one-third of all wool in the province. In Xinjiang, the Supply and Marketing Co-operatives (in the original form) traded about 11 000 tonnes of wool or 16 per cent of the total wool. In other major wool growing regions such as Inner Mongolia, Supply and Marketing Co-operatives have all but been dissolved and trade negligible amounts or less than 1000 tonnes per year. Cases discussed below highlight where Supply and Marketing Co-operative structures have been dramatically restructured. For example a company restructured from the Supply and

Marketing Co-operative system in Xinjiang trades 5300 tonnes or 8 per cent of the Xinjiang total, while another restructured Supply and Marketing Co-operative company operates in Inner Mongolia.

Image 7.1   Private dealers assembling wool in western China

Private dealers have replaced State procurement agencies as the dominant players in domestic wool marketing. They operate in a loose hierarchy extending from grassroots purchasers to large eastern dealers. In between, intermediate-level dealers (pictured) are responsible for assembling wool, packing and transport and some crude grading. The fragmented nature of private dealers and lack of price-grade differentials embodied in the system may be suitable for low grade wool but has contributed to the demise of the fine-wool sector.

The demise of the Supply and Marketing Co-operative system has major consequences for the industry. It was a vast network consisting of over 11 000 purchase points at village and township level, an extensive (if not overly sophisticated) technical infrastructure, a workforce with at least some training and experience in wool and wool marketing, and a huge distribution and logistics network. Thus Supply and Marketing Co-operatives had the infrastructure and wherewithal to assemble small heterogeneous lots of wool from the multitude of herders for interlotting into relatively large lots of homogeneous wool needed by wool textile mills, even if in practice they did not make full use of this potential. Furthermore although price-grade differentials were administratively established, premiums for better-quality wools were embodied in the system.

The Supply and Marketing Co-operative system was far from perfect, especially in regard to the administratively created inefficiencies and large debts accrued by the system. However in terms of its potential to apply industry standards and deliver to mill requirements, it surpassed the private trader system of today. Thus even in the deregulated market of the early 2000s, Supply and Marketing Co-operatives still hold a number of competitive advantages and have access to niche market opportunities. These opportunities have not been accessed by most local Supply and Marketing Co-operatives, which have buckled under the weight of debt or been unable to make the necessary changes. Others however have found a niche in mid-value wool markets. That is they lie somewhere in between the plethora of private dealers in the low-value market and the large Dragon Head marketing organizations and State Farms that dominate the high-value fine-wool market.[5]

7.2.2 Emergence of Private Dealers

By the end of the 1990s, Supply and Marketing Co-operatives had been overwhelmed by private wool dealers. In Xinjiang, private dealers traded 70 per cent of the provincial wool clip, while the equivalent figure was 90 per cent in Inner Mongolia and around 50 per cent in Gansu. Although private dealers account for a lower proportion of the fine-wool trade, the proportion is not much lower and has been growing in recent years.

Private dealers have forged ahead for various reasons. First, they do not have the legacy of the overhead and debt repayments of the Supply and Marketing Co-operative system. Private dealers run low-cost operations as individual enterprises or small companies, with loosely organized procurement and distribution networks. Supply and Marketing Co-operatives also complain that they pay more taxes than the private dealers.[6] Second, private dealers tend to buy wool on a mixed average grade basis. This practice, combined with the asymmetric access to market information between dealers and small households, means that dealers often pay less for the wool than its true value. Third, even if household wool producers are aware of the information asymmetries, they often prefer to sell to private dealers because they offer immediate cash payments.

Some interesting spatial patterns have emerged in the private marketing of domestic wool in China. Despite the differences with Supply and Marketing Co-operatives outlined above, private dealers interact with each other to form a loose network that logistically at least is not unlike that of the Supply and Marketing Co-operatives. In particular a hierarchy of purchasers and dealers coordinate from grassroots level up to inter-provincial dealers and processors. The process is essentially run by larger inter-regional dealers. Every year before the short shearing season in summer, large dealers contact county-level dealers to specify the broad types and prices for wool for which they are looking. These county-level dealers then delegate the job of wool purchasing to local buyers.

At the grassroots – village or township – level, small local buyers interact directly with sheep households. These households sell all of their wool (unsorted and unclassed) to the local buyer for a negotiated price with payment on the spot.[7] These dealers have small vehicles – such as small three-wheeled motorbike trucks – to transport the wool.

The wool is transported to collection points that are organized by the next tier of (county-level) dealers.[8] The county-level dealers trade about 50 tonnes per year each, though there is significant variation. Dealers at this level spread the wool out over a large area and perform crude sorting, at least differentiating between fine and semi-fine wool. It is at this level of sorting and scale that the dealer can trade commercial-sized lots. The dealers sometimes operate independently and sell to scours or mills within or outside the local region. Usually however they act as intermediaries for the larger inter-regional traders that operate at the next level up. Indeed larger inter-regional dealers often visit the county-level collection points to organize the sorting and transport.

The large dealers base themselves in east coast areas, especially Heze Prefecture in southern Shandong Province. Registered as private or shareholder companies, they undertake a range of trading activities. For example, many of the dealers interviewed primarily acted as hide and skin traders and engaged in wool trading only over the summer shearing season. However because the Chinese shearing season varies by area depending on the temperature and altitude of the region, it can last for several months on a nationwide basis. So after the purchasing season in a particular area, the inter-regional dealer moves on to the next wool production area which has a different shearing and buying period. Large dealers can purchase up to 500 tonnes per season in this manner.

The wool journeys back to the east coast, but through various routes. Most wool is probably delivered in raw (greasy) form. However some dealers have the wool scoured on a service processing basis near the place of purchase. Given the low clean yields of Chinese wool, this will reduce the weight of the wool by more than 50 per cent, substantially reducing transport costs. Some dealers also have the wool combed into tops and even spun into yarn on a service processing basis (where the dealers retains ownership). These processed wool products are then sold to later-stage carpet making and other woollens processors on the east coast.

The decentralized nature of private trading, the lack of registration and reporting procedures, and the multiple stages of product transformation undertaken makes it difficult to follow – let alone quantify – the wool marketing chain for private trading. Another complicating factor is that low-value wool derives not just from fleece wool (shorn from live sheep), but also from sheep skins (as a by-product of sheep slaughter). This fellmongered wool from sheep skins is marketed along a series of slaughter and hide processing operations, where markets and private dealers play important marketing roles.

For an insight into the destination and processing of low-value wool in China, consider the case of Li County in the eastern province of Hebei, which is similar to the nearby counties of Xinji and Wuji. In 2003, Li County alone had more than 20 wool scours (with a combined scouring capacity of 100 000 tonnes), 210 small private woollen textile mills (150 000 spindles and 100 000 tonnes woollen yarn), housed a large leather market and skins processing companies, and had a large raw wool market. Much of the low-value wool from Western China is destined for markets like the one in Li County, which was said to have a turnover of 100 000 tonnes of wool per year and cover more than 400 *mu* (26 hectares) of land. The land is leased out by local farmers (to compensate for lost grain production) to individual wool dealers. The raw wool is simply piled on the cultivated ground, where it becomes very dirty and tangled, and is loaded (along with dirt) into small trucks with pitchforks (see Image 1.4).

This wool is purchased directly by local scours or, increasingly commonly, by woollen mills that then have the scours process the wool on service basis. Either way, the scour sorts the wool into broad categories (such as 58 count wool and below and 60 count wool and above). However this sorting is extremely crude. One scour visited, with a capacity of 6000 tonnes per annum, contracted 500 women from agricultural households every year to sort the wool at a wage of Rmb1 per hour. Although some specialized wool graders were said to be present, the mass of untrained and poorly paid graders could not hope to grade the wool effectively. Furthermore, the primitive scouring equipment and methods used in the county produced irretrievably tangled scoured wool. The mixed-grade, matted scoured wool may be suitable for the lower-value woollen mills in the region, but precludes access to the higher-value woollen or worsted sectors.

The analysis of domestic sheep and wool production systems in Chapter 8 suggests that many of these systems may be suited to the lower-value segments of the wool textile industry. Consequently, having low-cost, rudimentary, but effective channels for marketing this wool such as that described for private dealers in this section, may be appropriate and aligned with the current economic incentives and biophysical conditions.

However sheep and wool production systems in China are extremely diverse and there are some regions and systems that are suited to higher-value segments of the wool and wool textile industry. Problems arise therefore when marketing channels do not exist to allow these particular growers, regions and systems to access the higher-value segments, or where clear signals are not available that enable appropriate decisions about which segments should be targeted. The following sections explore some of the efforts to improve the marketing channels for fine wool.

7.3   EFFORTS TO DEVELOP DOMESTIC FINE-WOOL MARKETING

An effort to revive fine-wool marketing in recent years has seen the emergence of new marketing organizations. These new organizations are insignificant players in the context of the total domestic wool – and even fine-wool – marketing sector and only exist in Xinjiang and Inner Mongolia. However as "Dragon Head" enterprises designed to lead along the rest of the industry, they are heralded as models of vertical integration and the future of fine-wool marketing in China.

Several major themes emerge from an investigation of these new marketing organizations. First, it shows how certain traditional governmental institutions have restructured their operations to survive in the reform era. Second, it reveals the complexity of the new institutional alliances that are emerging. Third, it highlights the manner in which China is developing more sophisticated institutions for the premium fine-wool market, including centralized wool assembly, the development and application of standards, vertical integration, and information systems. Fourth, it indicates the significant level of replication and lack of coordination both within and between provinces that acts as a major obstacle to the development of a national fine-wool marketing system in China.

7.3.1   Xinjiang Uyghur Autonomous Region

Xinjiang is China's largest fine wool producing province and where the country's most sophisticated set of wool marketing institutions has been created. A feature of this new marketing environment has been the new alliances and relationships that have emerged among some of the traditional wool market participants. Competition in wool marketing has shifted from that between agencies to a competition between alliances. Nonetheless the legacy of the old institutions means that some elements of coordination exist in the midst of otherwise fierce competition.

Xinjiang Fine Wool Producers Association

Leading the charge is the Xinjiang Fine Wool Producers Association (also known as Sapale). Although established as late as 1998, it is now the best known domestic fine-wool marketing organization in China. Originally scientists-cum-entrepreneurs from the Xinjiang Academy of Animal Science established the association with cross-institutional support from various organizations. Association members are fine-wool production organizations that undertake to sell their wool to the association on the basis of Sapale grading standards which are more rigorous than the National standards. In 2002, there were 40 "base production areas" – of which 18 were State Farms and 22 were townships – that had contracts with the association. Another 49 areas (farms and townships) had a non-binding option to sell to the association.

In coordination with the association, the base production areas organize and support thousands of households under their jurisdiction to fill the contracts. The support includes the provision of extension services (breeding, feeding and veterinary care), centralized wool assembly services (mechanical shearing, classing and baling) and some financial services (including credit). Household producers receive payment based on the clean-wool yield, objective measurement results, and prices received at the auctions. That is, Sapale acts as a broker. This contrasts starkly with private dealers who take ownership of the wool they buy on a cash basis from households on a subjectively assessed, mixed-grade basis. The association and base production areas take some fees and commissions for their services. The majority of the wool is sold at auctions organized by the Nanjing Wool Market in the Yangzi River Basin where most of China's worsted mills are located.

This model has considerable potential to deliver better-quality and more homogeneous lots to worsted mills, to generate price premiums for better-quality wool, and for these to be delivered back to association members and ultimately to household producers. From an industry-wide perspective, the objective standards used by the association can reduce the costs and risks for worsted mills and promote industry integration and modernization.

Against these perceived positive developments, some cautionary signs are emerging. First, the amounts marketed by the Sapale association are negligible. Volumes peaked at 1100 tonnes in 2001 but fell to 600 tonnes in 2002 and only a few hundred tonnes in 2003. The Sapale system must compete with other domestic fine-wool marketing systems (especially direct sales between State Farms and mills that bypass Sapale) and with imported fine wool. The organization has also begun to pay households on the basis of wool assessment at classing time, rather than on prices received at auction. This may be a response to households' preference for up-front payment, but may also be an attempt to extract more rents from a contrived auction system. The organization is also in the process of changing its status from that of an association to a shareholder company (called Sapale) and is branching out into the related but potentially more lucrative mutton business. Further information about the association and the Sapale Company can be found in Chen and Chen (2002), Chen et al. (2001) and Zhang (2001).

Image 7.2   Private dealers deliver wool to scours in eastern China

Private traders deal mainly in lower value wool that is sorted only into broad types. This is suitable for lower-grade scours that produce for the woollens industry, although they are likely to do more sorting at the scour.

The association is linked to other organizations also regarded as "Dragon Head" organizations in the integration of China's and especially Xinjiang's fine-wool industry, namely the Nanjing Wool Market, the Kuitun Storage and Transport Company, the Xinjiang and Jiangsu Fibre Inspection Bureaus (see Chapter 3), and the Stud Sheep, Wool and Cashmere Quality Supervising, Inspecting and Testing Center of the Xinjiang Academy of Animal Science.

Because of its institutional connections, the association has received funding from sources such as Nanjing Wool Market and the National and Xinjiang Science and Technology Commissions as well as policy support from the Xinjiang Animal Husbandry Department and the Animal Husbandry Division of the Production and Construction Corps.[9]

Kuitun Storage and Transport Company

The Kuitun company was established with involvement from the Ministry of Agriculture, the (former) Ministry of Foreign Trade and Economic Co-operation and the Xinjiang Production and Construction Corps. It is closely involved with the Production and Construction Corps Supply and Marketing Co-operative (which is quite distinct from the Supply and Marketing Co-operative system described in Section 7.2) and is still subsidized to store and stockpile strategic commodities such as grain, flour, cotton and limestone in Kuitun, a strategically important region of Xinjiang. The company headquarters and storage facilities are located strategically on the major Asia–Europe rail line which also connects the fine-wool growing areas of Xinjiang (Bole, Yili and Tacheng) to the eastern areas of China.[10] The company compound covers a vast area, although most of it is not under cover.

Because wool is not a commodity subsidized for stockpiling, wool marketing activities have to be undertaken on a commercial basis. The company aims to store up to 2000 tonnes of wool and to provide repacking, compression (from three bales to one to reduce transport volumes) and interlotting services. The margins on these wool marketing activities however are low, and there are also other more important strategic reasons behind the efforts to develop the centre. The facility plans to conduct wool auctions in Kuitun rather than at Nanjing, and to extend its links beyond the Xinjiang Fine Wool Producers Association and the Nanjing Wool Market. One stated reason was to reduce costs for mills located in Xinjiang and Gansu as the wool would not have to be transshipped to Nanjing and back again (as is the case when the wool is sold at auction in Nanjing). A more compelling reason is that auctions on the east coast place sellers in a "passive" position because there are few alternative avenues to sell the premium wool if it is passed in (not sold) at the auction. However these arguments depend on the notion that Chinese wool cannot be sold by description or even by sample (which would alleviate the need to physically transport the wool to the site of the auction on the east coast). This argument illustrates how the lack of widely accepted product standards and a system of objective measurement continue to be key obstacles to the development of wool marketing in China.

The notion of having ideally located transshipment points, which form the nexus of a range of distribution and marketing services including sale by description, aligns with efforts to modernize domestic wool marketing.

Kuitun has much to offer in this regard, but the problems experienced in operating in this manner and in extending its marketing activities highlight some of the problems associated with modernizing domestic wool marketing in China.

Xinjiang Merino Fine Wool Sheep Science and Technology Company

Other organizations in Xinjiang have sought to emulate and compete with the vertically integrated model of the Xinjiang Fine Wool Producers Association. One such company is the Xinjiang Merino Fine Wool Sheep Science and Technology Co. Ltd. (otherwise known as the Merino Company). The company is based in Yili Prefecture which is one of Xinjiang's foremost and famous fine-wool growing areas. Shareholders and participants in the company include the Xinjiang Supply and Marketing Co-operative (75 per cent share of the company and initial investment of Rmb15 million), the Xinjiang Agricultural University, the Yili Supply and Marketing Co-operative, and the Yili Animal Husbandry Bureau (which have contributed significantly in the form of farms, breeding sheep and extension facilities). The participants have been chosen strategically so that the company can draw on their facilities and resources, especially with respect to purchase points, storage facilities, skilled classers and shearers of the Supply and Marketing Co-operatives, and the sheep extension capabilities (feeding, breeding and veterinary) of the Yili Animal Husbandry Bureau system.

The Merino Company currently operates in three counties in Yili Prefecture but has plans to expand to seven counties. It owns 7000 "core breeding sheep". Because of the small number of sheep, the company produced just 30 tonnes of fine wool in 2001 which was sold through the Nanjing Wool Market. The long-term plans of the Merino Company involve the development of a core breeding flock that will produce tens of thousands of fine-wool sheep that will be distributed to households. The households will raise the sheep for a commission, buy them outright, or in lieu of shares with the company. In return the company will buy wool from the households at a floor price, and pass on above-reserve prices from the auction back to the household after deducting costs. Future plans involve bypassing the auction system and selling direct to mills.

Xinjiang Tianling Animal By-products Company

The Xinjiang Supply and Marketing Co-operative system has responded to reforms in the premium wool sector not only by branching out into the Merino Company as discussed above, but also by establishing another parallel marketing company called the Xinjiang Tianling Animal By-products Company. Tianling Company is closely connected with the Merino Company. The manager of the Merino Company was formerly the deputy manager of the Tianling Company – which is purely a commodity marketing company. In addition the Tianling Company acts as the Xinjiang branch of the National Tea and Animal By-products Export–Import Company, formerly under the Ministry of Foreign Economic Relations and Trade. In 2002, the manager of the Tianling Company was also in the process of establishing the Xinjiang Tonghui Animal Husbandry Products Market at Miquan near Urumuqi, as discussed in Section 7.4.3.

The original Xinjiang Supply and Marketing Co-operative owns 20 per cent of the shares of the Tianling Company, while employees own another 40 per cent with the final 40 per cent owned by outside investors. However the company remains essentially a reincarnation of the old Supply and Marketing Co-operative system. Tianling utilizes the old Supply and Marketing Co-operative purchasing stations to buy from herders. It is prohibited from dealing with purchasing stations that have "policy losses", but this is not a major issue as these stations have few if any staff and minimal or no activity.

Tianling traded about 5300 tonnes of wool in 2001, much of which was said to be mid-grade and mid-value wool. Whether these volumes can be sustained under pressure from the other Dragon Heads in the fine-wool market, namely Sapale and Merino, and from competition with private dealers in low-value markets, remains to be seen especially as the Tianling Company is no longer eligible for subsidized loans to finance their wool buying activities.

7.3.2 Inner Mongolia Autonomous Region

The growing and perhaps destructive competition within provinces like Xinjiang is magnified by inter-regional competition from provinces like Inner Mongolia that have also developed structures to promote vertical integration in the fine-wool industry. Because of the similarity in these new structures, the Inner Mongolian situation will not be elaborated on in detail here.

The equivalent of the Sapale or Merino Company in Inner Mongolia is the Inner Mongolia Livestock Economic and Technological Development Company which comes directly under the Inner Mongolia Animal Husbandry Bureau. In addition to marketing activities through its brand name (Saiaosi), the company also runs its own Inner Mongolian wool auctions, where 500 tonnes of fine wool were sold in 2002 although no wool was sold in 2003 due to the outbreak of Severe Acute Respiratory Syndrome (SARS). Through organizing their own auctions, Inner Mongolian officials seek to capitalize on their extension and wool assembly services for fine wool, rather than see "outside" organizations such as the Nanjing Wool Market unduly benefit from these efforts. The major problems facing both Inner Mongolia and the Nanjing Wool Market as they seek to establish viable and sustainable auction

*Images 7.3 and 7.4   Centralized wool grading and assembly at a State Farm
in Xinjiang.*

*One of the advantages that State Farms is that they have sufficient quantities of
homogeneous fine wool to justify integrated shearing (Chapter 8), grading (top
image) and baling, storage and transport facilities (bottom image).*

systems suggests that a strong degree of coordination is needed between the two auction systems.

The restructured Supply and Marketing Co-operative company in Inner Mongolia is called Muwang, but in 2002 this organization traded only 1000 tonnes of fine wool.

Most of the State Farms in Inner Mongolia were under control of the Ministry of Agriculture/Animal Husbandry Bureau as compared with the dominant Production and Construction Corps system in Xinjiang. The most famous fine-wool State Farms in Inner Mongolia are Aohan, Erhongji, Jinhong, Erduosi, Wuyi, Gadasu and Jinfeng. Each of these farms have core fine-wool breeding sheep flocks (owned by the farms) of between 2000 and 8000 head.

7.4   OTHER MARKETING CHANNELS

The main elements of the transition in domestic wool marketing involve the replacement of State marketing agencies by private traders, and the efforts of various organizations to raise marketing standards through the establishment of Dragon Head organizations. However, other marketing channels including State Farms, direct sales, physical markets and auctions also play significant roles in Chinese wool marketing.

7.4.1   State Farms

The discussion in Chapter 8 reveals that as State Farms undergo reform, the incentives for them to produce fine wool are also changing. Nevertheless many State Farms still have large numbers of fine-wool sheep, either as breeding flocks run by the farm, or as commercial flocks run by households on the State Farm. Many State Farms also conduct centralized shearing, grading and baling.[11] As a result, State Farms can produce relatively homogeneous and large lots of fine wool – between 30 and 100 tonnes of fine wool per farm per year.

Because of the homogeneous and large lots of fine wool, State Farms tend to enter into relatively direct forms of exchange. They rarely sell through the Supply and Marketing Co-operative system and do not sell the wool from core breeding flocks to private dealers. However there has been a strong trend since the late 1990s for households on State Farms that run commercial sheep not in the core breeding flocks to exercise their right to sell their wool through private dealers. State Farms remain as the main supplier of fine wool for Chinese auctions. As discussed below however they also often bypass the auction systems and sell direct to mills.

7.4.2   Direct Purchases by Mills

Changes occurring in the wool marketing system adversely impact upon the ability of worsted mills to source domestic wool to specification. In particular, the demise of Supply and Marketing Co-operatives and the growth in private dealers has fragmented the marketing system and caused specifications to be lost through intermediaries in an undeveloped wool marketing system. This void is yet to be adequately filled by the new Dragon Head marketing organizations or by developed market systems such as auctions. Consequently many east coast worsted mills rely almost exclusively on imported wool even if some of the Chinese fine-wool clip is suitable for their purposes.

On the other hand, some worsted mills – especially in western China – may perceive a competitive advantage in sourcing wool domestically especially in periods of higher imported wool prices. Due to inadequacies in the domestic wool marketing system, many of these worsted mills have resorted to purchasing wool directly from wool growers. This form of direct exchange has occurred since the liberalization of wool marketing in the early 1990s, but has become more pronounced in recent years. These mills consider it to be more reliable and cost effective to travel to and buy direct from production areas.

The heterogeneous and fragmented nature of Chinese wool production systems however severely limits the scope of direct purchases. Absolute limits apply on how many suppliers there are that mill buyers can approach, while the capacity and economics of mill sorting and grading systems effectively limits the number and source of suppliers. Thus direct purchases have been confined mainly to exchanges between the larger mills and larger State Farms with homogeneous lots of sufficient size for the mills.

Even with State Farms however there are too many State Farms for an individual mill to approach separately. And there are few sources of systematic information about the type of wool that particular State Farms have to offer. Thus mills tend to deal with a select group of State Farms with which they are familiar. Alternative marketing channels such as wool auctions have served as a de facto source of information to bring mills and State Farms together. State Farms and mills that initially participate in auctions – and signal each other's requirements and wool characteristics – may subsequently bypass the auctions in direct exchanges. However there are undoubtedly more effective means of information exchange and communication for increasing awareness and bringing mills and State Farms together.

Mills can purchase directly in the wool production areas in various ways. The central administration of State Farms sells wool from core breeding flocks and also organizes the households on the farm to sell wool from their commercial flocks. Alternatively, mill buyers purchase from dealers that buy from households on the State Farms. The amount delivered in a single lot averages 30 tonnes but can be as low as 10 tonnes. In the latter case, the wool is rarely graded, although some skirting may occur. Mills grade the domestic wool themselves, but the lack of grading at the point of purchase makes wool buying riskier and more expensive.

7.4.3 Markets

Physical market places – called rural trade (*nongmao* or *jimao*) markets – are important for the trade of most agricultural products in China, including sheep, sheep skins and mutton. Wool trading normally does not occur through these markets. However there is evidence to suggest that large quantities of lower-grade wool pass through some market places, some of which were established especially for the purpose. Trading in these market places is closely associated with the activities of the private dealers discussed above.

Wool markets in China have concentrated around intensive areas of skin and hide markets and wool scours. One such area is Sanjiaji in Linxia County in the south of Gansu Province. The area represents a major gateway for sourcing sheep and goats, their skins, wool and cashmere from the provinces of Gansu, Sichuan and Qinghai, and also sits beside a major rail line from western to eastern China. The other example of Li County (and neighbouring Xinji and Wuji Counties) in Hebei Province was discussed in Section 5.7 and reported in Box 5.4 in Chapter 5.

Given the scale of these markets relative to the number of sheep (77 million in 2002) and goats (144 million in 2002) sold in China, the amount of animal fibre that passes through these channels is huge and accounts for a large proportion of China's wool trade.[12] However virtually all of this wool is coarse or semi-fine wool destined for use in the woollens trade. This type of wool is not suitable for the worsted mills discussed in Chapter 5.

Some attempts have and are being made to establish physical market places for wool shorn not only from sheep skins, but also fleece wool from live sheep. In 2002 for example the manager of the Xinjiang Tianling Animal By-products Company, mentioned in Section 7.3.1, was in the process of establishing a wool selling facility in the Xinjiang Tonghui Animal Husbandry Products Market in Miquan County on the western outskirts of Urumuqi. The market sold live sheep and sheep skins,[13] and was located close to compounds from which wool dealers operated. Large dealers based in Miquan County but sourcing their wool from well beyond Miquan claimed that they sold hundreds of tonnes of wool per year to eastern mills, while smaller local dealers traded only a few tonnes and sourced wool from within the county. The wool was all coarse or semi-fine wool, although similar dealers of fine wool operated out of a large rural trade market in nearby Changji City.

These examples may provide insights into the way that larger and more specialized wool markets may develop in the future. The Tianling Company envisioned that wool sold through the market would be graded and that market information (especially prices) services would be provided.[14] That is, the market was intended as a "Dragon Head" for the integration of the wool supply chain. The extent to which these physical market places facilitate efficient marketing and accurate pricing of lower value wool remains to be seen.

7.4.4   Auctions

One of the more innovative aspects in the early stages of wool marketing reform in China in the 1980s was the introduction of wool auctions. Strongly supported by an alliance between the Ministry of Agriculture and the Ministry of Textile Industry – and with equally strong opposition from the Ministry of Commerce – the auctions promised to bring buyers and sellers together, improve the accuracy of price determination, and focus attention on issues such as grading, objective measurement and quality improvement.

The first round of auctions occurred between 1987 and 1992 and failed to live up to expectations. Brown (1997) and Longworth and Brown (1995, Chapter 8) provide a detailed account and critique of these auctions, and highlight some fundamental shortcomings and systematic failings in the conduct of these auctions. Some of these shortcomings included: the small amounts and proportions auctioned; the contrived nature of auctions; the relatively high cost and inconvenience of selling through auction; and the lack of throughput in the auctions as State Farms and buyers bypassed the auctions once the type of wool and buyer requirements had been signalled.

The rapid demise of the first round of auctions meant that efforts to restart auctions did not occur until 1999. It may have been expected that industry transition and a more sophisticated agribusiness environment of the late 1990s may have been more conducive to effective operation of the auctions. However this has not been the case. Indeed the latest round of auctions has followed a remarkably but disturbingly similar pattern to the auctions a decade previously, where modest initial trials were followed by slightly larger sales, then a rapid decline and suspension of trade. For instance the Nanjing Wool Market auctioned 275 tonnes in 1999, 750 tonnes in 2000, 1100 tonnes in 2001, and 500 tonnes in 2002, while trade was negligible in 2003 due to SARS. A close investigation of the operation of wool auctions in the 1999 to

2003 period reveals that they embody many of the fundamental problems and features that Brown and Longworth highlighted. To make the prospects of success even more difficult, an additional set of adverse factors feature in the auctions in the 2000s compared with the auctions in the early 1990s. There are many organizations (the Nanjing Wool Market, Saiaosi in Inner Mongolia and plans for Kuitun in Xinjiang) that want to develop their own auctions which will rapidly overcrowd an already limited marketing channel. There are also now more marketing channels that compete with the auctions for a limited amount of high-value wool, including the Dragon Head enterprises and direct sales.

Auctions are central to wool marketing in many major wool producing countries, and an effective auction system would seem an important aspect of the modernization of the high-value fine-wool marketing sector. Though the organizations conducting the auctions are well intentioned and knowledgeable about wool, there are several fundamental aspects that need refining. These include the need to introduce competitive bidding among mills and other buyers for auction lots,[15] and sale by (accurate) product description without the cost of transporting the wool to the auction site. The latter point will become important if China is to develop trials of e-commerce and other forms of virtual exchange for wool.

NOTES

1   For a detailed discussion of wool production and marketing in China prior to the mid-1990s, see in particular Longworth and Brown (1995) and Longworth and Williamson (1993).

2   The China National Animal By-products Import–Export Corporation had provincial branches in Xinjiang, Inner Mongolia, Gansu, Hubei, Ningxia and several other provinces. These provincial trading companies operated under various names but in Xinjiang were known as the Tea and Animal By-products Company. They differed from the similarly named Supply and Marketing Co-operative companies not only in their ability to engage in international trade but also in that they did not have subsidiaries below the provincial level.

3   In Xinjiang alone, State agencies were said to require Rmb250 million in capital per year to purchase wool – Rmb300 million if they were to purchase all the cashmere as well.

4   For further information on the reform of the Supply and Marketing Co-operative system in general, see SMCCFB (2002) and Zhu (1998).

5   There are strong parallels in this regard with State marketing agencies in other agricultural industries. In particular, the vast network of General Food Companies that also operated under the former Ministry of Commerce monopolized the marketing and processing of China's massive non-staple foods sector. The network includes hundreds of beef and sheep abattoirs located throughout China that are under reform and being forced to compete in a liberalized market environment. The abattoirs have been squeezed on low-value markets by a multitude of low-cost individual private slaughter households and cattle and beef traders and on high-value markets by new modern vertically integrated abattoirs (see Longworth et al. (2001, Chapter 9). However some General Food Companies have been

able to utilize their mechanized slaughter lines, cold storage, distribution and food safety and inspection capacity to establish a niche in mid-value beef and mutton markets.

6   The taxes and fees local Supply and Marketing Co-operatives had to pay in 2002 included a 10 per cent product tax to the county government, a quality testing fee to the local Fibre Inspection Bureau, a grassland development fee to county government, the Industry and Commerce Administration Bureau management fee, and VAT paid to central government of 3 per cent for greasy wool and 7 per cent for clean wool.

7   In some cases – such as Wushen County famous for its fine wool – the dealers also have shearing teams and purchase the wool in advance.

8   These collection points can be in anywhere from the courtyards of factories to schoolyards in the school holidays.

9   In Xinjiang there are two separate administrative structures responsible for agriculture and animal husbandry activities, namely the usual Ministry of Agriculture provincial hierarchy and the Production and Construction Corps. For a detailed discussion of the origins and importance of this dual system of administration, see Longworth and Williamson (1993, Chapter 7).

10   A single freight train carriage can hold 48 to 52 tonnes of wool. The cost of transport to Nanjing using the compressed bales is about Rmb450 per tonne, which is significantly cheaper than the costs of moving wool by truck.

11   About 30 per cent of the Production and Construction Corps farms in Xinjiang use mechanical shearing. The Production and Construction Corps farms organize unified shearing, classing, packaging, transport and selling of the fine wool.

12   Under the assumption that local breed, cross-breed or mutton sheep yield 2 kilograms of unskirted wool, these channels handled around 154 kt of wool in 2002 (which accounted for most of China's coarse and semi-fine wool production of 195 kt in 2002). However yields can be lower when shorn from the skin while many of the sheep skins are not shorn at all.

13   Two designated slaughter points located in Miquan also promote the need for a market for live sheep and goats, skins, and wool and cashmere sales.

14   The manager of the Tianling Company is vice president of the Animal Husbandry Marketing Association and, under this, the head of the Special Committee for the Marketing of Cashmere and Wool. The association holds two conferences each year, one to discuss prices, and one for companies to exchange experiences. Mills and trading companies from throughout China were said to attend.

15   As an indication of this, despite the fact that up to 20 mills can attend the auctions, final exchange auction prices inevitably are virtually the same as the starting floor price (to within Rmb1/kg). Some lots can attract several bids at auction but it is well known that the mills continue to trade the lots among themselves after the auction. Against this, the Nanjing Wool Market argues that average auction prices increased from 1999 to 2002, but it is unclear whether this is due to more competitive bidding or associated with increasing imported wool prices.

8. Reorganizing Domestic Raw Material Production

China is renowned for its position as the world's largest wool textiles producer and importer of wool. At the same time, China also had the largest sheep flock of any country and produced almost 300 kt of greasy wool in 2002. In particular China has a long history of efforts to develop a fine wool growing industry.

The traditional reasons for placing considerable emphasis on fine-wool production were related not just to import replacement and the desire to secure supplies for the wool textile sector, but also on the improved income-generating opportunities fine-wool growing could offer households. Traditionally, sheep raising and wool production represented one of the few commercial activities for households in the remote pastoral areas of China. Given the severely constrained resource base – badly degraded rangelands – it made sense to maximize the returns from individual grazing animals and hence the interest in higher-value fine wool.

Thus the domestic wool production sector is of interest not only because it is a source of raw materials for the textile industry but also because of its traditionally perceived potential to contribute to rural development in some of the poorest and most remote parts of China.

Despite the past emphasis on expanding fine-wool output, the most notable change that has occurred in Chinese wool production in the 1990s has been the switch out of fine-wool production and into semi-fine wool production. The switch is reflected in aggregate official statistics but, for the reasons discussed in Section 8.1, the official statistics probably significantly understate the decline in genuine fine-wool output.

Part of the reason for the switch out of fine-wool production relates to the elimination of policies that previously artificially supported fine-wool production. These policy changes and the resultant fragmentation of extension services supporting fine-wool growing are covered in Section 8.2. Finally, Section 8.3 outlines how some of the production units still oriented towards fine-wool production, as well as some new production structures that have emerged, are seeking to thrive in the new economic environment.

8.1   STRUCTURAL CHANGES IN CHINESE WOOL PRODUCTION

This section overviews greasy wool production trends between 1982 and 2002 and explains some of the factors behind the trends. In this context it is important to note that "greasy wool" is the term for raw wool as it is shorn from the sheep. Once wool grease, vegetable matter, dirt and other impurities have been scoured out of the wool, the wool is referred to as "clean scoured wool". The percentage of clean scoured wool obtained from greasy wool would average between 40 and 45 per cent in China. The average clean scoured yield in Australia would be closer to 65 per cent or more. It is important to recognize the potentially major differences in clean scoured yields when comparing greasy wool output in China with that of other major wool growing countries.

Aggregate official statistics record the steady growth in total greasy wool production between 1982 and 2002 and also a discernable shift out of fine wool and into coarser wool production since the mid-1990s. These trends are evident for China as a whole and for nearly all major wool producing provinces.

However Chinese livestock statistics are notoriously unreliable. For example following the Agricultural Census of 1997, official beef production was significantly adjusted downwards with some provinces such as Shandong recording adjustments as large as 50 per cent. Appendix A in Longworth et al. (2001) provides a full discussion of how livestock statistics are collected in China and the "corrections" to official statistics following the census.

In the case of wool output, official data collected when the Supply and Marketing Co-operatives procured almost all the clip would have been reasonably accurate since they needed to reconcile with the actual amount of wool flowing through the Supply and Marketing Co-operative system. Nowadays there is no means of checking the estimates of wool output made by local officials and on which provincial and national figures are ultimately based. Given the historical policy emphasis on increasing fine-wool production, it might be expected that local officials have been reluctant to reveal fully the decline in fine-wool production in recent years.

8.1.1   Sheep and Wool Production in China[1]

Keeping in mind the potentially serious deficiencies in the official data, Figure 8.1 illustrates sheep and greasy wool production for China between 1982 and 2002. Sheep numbers increased by 35 per cent over this period, with total wool production increasing broadly in line with sheep numbers.

However there have been significant changes in the proportion of the total wool clip in each of the three broad categories in recent years. The three broad categories each now contribute about one-third of China's greasy wool.[2]

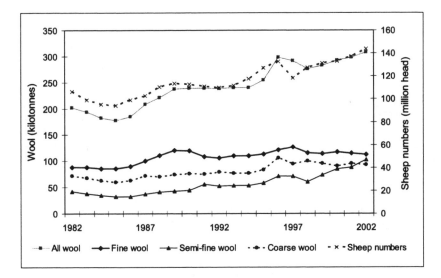

Figure 8.1 Greasy wool production and sheep numbers in China: 1982 to 2002

Fine wool output – defined in the 1993 standards (see Section 3.2.1) as the production of wool with an average fibre diameter of 25 micron or less – increased relatively little between 1982 and 2002. An increase during the buoyant period of the second half of the 1980s has since been partially offset by declining production between 1997 and 2002.[3] As Longworth and Williamson (1993) emphasize, the "fine" wool category in Chinese official statistics includes genuine fine wool and "improved" fine wool. Improved fine wool is produced by sheep that are being upgraded from native coarse wools by mating to merinos or genuine fine-wool rams. While improved fine wool may have an average fibre diameter of less than 25 micron, it also contains coloured and/or medullated (hairy) fibres and exhibits large variation even within the one fleece. Therefore although on the basis of average fibre diameter this wool is of a fineness suitable for worsted production (see Figure 2.3 in Chapter 2), because of the other attributes of the wool, only a small proportion of this wool can actually be used by worsted mills.

Official statistics do not distinguish between genuine fine wool and improved fine wool. In recent years however, the proportion of improved wool in the statistical category "fine" wool would have increased significantly. This is because many sheep herding households have mated their genuine fine-wool ewes to native breed rams or to imported mutton-breed rams. This regression in the genetic composition of the Chinese sheep flock has been widespread as herders respond to the market incentives to raise hardier sheep primarily for mutton production. Consequently the output of genuine fine wool will have declined much faster since the mid-1990s than the modest decline in the statistical category "fine wool" shown in Figure 8.1. According to these official statistics, "fine wool" accounted for 44 per cent of China's total output of greasy wool in 1982 but this percentage had dropped to 36 per cent in 2002.

"Semi-fine" wool – defined as having a mean fibre diameter between 25.1 and 40 micron – is suitable for the woollens industry which produces items such as bulky apparel goods. Since the mid-1990s, semi-fine wool production has expanded significantly and has accounted for all of the increase in total wool production.

"Coarse" wool is essentially wool with a great many medullated fibres that is processed in local towns and villages for traditional woollens products. Better-quality coarse wool can be used to make carpets on a commercial basis. Coarse wool production has been steady since the 1970s.

8.1.2   Changes in Provincial Greasy Wool Production

National-level statistics can mask some of the regional changes that have occurred in Chinese greasy wool production.[4] Eight major wool producing provinces that span production systems and geographical regions are examined in Table 8.1. Together, these eight provinces accounted for 82 per cent of China's total greasy wool production in 2002. Table 8.1 shows the volume of greasy wool produced by these provinces as well as their share of Chinese greasy wool production for the years 1982, 1992 and 2002.

Table 8.1 reveals the growth in both absolute and relative terms in wool production in provinces like Xinjiang, Hebei, Shandong and Heilongjiang. As highlighted in Figure 8.2, it is precisely these provinces that have been switching from fine to semi-fine wool production. Several provinces, most notably Inner Mongolia and Gansu, have experienced a more modest decline in the proportion of fine wool produced since 1992. Only one province, Jilin, has increased its proportion of fine wool but this has not offset the declines in other provinces because the total output of wool in Jilin is relatively small (Table 8.1).

Table 8.1   Greasy wool production by key wool- growing provinces: selected years

Region	1982		1992		2002	
	kt (% of Chinese production)					
Xinjiang	38	(19)	50	(21)	74	(24)
Inner Mongolia	52	(26)	58	(24)	59	(19)
Hebei	7	(3)	11	(5)	29	(9)
Jilin	5	(2)	9	(4)	22	(7)
Shandong	10	(5)	22	(9)	20	(6)
Heilongjiang	13	(6)	12	(5)	18	(6)
Qinghai	17	(8)	18	(8)	16	(5)
Gansu	9	(4)	15	(6)	15	(5)
Subtotal	*150*	*(74)*	*195*	*(82)*	*252*	*(82)*
All China	**202**	**(100)**	**238**	**(100)**	**308**	**(100)**

Source: EBCAY (various years) and MOA (various years).

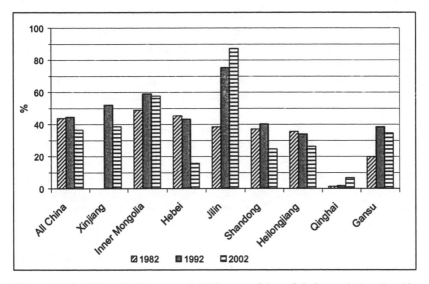

Note: Data for 1982 for Xinjiang are excluded because of the statistical anomaly (mentioned in note 3) of classifying semi-fine wool as fine wool at that time.

Figure 8.2   Fine wool as a percentage of all wool in major wool-growing provinces

8.1.3   Key Determinants of the Swing Away from Fine Wool

Several explanations for the decline in fine-wool production in China are discussed below. However two broad explanations – related to competing products on the supply side and to the location of users on the demand side – are the most important.

On the supply side, there has been a strong shift from wool sheep to meat sheep production. Mutton production statistics in China – which aggregate sheep and goat meat production – increased more than sixfold from 52 kt in 1982 to 316 kt in 2002. Although much of this growth arises from expansion of China's goat herd, Waldron et al. (2004) estimated that sheep meat output rose by several hundred percent over the period, representing double-digit annual growth.

The single most obvious reason for the swing to mutton production has been the major change in relative prices. Mutton prices have risen much faster than wool prices. Another key factor has been the increase in the costs of raising fine-wool sheep compared with hardier dual-purpose sheep. Sheep-raising households have responded to the higher profitability of dual-purpose sheep.

The switch from wool to mutton production has not resulted in a geographical shift in raising sheep from pastoral areas to agricultural areas.[5] Indeed with only modest exceptions, the distribution of the total sheep flock across provinces in China has remained similar since 1980.[6] On the other hand, even within the traditional (pastoral) wool production provinces of Xinjiang and Inner Mongolia, there has been a substantial move into meat sheep production.

The shift from wool to meat sheep production is reflected in sheep production practices including breeding, feeding, shearing and slaughtering practices. However producers still shear their sheep on an annual basis in what can best be described as dual-purpose sheep production systems. Furthermore producers often enter into meat or dual-purpose sheep production on the basis of their wool sheep. That is, producers cross their female wool sheep to rams belonging to local or introduced mutton breeds. The offspring crossbred sheep usually produce semi-fine wool, the output of which, as outlined above, has grown faster than the output of other types of wool since the early 1990s.

The relationships between wool and sheep meat may change as the breeding programme continues over time. If China develops a sizable lamb as opposed to mutton industry, the young sheep will not be shorn before slaughter. Furthermore the growth in semi-fine wool output may subside if crossbreeding programmes lower fleece weights. In the short to medium term however, mutton production can be seen as competing with fine-wool production but being complementary to semi-fine wool production.

Demand-side forces have also been a key factor in the decline of fine-wool production in China. Industry modernization has seen Chinese worsted mills, particularly mills located in eastern China, become more demanding in their wool input specifications. Under normal market conditions, mills find it more cost effective to import fine wool than to buy heterogeneous lots of domestic wool through the inefficient domestic wool marketing channels (see Chapters 6 and 7).

Furthermore the traditional major users of domestic fine wool – the worsted mills and early-stage wool processors in the north-western wool production areas – underwent drastic rationalization in the 1990s (see Chapter 5). Many of the more progressive worsted mills that remain in western China now import most of their raw wool. The breakdown in the relationship between fine-wool producers and worsted mills in the western pastoral regions has had detrimental implications for domestic fine-wool production.

8.2 POLICIES AND SERVICES IN WOOL PRODUCTION

While the higher returns from dual-purpose sheep have been an obvious key factor in the changing composition of the Chinese wool clip, changes in the policy environment have also been important. Policies directed specifically at wool production have become less and less interventionist. At the same time, the broader policy environment has become more and more liberalized giving sheep-raising households almost complete freedom to respond to economic incentives. The role of government in the production sector is now confined primarily to areas such as grassland protection and service provision.

8.2.1 Policies Toward the Wool Production Sector

Government in China still adopts a strong interventionist role in agricultural industries deemed as either strategically important or as "sunrise" industries eligible for "fast tracking". Historically the wool industry has been subject to strong intervention because of its importance in pastoral areas that are located on national boundaries and populated by ethnic minorities. Targeted policies in the past have taken the form of: rigid production plans; price support and stockpiling schemes; influence over processing capacity (mills and scours); inter-regional marketing controls; support for State Farms; and coercive powers over sheep-raising households. Although corresponding policies and interventions remain in place for staple agricultural industries like grains and cotton, such interventionist policies have now been phased out in relation to wool production.

The wool industry has also missed out on a range of more recent industry policies that have targeted emerging livestock industries. These include the Straw for Ruminants programme and the Advantaged Areas programme that have been instrumental in the development of the beef and mutton industries.[7] A strong suggestion that the industry would recapture policy attention occurred in 1999 when the Ministry of Agriculture issued the document *Opinion of Accelerating Livestock Development*.[8] Along with the dairy sector, fine wool was identified for development over other livestock industries primarily because China was a large net importer of these commodities and, in the wake of WTO accession, domestic targeting was designed to replace imports. In practice this programme has provided little special funding or other tangible benefits for wool production.

For China as a whole, the wool production sector has lost the strategic importance attached to it in the pre-reform and early reform periods, and indeed receives far less policy attention than competing industries such as cotton, mutton and beef. This national outlook is generally mirrored in policy toward the industry at the provincial level and below.

On a more localized level however, a relatively proactive policy stance toward the industry continues to be adopted by some intensive wool production areas in Inner Mongolia and Xinjiang. These areas are reluctant to see their many decades of work invested in building up a fine-wool growing industry unravel in a relatively short period of time. In addition these areas have relatively few development options and see fine wool as one of their few sources of comparative advantage. The local more proactive policies towards fine wool take a number of forms including:

- Production targets (including wool output and proportion of sheep that are fine wool). For example the Tenth Five Year Plan (2001–2005) of Changji Prefecture in Xinjiang included a plan to have 1 million genuine fine-wool sheep.
- A number of "base" or "specialized" areas have also been identified. For example, Inner Mongolia is planning to invest Rmb15 000 in 30 "base" fine-wool counties. In Eastern Inner Mongolia, fine-wool sheep are one of the livestock types targeted for development in "specialized small areas" (based around household groups within villages). These areas hold at least 500 fine-wool sheep.
- Local tax breaks such as exemption on wool purchase tax for households with more than 100 fine-wool sheep.
- Poverty alleviation funds can also be used to support fine-wool production. The Inner Mongolia Animal Husbandry Bureau

administers approximately Rmb10 million in poverty funding per year, about one-third of which is directed toward fine-wool producers.

Although officials in these areas often have a desire to revive their fine-wool industries, their ability to do so is severely constrained by a lack of funding both from higher levels and from within these relatively poor areas. Local officials keen to promote fine-wool production are also hampered by a lack of strong policy direction from higher levels. Even when special resources and policies can be put in place by local officials, these are generally insignificant compared to market forces. Indeed officials under pressure to raise household incomes through livestock production, even if reluctantly, must accept that market forces should ultimately forge industry development.

Image 8.1   Breeding rams on Gadasu State Farm in Inner Mongolia

Dr Colin Brown and an Inner Mongolia Animal Husbandry Bureau official with fine-wool Merino rams at one of China four national-level sheep breeding studs. Core breeding flocks remain on many State Farms but commercial flocks have been distributed to households, many of which are switching out of fine wool.

8.2.2   Service Provision in the Wool Industry

With the demise of strong interventionist policymaking toward the wool industry, the role of government has been largely confined to service provision, especially extension services. As outlined in Chapter 3, a distinction between administering policy and service provision can be drawn because they involve different activities and are run by different types of organization.[9] However the distinction between the two forms of government activity can be blurred because agricultural extension is commonly used as an instrument of policy in China. Extension activities can have a strong element of policy administration as well as providing the normal technical and educational services.

China has an enormous livestock extension service that, in 1999, comprised more than 56 000 units (mainly at village levels) and employed more than 1.1 million people. The logistics of providing extension services in pastoral areas where most wool is produced are particularly demanding because of the vast distances and extreme climatic conditions. These services are seen by all levels of government as essential not just from an industry perspective, but also for the livelihoods of the herders. As a result, despite the increasing pressure on fiscal budgets, government continues to subsidize certain extension services relevant to wool growing:

- *Breeding* is a major focus in all livestock industries, but especially so in fine wool.[10] Breeding activities include the purchase of breeding sheep from overseas, breed development and support for logistics of operating an enormous breeding network. For example in the mid-1990s, Xinyuan County in Xinjiang Province had 82 artificial insemination points that provided fine-wool ram semen. However there were major difficulties in getting both the female sheep and the semen (and liquid nitrogen) to the artificial insemination points.[11] Some of the costs to the extension system are offset as State Farms do a significant amount of breed development work and artificial insemination, while households specializing in raising rams provide much of the service at grassroots levels as a sideline business. However these activities are still heavily subsidized by government.
- *Veterinary services* are important in pastoral areas where disease, pests and climatic extremes can have devastating effects on households and local economies. Most veterinary technicians are also household heads that provide their services as a sideline activity. However these people need to be provided with training, veterinary products and information.
- *Grassland management and supplementary feeding practices* are highly complex. The development of better systems of grassland and livestock management for the extremely harsh conditions and the encouragement of herders to adopt these improved practices is a massive, ongoing extension task.
- *Investment in and the education of herders in the use of supporting infrastructure* such as livestock sheds, fencing, feed and water storage

and livestock dipping facilities are essential if the wool growing sector is to modernize.

- All of the activities listed above involve significant training of the personnel involved. For instance half of the entire Gansu provincial livestock extension budget is devoted to training activities.

In addition to livestock production activities, the Animal Husbandry and Veterinary Bureau in several regions has undertaken to train and equip people and units in wool assembly, including shearing, baling and grading.[12] However these activities are insignificant compared to other production-oriented extension activities discussed above, and have been limited to some State Farms and highly specialized areas.

Although these extension activities play a crucial social, economic and development role in China, extension providers are severely under-resourced. For example the total Gansu provincial budget for livestock extension fell throughout the 1990s to total only Rmb1.3 million in 2001. In many areas, extension agencies struggle to provide even rudimentary services, let alone services to help households develop systems to produce and access higher-value product markets. Resource availability problems are magnified by institutional problems. The extension service has yet to develop "fee for service" arrangements even in situations where such an approach might be commercially viable. Fees, or even partial fees, for certain high-demand services could help them recoup some of the additional costs of providing better services. The large cumbersome system is also run on a top-down and bureaucratic basis and has trouble orientating to the needs of producers looking to move up the value chain.

The decline in, and in many cases the total lack of, extension support services also helps explain the switch out of fine wool. In the absence of a highly developed extension system and significant price premiums for high-quality wool, it is less risky and costly for households to use their own local rams in natural mating to produce hardier crossbreed sheep that do not require the same high level of inputs and costs, many of which are extension service related. Thus along with the underdeveloped wool marketing system, the lack of an appropriate extension system explains why herders have difficulty in integrating with the fine-wool segment of the industry.

In response to these underlying problems, governments in some of the better fine wool-growing areas in Xinjiang and Inner Mongolia are in the process of transferring to new corporate structures the responsibility for the provision of many extension activities for a range of high-value products. For example the companies designed to take fine-wool production into the next century in Xinjiang include the Xinjiang Fine Wool Producers Association and the Merino Company. In addition to preproduction and extension activities, these companies are integrated across industry sectors and so are discussed in more detail in Chapter 7 (wool marketing) and Section 8.3.3 (wool production). These companies have been conceived, developed and invested in by a diverse group of government departments, including the Animal Husbandry and Veterinary Bureau, research institutions and marketing agencies. In the case of Animal Husbandry and Veterinary Bureau involvement in the Merino Company in Yili Prefecture in Xinjiang, this has involved a transfer of extension infrastructure incorporating breeding stock ("core flocks"), breeding infrastructure (pens, semen collection, artificial insemination points), and Animal Husbandry and Veterinary Bureau farms, grasslands and sheds. The companies dictate breeding, veterinary and feeding regimes as well as wool assembly and marketing activities, regardless of the actors that actually grow the wool (households, State Farms or local groups). In Chinese terms, these new companies are the "Dragon Head" enterprises that are intended to lead the rest of the industry.

Image 8.2   Flock of State Farm breeding sheep in Xinjiang

China has spent decades developing fine-wool sheep genetics. With the exception of only a few areas in China such as that pictured, the breeding programme has regressed enormously in recent years.

8.3 WOOL PRODUCERS

Against the background of changes in the economic and policy environment, there has been a major shift in the incentives that face wool producers. Three major categories of wool producers can be identified, namely State Farms, households and Dragon Head enterprises. Quantifying the relative importance of these actors is problematic because of the lack of data, blurred categories and the rate of change in the sector. However economic reform and liberalization has meant that private households now represent the major group of producers for all wool types. An important aspect of the reform is that the "households" category includes those that act either independently or within larger forms of organization, including State Farms, Dragon Head enterprises or local groups.

8.3.1 State Farms

State Farms have long been important players in China's fine-wool production sector. There are several types of State Farms, but those of most interest are the Production and Construction Corps[13] farms in Xinjiang and Animal Husbandry Bureau farms throughout China.[14] Longworth and Brown (1995) estimated that in 1992, sheep on State Farms produced only 10 per cent of China's greasy wool, about 20 per cent of fine and improved fine-wool production, but up to 50 per cent of all genuine fine wool grown in China.[15]

In general, State Farms are following the broader industry switch out of fine-wool production. However the underlying reasons why State Farms dominated genuine fine-wool production remain in place. First, many State Farms, especially those under the control of higher levels of government, run pure-breed fine-wool core breeding flocks. Breeding stock and genetic material from these core flocks are distributed to lower-level State Farms and throughout the livestock extension system. Second, households on State Farms run large commercial flocks, a large proportion of which are fine-wool sheep. Third, compared to other production systems, a relatively large proportion of State Farms conduct centralized shearing, grading and baling.[16]

Consequently State Farms are one of the few types of production units capable of producing relatively large and homogeneous lots of fine wool. The amount of fine wool for offer on individual State Farms now varies between 30 and 100 tonnes per year. Thus these farms are better positioned to market to higher-value markets and marketing channels including direct sales to mills and through the auction system. Indeed just 18 State Farms in Xinjiang have accounted for most of the wool sold through Xinjiang Fine Wool Producers Association and the Nanjing Wool Market auctions in recent years.

Despite their relatively favourable position in the industry, State Farms are withdrawing steadily from fine-wool production in Gansu, Inner Mongolia and Xinjiang. The shift is most pronounced for the Production and Construction Corps system in Xinjiang where total sheep numbers and wool output have increased but fine-wool sheep numbers and fine-wool output have decreased. Fine-wool output in the Production and Construction Corps system fell from 7946 tonnes in 1990 to 6200 tonnes in 2001. The proportion of fine and improved fine-wool sheep to all sheep in the Production and Construction Corps system declined from 79 per cent in 1991 to only 51 per cent by 2001.

Image 8.3   Shearing on a State Farm in Xinjiang

State Farms retain centralized shearing infrastructure that (as depicted in Images 7.4 and 7.5 in Chapter 7) are integrated with other wool assembly activities. The shearers are either "roving shearers" that move between State Farms or are from the State Farm itself. Significant resources and training have been invested into developing mechanical shearing, but hand clippers still predominate.

State Farms are shifting out of fine-wool production for several reasons. The reform of State Farm systems has placed increasingly hard budget and commercial constraints on individual farms and farm managers have been given increasing freedom to choose the more profitable economic activities. Individual Production and Construction Corps farms and divisions oriented toward fine-wool production lost money throughout the 1990s. Indeed State farms are scaling down all animal husbandry activities – not just fine-wool production – and moving into industrial and agricultural activities, especially cotton.[17] By 2001, the animal husbandry activities of the Production and Construction Corps in Xinjiang generated only 15.7 per cent of the Production and Construction Corps gross value of agricultural production.

The unprofitability of fine-wool sheep production on State farms is also related to the decline in demand for their breeding sheep, both within the various State Farm systems and in the public Animal Husbandry and Veterinary Bureau extension system. Consequently, breeding stock prices have fallen. For example "Gongnaisi", the major Animal Husbandry and Veterinary Bureau State breeding Farm in Xinjiang and one of the four central-level fine-wool sheep breeding farms in China, sold about 5000 breeding rams per year at the end of the 1980s for an average of Rmb1500 each. By 2001, the number of rams sold each year and the prices received were about half of these values. That is, the fine-wool sheep breeding business on State Farms has become increasingly less economically attractive.

Another key area of State Farm reform has been to transfer the ownership of land and livestock to households residing on the State Farms. In the early 1990s, 85 to 90 per cent of the sheep on the Production and Construction Corps State farms were owned by the central farm administration (and so ultimately by the State). A decade later, the Production and Construction Corps farms own just 15 per cent of the sheep which represent the core breeding sheep flocks. Even the raising of these core flocks is now often contracted out to households. The State Farm controls the breeding programme, feed and veterinary regimes for these core flocks and has rights to select replacement breeding stock. The households receive an annual fee for looking after the flocks and are fined for deaths over a predetermined rate (usually about 4 per cent).

Households living on the Production and Construction Corps farms privately own the remaining 85 per cent of sheep and have full decision-making rights over the stock.[18] Notionally households on State Farms appear to be well placed to enter into fine-wool production because the sheep allocated to them are from good bloodlines and they have access to the shearing, grading and marketing arrangements of the State Farms. Some households on State Farms have taken up these opportunities. However many other fine-wool producing households on State Farms – about half in Xinjiang – sell their wool instead through private traders. In addition, large numbers of households have exercised their right to move out of fine-wool sheep production and run mixed-breed flocks. That is households on State Farms now act as autonomous units. Even with their advantageous access to

State Farm production and processing infrastructure, they have elected to turn away from fine-wool production.

8.3.2 Household Production

Households not associated with State Farms raise the vast majority of sheep in China, and at least half of the fine-wool sheep. A fundamental distinction exists between specialized and unspecialized households in fine-wool sheep production. Specialized fine-wool households raise larger and more homogeneous flocks of fine-wool sheep.[19] Formally, the distinction centres on the proportion of resources that households devote to a particular activity – in this case fine-wool production – which is usually set at 60 per cent. In practice at regional levels, the distinction depends on absolute numbers of livestock raised by the household unit. In the case of fine-wool sheep production, this level is set at 50 head of fine-wool sheep in most regions. Total household sheep flock sizes in pastoral areas are often higher than this, but these flocks usually include various types of sheep (fine-wool, local breeds, mutton sheep) and goats run as a mixed flock.[20]

Unspecialized households raise most of China's sheep as mixed flocks of sheep (various lines and breeds) with other livestock types including cattle and goats. Unspecialized households are unlikely to produce fine wool and sell their wool on a mixed-grade basis.[21] Thus the switch out of fine-wool production manifests itself as an increase in unspecialized households relative to specialized fine-wool producing households.

The trend toward households raising mixed flocks has occurred in an environment that has afforded them increasing independence and even isolation on a number of levels. First, local government has become less coercive in dictating household production activities. Section 8.2.1 outlined the less interventionist policies toward the industry and the decline in extension subsidies and local policy inducements. Some exceptions occur where local governments seek to encourage households to enter into fine-wool production arrangements through the establishment of Dragon Head enterprises which are discussed in the following section. Second, households have gained increasingly secure property rights over livestock and land. In the 1990s, this occurred through extending contracts (and some fencing) of winter and spring land, and the extension of land allocation and grazing rights to incorporate autumn and sometimes even summer grazing lands.[22] Third, households have an increasingly wide variety of viable choices of livestock activities and marketing channels available to them, especially with the rapid development of the mutton and beef industries in recent years.

The delegation of decision making about sheep – including fine-wool sheep – production to increasingly independent households has important implications. In the absence of strong intervention, households respond to economic and market incentives, which are to switch out of specialized fine-wool production and into local-breed, mutton, dual-purpose or mixed-herd sheep production.[23] Relative commodity prices and costs, adaptability to agroclimatic conditions and risk minimization contribute to these decisions.

Image 8.4   Household mixed flock in semi-pastoral area

Households raise the vast majority of China's sheep, usually in mixed flocks of different sheep breeds and goats. It is highly unlikely that fine wool will be produced from household mixed-flock systems because of breeding and fibre contamination. Many parts of western China are semi-pastoral and have a significant amount of cropping. Transport infrastructure has also improved in these areas, opening up new opportunities such the marketing of mutton.

Increasing household independence has also fragmented fine-wool production structures. In the 1980s, a centralized wool procurement, extension system, policy regime, and production units held household production systems together. Since the 1980s, an extreme type of household individualism has emerged in Chinese agriculture, including the fine-wool production sector. Fragmented household producers sell their wool to independent private wool traders and shear their own wool in uncentralized systems. Some responses to the problems associated with a highly decentralized system are already emerging with some fine-wool household producers organizing into groups, associations, "small livestock raising areas" and, as detailed below, Dragon Head enterprises. However these forms of organization are limited relative to the size and geographical distribution of the wool production sector.[24]

8.3.3 Dragon Head Enterprises

The development of Chinese agriculture has been constrained by unstandardized (*bu guifan*), fragmented (*fensan*) and chaotic (*luan*) production and marketing structures. Problems in fine-wool production in terms of fragmented household production structures, lack of capacity in extension service provision for fine-wool production, and the decline of fine-wool production on State Farms have been outlined in this chapter, while problems of fragmented wool marketing structures and underuse of wool standards and inspection services were outlined in Chapters 3 and 7. Dragon head enterprises have been one of the instruments used in the attempt to link producers with higher-value industry segments. Some areas of China have applied the model to fine-wool production to overcome some of the problems associated with fragmented production and marketing structures.

A description of Dragon Head enterprises active in the fine-wool industry appears in Chapter 7 because of their primary role as wool marketing organizations.[25] However some of these organizations are also extremely active in production aspects of the industry, especially the Merino Company and the Sapale Company in Xinjiang. One feature in the development of these enterprises is that they have adapted and extended existing State production structures. That is while the Dragon Head enterprise idea may seem a product of the new era, it also involves an element of continuity and participation from existing State-owned participants, albeit in a different form.

The Xinjiang Merino Fine Wool Sheep Science and Technology Company (otherwise known as the Merino Company) is based in Yili, which is the major fine-wool producing prefecture in Xinjiang. The company was formed by Supply and Marketing Co-operatives and Animal Husbandry Bureaus at various levels, as well as the Xinjiang Agricultural University. Each of these participants has invested or transferred resources from their old structures. The Supply and Marketing Co-operative participants have invested purchase points, storage facilities, skilled classers and shearers of the Supply and Marketing Co-operatives. On the production side, the Yili Animal Husbandry Bureau – and three county-level Animal Husbandry and Veterinary Bureaus in Yili – have contributed farms, breeding sheep, technicians and extension facilities, including breeding, feeding and veterinary facilities.[26] The Company also has access to large tracts of land – over 50 000 *mu* or 3333 hectares of grasslands – in a number of counties.

Furthermore fine-wool sheep production structures operated by the Merino Company have taken a form similar to that of State Farms. In 2002, the company had 7000 "core flock" sheep owned by the company. From this core flock, the company plans to build the largest fine-wool sheep flock in China.[27] This is reflected in the production structures described below and includes the development of a non-core flock over the longer term. Both the core and non-core flocks are to be raised predominantly by contracted households under three models:

- Sheep are owned by the company and household are paid a fixed salary (either by wages or per head) to raise the sheep with a penalty for death rates over a set limit.
- Sheep are half-owned by the company with the household receiving a half-share of the revenue from the wool or lambs. Alternatively, households can use the revenues (from wool and lambs) to buy the full share in the sheep.
- Sheep are fully owned by the household, with the household deciding on whether or not to sell wool and lambs back to the company. In this case, the company provides services to the household.

Under the first two models, the company has claim on all the products – lambs and wool – and hence controls all aspects of the raw wool supply chain. In all models, the company provides extension services, some inputs and wool assembly services such as shearing, grading and baling. In return, the company receives revenues for some of the marketing services it provides. The company has also set up its own fine-wool grading and branding scheme.

Some counties in Yili Prefecture involved in the Merino Company set targets for household participation. For instance, participating townships aimed to have five households with more than 300 fine-wool sheep (supplied by the Merino Company). Counties also encouraged households that run mixed flocks (that might total 300 sheep) to run their fine-wool sheep (about 50 head) in separate flocks. These smaller flocks of fine-wool sheep would be combined and run by specialized households. Such plans were complemented by preferential policies. For example households where fine-wool sheep constituted more than 80 per cent of their flock were given a 20 per cent reduction in grassland fees and free artificial insemination services. Herders also received a Rmb300 grant to buy part of a ram, which might be worth about Rmb1000. The county provided cash incentives of around Rmb500 to Rmb3000 for township officials to carry out the programme.

Another Dragon Head enterprise in Xinjiang associated with fine wool is the Xinjiang Fine Wool Producers Association. Otherwise known and registered as a company and brand name called "Sapale", it is again primarily a marketing organization but with deep roots in production structures. Scientists-cum-entrepreneurs of the Xinjiang Academy of Animal Science originally established the association or company in 1998 with cross-institutional support from the various organizations discussed in Chapter 7. It is especially interesting that the Xinjiang Animal Husbandry and Veterinary Bureau provides support to Sapale, while its lower-level equivalent, the Yili Animal Husbandry and Veterinary Bureau, supports the Merino Company which competes with Sapale.

In 2002, the Sapale Association consisted of 89 members that were fine-wool producer organizations. Of these, 40 were "base production areas" with contracts to produce and sell their wool under the Sapale brand and marketing channels. Some 18 of these base production areas were State Farms, nine of which were Production and Construction Corps farms and nine local Animal Husbandry and Veterinary Bureau breeding stations.

Image 8.5   The sheep-raising facilities of a Dragon Head enterprise in Xinjiang

Efforts to revive China's fine-wool industry have seen the rise of Dragon Head enterprises that have large, centralized sheep-raising facilities. Core breeding flocks and lambs are fed intensively for much of the year in this cold, high-altitude part of Xinjiang. Commercial flocks are raised by households under contract to the Dragon Head enterprises.

The other 22 base production areas were townships, with several township members in each of the major fine-wool producing counties in Xinjiang spanning eight prefectures. In principle, the association provides services to the townships, and makes an advance payment (or loan) for the wool to be supplied to Sapale in the next shearing season. Townships are responsible for repaying the loan and filling the contract, which they do for a management fee of Rmb500 per tonne of wool sold to Sapale. To fulfil these obligations, township officials establish contracts with between 20 and 30 households and, together with the local Animal Husbandry and Veterinary Bureau, organize households to produce Sapale-grade fine wool. The contracted households each raise between 200 and 300 sheep each. If everything goes to plan, the townships produce about 30 tonnes of Sapale wool per year which is similar to the amount produced on many State Farms. The townships are also recognized as model or demonstration townships under the "fine wool vertical integration" project of the Ministry of Agriculture.

The association is seeking to expand the farms and townships with which it has relations. In 2002, loose relationships had been established with another 49 production areas (farms and townships) that had the option but not the obligation to sell to the association. Despite these efforts, in practice Sapale has struggled to attract producers to buy its wool. In 2001 Sapale marketed 1100 tonnes but volumes fell to 600 tonnes in 2002 and only a few hundred tonnes in 2003. Local production areas and State Farms choose to circumvent Sapale by selling direct to mills or dealers. Various reasons are behind this trend, including the shortcoming of the existing high-value marketing channels for fine wool such as the auction system (as discussed in Chapter 7). However a key element is also the switch out of fine-wool production by production bases and so their disengagement from the association.

NOTES

1   For a comprehensive discussion of sheep and wool in China, see Longworth and Williamson (1993).
2   Although it would be desirable to have more differentiated data, such as that based on the Chinese wool types, the data is limited to three broad categories of wool: namely fine, semi-fine and coarse.
3   One major statistical anomaly described in Longworth and Williamson (1993, Section 4.3) is that prior to 1991, semi-fine wool in Xinjiang was classed as fine wool. Because of the importance of Xinjiang as a wool producing province, the correction of this anomaly in 1991 impacted significantly upon the overall statistics. According to the statistics, Chinese fine-wool production declined in 1991 while semi-fine wool output increased in that year.
4   From the perspective of sheep and wool production, important distinctions exist between production systems in pastoral, semi-pastoral and agricultural areas of China, and between geographical zones such as the north-western, north-eastern, south-western and central plains regions. Background data analysis however revealed that aggregating up provincial

data into these production systems or zones can be misleading. Trends within these zones can be dominated by major provinces and other provinces often display contradictory patterns. Wool production, especially fine-wool production, can be a very geographically specific activity that does not match administratively set boundaries. For instance large tracts of land in Jilin, Liaoning (north-east China) and Hebei (central plains) are pastoral or semi-pastoral and share much in common with Inner Mongolia (north-west China). A detailed understanding of the production systems therefore requires analysis on a prefecture or county level (see Longworth and Williamson 1993).

5   This is in marked contrast to the beef industry, where the massive expansion in beef output has seen a major shift in beef production from pastoral to agricultural areas (Longworth et al. 2001).

6   Some Central Plains agricultural provinces such as Anhui and Jiangsu have moved virtually entirely out of sheep and into goat production. There has also been a move out of sheep in southern provinces such as Yunnan. Conversely, in a relative sense, sheep numbers have increased in the pastoral autonomous regions of Xinjiang and Ningxia, as well as central plains provinces such as Hebei and Beijing.

7   Unlike the processing sectors of many other agricultural industries – meat, grains, dairy, fruit and vegetables for example – the wool processing sector lies outside the traditional realm of agriculture. Thus the wool industry has also missed out on programs that explicitly target the agricultural processing sector.

8   This document was closely associated with the Strategic Adjustment of Agricultural Structures Programme.

9   The broad Animal Husbandry and Veterinary structure is divided between administrative units (Animal Husbandry and Veterinary Bureau) and service units (National Animal Husbandry and Veterinary Service, or Station).

10   Because wool breeding is so heavily emphasized, there are multiple funding channels such as the Ministry of Agriculture/Animal Husbandry and Veterinary Bureau, Science and Technology Commission, and Planning Commission. Inner Mongolia has received up to Rmb20 million per annum from the Ministry of Finance to invest in wool sheep breeding, with even higher funding levels in Xinjiang.

11   Despite the large number of artificial insemination stations and other forms of official encouragement, the production of fine wool in Xinyuan County declined sharply in the second half of the 1990s.

12   For example in 1999, the Inner Mongolia twice invested Rmb2 million in baling and shearing equipment and the training of wool graders, mainly for breeding farms.

13   The Production and Construction Corps system in Xinjiang has 11 divisions and three farm management bureaus all of which raise fine-wool sheep. Longworth and Williamson (1993) outline the Production and Construction Corps system in detail and explain its substantial role in fine-wool production.

14   For example in Gansu in 2000, 17 State-owned farms bred sheep of which ten bred fine-wool sheep.

15   In 1990, State farms produced 16 500 tonnes of wool or one-third of the Xinjiang total. State Farms produced 2700 tonnes in Inner Mongolia, 750 tonnes in Heilongjiang, 530 tonnes in Qinghai and Jilin, and 350 tonnes in Hebei and Gansu.

16   About 25 to 30 per cent of the Production and Construction Corps farms in Xinjiang use mechanical shearing. Four or five shearing teams go from farm to farm over the very short shearing season (about one month). The Production and Construction Corps system has trained 89 graders (an average of three on each farm).

17   Cotton prices increased throughout much of the 1990s. In addition it is tacitly acknowledged that Production and Construction Corps farms have a mandate to increase cotton production as a means of populating Xinjiang with ethnic Han migrants (Becquelin, 2000).

18   The arrangements between State Farms and households can vary. For example Ziniquan State Farm in Xinjiang (the top Production and Construction Corps fine-wool breeding farm) allocated ewes to households in 2002 at a cost of Rmb180 per head. In lieu of the cash payment however households pay the State Farm in the form of lambs every year.

19 In Gansu, there are about 94 000 specialized sheep-raising households that raise 4.5 million head (or an average of about 50 head per household). The vast majority of these households are raising sheep for mutton.

20 For example Ministry of Agriculture scale of production data for sheep and goat numbers per household in Inner Mongolia in 2002 is: 1 to 4 head – 10 per cent; 5 to 49 head – 34 per cent; 50 to 199 head – 28 per cent; 200 to 499 head – 15 per cent; 500 to 999 head – 9 per cent; and greater than 1000 head – 5 per cent.

21 From a production perspective, fine-wool sheep breed regimes and bloodlines cannot be retained if sheep are run together and joined through natural mating with local or meat-sheep rams. Local breed or meat sheep also rub against fine-wool sheep, inevitably resulting in fibre contamination. The breeding cycles and production regimes for meat and wool sheep also differ, especially given the need to reduce stress (from lambing, weather and feed) on fine-wool sheep in periods when they are growing the middle section of their staples. For these production related reasons alone, fine-wool production is best done as a dedicated activity.

22 Collective grazing between groups of households still occurs on summer and autumn land and stocking rates are still notionally subject to locally set levels. In addition there has been a series of new laws and regulations that reduce extensive grazing and increase intensive feeding in sheds.

23 Zheng et al. (2003) examine the incentives to pastoral households in more detail using survey data from the "National Agricultural Products Cost and Revenues Material Collection" of the China Price Bureau (Department).

24 This relates partly to the lack of legal framework for the development of independent groups, such as a National Co-operative Law. However this legal framework is also absent in agricultural parts of China where the number of local groups – including livestock associations and specialized small areas – has proliferated. It may be that the more recent implementation of market-oriented reform and the geography and distances involved in the north-western pastoral regions of China make local-level cooperation more difficult. Major wool producing counties in China such as Sunan (in Gansu Province) and Wushen (in Inner Mongolia) were said by officials to have sheep-raising groups (collectives and associations); however fieldwork revealed little evidence of household cooperation.

25 These include: the Nanjing Wool Market in Jiangsu; the Xinjiang Fine Wool Producers Association; the Kuitun Storage and Transport Company in Xinjiang; Xinjiang Merino Fine Wool Sheep Science and Technology Company; Xinjiang Tianling Animal By-products Company; the Inner Mongolia Livestock Economic and Technological Development Company; and the Muwang Company in Inner Mongolia.

26 For example one of the county Animal Husbandry and Veterinary Bureaus in Yili is investing an average of Rmb300 000 into the Merino Company every year, including in-kind provision of artificial insemination stations and services, breeding sheep, sheds and land. Some Animal Husbandry and Veterinary Bureau breeding farms, such as Chabuchaer, and their sheep were virtually transferred in total to the Merino Company.

27 The largest flock in Xinjiang is Production and Construction Corps Division 5 (Bortala) that had 200 000 fine-wool sheep in 2002.

9. Understanding and Improving Industry Transformation

The analysis of modernization and transition in the wool and wool textile industry in Chapters 4 to 8 revealed the numerous and profound changes occurring within this particular industry as a result of a series of mega-forces. Those same forces impact on many other Chinese industries with similar consequences. This final chapter generalizes the findings in relation to the wool and wool textile industry so that the lessons learned about modernization in relation to this industry can be applied to other Chinese industries.

As pointed out elsewhere in this book, one way to clarify the transition process in China is to break it into three phases, namely: institutional and ownership reform; technical reform; and operational or managerial reform. Reflecting on industry transition in this way, Section 9.1 highlights that while reforms have been profound, substantial progress is still needed especially in connection with the third phase of the transition process. In particular, there is still a long way to go in China to develop industries in an integrated way and to improve management and operational practices within enterprises.

Based on this assessment of where China is at in its transition process, Section 9.2 presents a broader discussion of where China should be heading to make industry transition work more effectively. The suggestions are made with reference to the mega-forces and mega-consequences outlined in Chapter 1. The final section (Section 9.3) draws together the descriptive and prescriptive discussion in a series of concluding remarks.

9.1 CLARIFYING INDUSTRY TRANSITION

Much of the apparent complexity in China's transition process can be better understood if the process is broken down into the three phases depicted in Figure 9.1.

The first phase relates to transforming ownership and governance structures at both the enterprise and industry level; the second phase involves

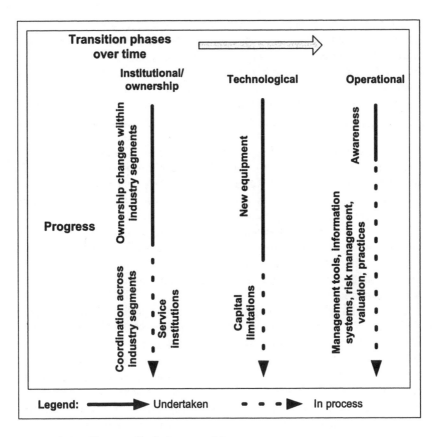

Figure 9.1   Phases of industry transition

an upgrade of equipment and technology; while the third phase concerns modernizing practices and operational procedures. Considered together, a discussion of these phases reveals much about the status of industry transition in China. One feature to emerge from the discussion is that while the first two reform phases – ownership changes and technological upgrading – have proceeded strongly, micro-level managerial and operational reforms have lagged behind, and this is a major reason for the apparent lack of economic coordination described by many Chinese commentators as creating a state of *luan* or "economic chaos".

9.1.1   Administrative and Enterprise Ownership Reform

Administrative reform and the reform of enterprise ownership structures are interrelated. As the specialized economic government departments have been directed to divest themselves of their State-owned Enterprises and agencies, government and enterprises have notionally gone their separate ways. Specialized economic government departments (such as the Ministry of Textile Industry) have been abolished or restructured into associations. The State-owned Enterprises come under different institutional structures (especially State Asset Management Commissions) or have been reformed into different ownership types (such as shareholder companies).

Despite the profound nature of the changes, this process has taken place over a relatively short time and been pushed in a way that does not necessarily develop optimal structures. For example, State-owned Enterprises have been sold to enterprise "insiders" that are in a better position to know the real value of the enterprises, and procurement agencies have been split up in a way that does not make use of their skills and facilities. The claim is also often made in China that enterprise reform has been largely a shuffling exercise, where enterprise ownership has been shifted from line bureaus to a nexus of State Asset Management Companies and other structures (such as holding companies) in which the State at various levels often remains the major shareholder.

Along with enterprise reform, administrative reform has also been somewhat of a shuffling exercise. Officials of disbanded administrative units have been found jobs in State-owned Enterprises, in service units or in the associations that their units subsequently became. Consequently industry associations that have been formed in recent years inevitably have a close relationship with government – often more so than with the other industry participants. At the same time, when government departments with industry coordination functions were disbanded, insufficient thought went into developing the institutions that replaced them. That is the institutions themselves are either too close to government, under-resourced, or there has been insufficient attention given to the development of "bottom-up" non-governmental industry institutions. Consequently most industries now operate in an arena where large numbers of industry participants act independently with only indirect reference to the institutions that notionally govern them.

Another aspect of administrative and ownership reforms has been that they have taken place in different ways in different industry segments. In the processing segment, ownership reform has been most complete. In the agricultural production and marketing segments, government continues to play a strong role not only in policy setting but in direct participation in enterprises and agencies. Thus while government as a whole plays a more facilitative, macro-control role, the function of government varies by industry segments with implications for integration across industries or sectors of the economy as a whole.

Although the discussion above argues that institutional and ownership reforms have been implemented in a suboptimal way, they have been more successful than the alternatives used in many other transitional economies. Without political disruption, social upheaval or commodity shortages, China has ushered in wide-ranging structural reform measures. Enterprises now assume a profit- or value-generating role with fewer political, social and welfare obligations and less administrative interference. The government also now has the potential to implement policies and deliver services that are less discriminating between industries and which advance national interests, rather than negotiate between the interests of particular specialized economic government departments structured along industry-segment lines.

The measures to dismantle previous administrative structures and establish new ownership structures however should be seen as a first step in a larger transition process. The challenge now is to rebuild a set of institutions that are more responsive to the needs of a market economy. Previous chapters revealed several areas where stronger institutional capacity is needed, including regulatory and policy enforcement, inspection of adherence to standards, and information provision. These tasks are more likely to eventuate with less fragmented industry structures and if the larger and more progressive enterprises also see the benefit in conforming to industry-wide institutional developments.

9.1.2 Technical Upgrading and Reform

China places an enormous emphasis on upgrading technology. Although this is a major and necessary step toward modernization and successful economic transition, it is only one part of the overall process. To be effectively implemented, "hard" technology must also be accompanied by "soft" technology, that is the necessary skills and, most importantly, management practices. China's progress in this regard can be assessed by looking at two very different segments of the wool textile industry.

In the processing segment, technological upgrading usually takes the form of new and refurbished machinery. As discussed in Chapters 2 and 5, Chinese wool textile mills – as with many other Chinese factories – have imported increasing amounts of new machinery over the 1990s and into the early 2000s. Anecdotal evidence suggests that this trend has accelerated in the mid-2000s. The new machinery also requires that new production lines and processes are designed. In some cases this has been accompanied by an investment in research facilities (such as laboratories and testing equipment), new software, or the training of technicians in association with research institutions.

Image 9.1   A sign of the times

The sign above a worker loading spindles in one of China's wool textile enterprises indicates the harsh reality of ownership reform and labour downsizing by stating: "If you have intelligence, please use it; if you do not have intelligence, please sweat; if you have neither intelligence nor sweat, then please leave the enterprise".

The new technology and processing facilities have enabled mills to process more efficiently, to process new products, and to access potentially higher-value markets. However the technology must match the resources and skills and the market environment for the firm's inputs and products. In essence, a blind drive toward the technological frontier cannot, and should not, substitute for careful economic appraisal of the new technology and the opportunities it may create. Without rigorous analysis, overcapitalization associated with the uptake of inappropriate technology can be an overwhelming liability. Although this point may seem obvious, in the highly dynamic, new market environment in China, due diligence sometimes takes a back seat for fear of being left behind in the rush to modernize.

Wool production and marketing segments of the industry have also been subject to many decades of technical upgrading. China has long embarked on breed improvement programmes for fine-wool sheep with a strong scientific basis. The result is that China has large flocks of fine-wool sheep for breeding purposes and the human resources to implement a widespread breed improvement programme. Considerable effort has also been put into developing facilities and infrastructure and training to introduce mechanical shearing, clip preparation, classing, grading, baling, storage and transport along the lines seen in other major wool producing countries. The former State monopoly wool procurement agency had an enormous network of infrastructure for the assembly of wool for distribution to mills. The fact that these programmes – fine-wool sheep breeding and systematic wool assembly – are falling into disuse is not due to lack of effort to introduce new technology and practices. Instead it reflects that the technology does not match the incentives or market environment, or has not been introduced in a way that can take advantage of these new market conditions.

The desire to seek a "technological fix" and to be at the forefront of technological developments is pervasive in China and manifests itself in various ways. At the macro, national level, it is reflected in for example China's entry to the space race, while at a micro level it manifests as managers being "technological junkies" seeking the latest technological systems irrespective of their capacities to make best use of that technology or the relative profitability of these systems. In internally and externally funded projects, it manifests in the preference for "bricks and mortar"-type projects over potentially much more worthwhile, but less tangible, projects that seek to improve management systems. China's willingness to embrace technology and to access it in whatever manner possible has been a major factor helping it keep pace with the rest of the world where some other transition economies without the access to or the focus on technology have faltered. However the way in which technology is used, as outlined in the following section, will become much more important in the new market economy era.

9.1.3   Operational and Management Reforms

Administrative and enterprise ownership reforms – together with technological upgrading – have better equipped enterprises to face the challenges of a new economic era. However the "ownership fix" and the "technological fix" can be seen as vital but not sufficient for a successful transition. Indeed numerous examples in the book demonstrate that ownership and technological reforms have failed to turn around the fortunes of many enterprises. Specifically, a modernization of management practices and operational procedures are also needed. Operational and management reforms are closely related to ownership and technological reforms, but can also be seen as a separate, and challenging, phase in the overall transition process.

Chinese enterprises are at vastly different stages in their reform of operational and management practices. The so-called chaotic nature of industries or industry segments stems partly from the variation in successful uptake of better management practices among economic agents. Some enterprises that have successfully embraced new management practices enjoy an advantage over other enterprises irrespective of ownership and governance structures or levels of equipment and technology.

The "management fix" involves much more than broad-scale management of human and other resources within the enterprise to which most Chinese managers are accustomed. Specifically it demands that within a conducive management framework, a whole series of analytic tasks be capably performed. These tasks span technical, economic and environmental decisions. Within the economic field, Chapters 4 to 8 revealed a plethora of tasks that need to be performed including: decisions about input procurement and product selection; proactive identification and establishment of market outlets; identification of growth opportunities; product pricing and service charges; rigorous investment analysis; and analysis of cost efficiencies.

The uptake of a more analytic approach to firm decisions – as compared with a more instinctive ad hoc approach – depends on both the incentives faced by firms as well as their capabilities to perform such tasks. The increasingly competitive, dynamic and commercial environment (unfettered and unsupported by government edicts) provides a strong incentive to pursue a more analytical approach.

Traditional management systems
As described in Section 1.3 in Chapter 1, management systems within the wool textile industry developed in a traditional cultural and command economy context. High-level managers of State-owned Enterprises spent much of their time managing large human hierarchies, meeting political obligations, and reporting to higher authorities. Cultural factors also meant that interaction was heavily based on interpersonal relationships, mutual trust and reputation, rather than more formal mechanisms. Decision making also occurred on a largely intuitive basis, partly because under Confucianist systems, managers take responsibility for a wider range of decisions than can be cognitively handled.

Existing management systems are highly variable and under reform. A new generation of young, well-educated managers are taking on key management roles within many of China's enterprises. Many of these managers come from a training background in business administration while others have risen through their enterprises from a technical background. Although these skills are unquestionably important, they are no substitute for – and must be complemented with – broader analytic skills if Chinese enterprises are to forge ahead.

Image 9.2   Frontier technology

A Chinese wool production manager inspects state-of-the-art equipment imported from Italy in the early 2000s. An integral aspect of China's economic transition has been to modernize equipment and upgrade technology and allows mills to produce more specific products for higher-value markets. Technological upgrades require an upgrade in skills and management practices and the economic rigour to ensure such investments are both feasible and profitable.

Management tools

One aspect of a more analytical approach to management involves the use of formal management tools, including computer models and programmes. Formal management tools can add rigour and a more systematic approach to management systems traditionally employed by Chinese managers. They complement and enhance – rather than replace – the detailed understanding of the enterprise and industry operations already held by most managers. However these models and programmes can be both complex and data demanding, and so may require the outlook and computer skills of newer managers, or at least their delegation to information technology professionals.

A large number of software packages exist that can assist enterprise managers, including supply chain management programmes, risk management programmes, programmes that optimise input–output selection from a technical perspective, and programmes that identify the profitability of various products and orders. In addition there are various intermediate and computer-based systems that can enhance decision making, including price information systems and market reporting systems.

Purchasing and installing computer programmes and employing the people to run the systems is the easy part. Ensuring that they accurately reflect the decision-making environment and actually incorporating results into management decisions is much more difficult. The discussion below highlights some of the problematic implementation issues.

Information

A central aspect of the ability of managers to perform analytic tasks is their access to, and use of, information. In respect to access, significant variation arises across enterprises in the amount and types of information they collate. Because of reporting demands, State-owned Enterprises collate extensive information (in print form), especially in relation to production details but also in regard to financial details. Since the late 1990s, some of these enterprises have transformed their data-gathering systems from print to electronic form, potentially allowing for a much wider and more convenient use of the information for analytic purposes. One of the major tasks for these enterprises is reformatting this information in a manner suitable for analysis, rather than for tax accounting, production scheduling, and reporting to government officials and agencies for which the information systems were primarily designed.

Other enterprises such as former Township and Village Enterprises have less well-defined data collation systems, and so face the task of establishing information systems within the new environment. This affords an opportunity to design new information systems unencumbered by elements of previous systems or the need for upgrade from previous systems. However input into the design of these systems will be required from analysts to reveal precisely what information is required in order to perform the various tasks. Given that many enterprises are unaware of how to go about these analyses, then some external input – including from government or industry associations – may be needed to assist the enterprises.

Information can come from a number of sources within the enterprise. It can come from systematic recording of practices already undertaken, which in many cases has to be subject to statistical analysis. A lot of technical information may require a more experimental approach involving trials. In many cases, a hybrid approach incorporating statistical and technical approaches will yield the most accurate results. Various sources of information external to the enterprise, such as market and price information, will also be crucial in decision making.

With respect to the use of this information, many enterprises have embraced information technology to the extent of having information technology staff or even sections. Most of these staff have basic information technology and computing skills to ensure efficient collation, storage and integration of internal and external data, but of course still rely upon managers to indicate what information is needed, and on analysts to decipher and use the information.

China and enterprise-specific adaptation

A fundamental problem in the widespread use and dissemination of software based programmes is that they have been designed for use in other countries or for different, though related, production and manufacturing systems. The systems employed differ markedly between enterprises in China, and even more so with enterprises in other countries. Thus models or programmes based on homogenous production systems in other countries may have little direct application in the Chinese context. The "sinofication" of overseas models and software requires that they be flexible enough to allow for user-specified data as well as user specification of some of the underlying structural relationships. Information technology staff within enterprises may be able to perform this task in consultation with the appropriate analyst and with access to the source code needed to make the modifications. Given time constraints on enterprise staff to do this, again there may be a role for industry associations or research and development agencies to facilitate the modification of these generic programmes and their extension among industry enterprises.

Because of the problems of adaptation, it is often more straightforward and more accurate for enterprises to build analytical tools and calculations around existing data systems, many of which could be spreadsheet or database oriented. These self-built systems may have a much more profound impact on operational practices especially in the early stage of transition. Even with simple techniques and models however a role may exist for the collective industry-wide development and extension of these techniques and demonstration of how they can be integrated into existing management systems. The CAEGWOOL model described in Box 5.5 in Chapter 5 is an attempt to develop mill-specific analytical tools that draw on existing data systems and generate relevant information for managers of Chinese wool textile mills.

Valuation

One area of analysis of common concern to many of the economic agents discussed in this book, especially wool textile mills, was the appropriate valuation of final and intermediate inputs and outputs as well as suitable methods for allocating costs among different products and departments. Most of the current systems have emerged in response to tax and administrative reporting commitments. Tax accounting, however, employs very different methods to valuing inputs and outputs and allocating costs than the real values and costs. Most managers are aware that the valuations are inaccurate for managerial purposes and are seeking guidance on how to determine more accurate valuations within the existing structures and resources of the firm. Developing valuation and allocation approaches that integrate with existing management and information systems – and so employ enterprise specific data – is likely to be of major benefit to Chinese enterprises.

Risk management

Another underdeveloped area of operational practice is risk management. Reforms at higher administrative levels have transferred much of the risk to enterprises and other economic agents. Concurrently, as highlighted in Section 2.8 in Chapter 2, the new marketing environment is more volatile and exposes these production units to more lucrative but riskier outlets for their products. Although the risks cannot be avoided, various risk management and risk tolerance strategies can be adopted. Despite the options open to Chinese enterprises, risk management employed by many Chinese firms is poorly developed or non-existent. The "chaotic" nature of industry and volatile fortunes of some enterprises stems partly from inadequate risk management. Given that risk management is now a core aspect of business management in enterprises throughout the world, this is one area of industry modernization and transition that lags behind in China.

More fundamental shifts in management practices

The development of proactive management practices requires an even more fundamental shift in the outlook of enterprise managers. Changing management practices can improve existing practices by building efficiencies and making production decisions based on market trends and demand. However as highlighted throughout the book, a more proactive approach needs to be adopted by Chinese managers. This involves among other things the development of new or better products (product innovation), new ways to raise capital for the new ventures, and establishing new procurement and marketing channels.

To successfully undertake these tasks, proactive managers will need to call upon all of their entrepreneurial skills and interpersonal relationships. However these alone will not be sufficient, and will require more systematic processes. Some of the reluctance to consider new channels and employ new practices relates to a lack of awareness and uncertainty about outcomes. Thus increased market research and information, and more systematic use of analytic approaches may transform the way Chinese enterprises go about their activities. Risk and uncertainty will also be reduced with a greater reliance on longer-term contracts and relationships rather than one-off deals, and the tighter use of product specification instead of loosely defined standards based on subjective measurement.

9.2 MAKING TRANSITION WORK

Section 1.2 in Chapter 1 advanced the argument that industry transition was driven by the mega-forces impacting upon industries. The environment that Chinese industries find themselves operating in – and contributing to – was described in Section 1.3 in Chapter 1 as "chaotic". In this chapter, Section 9.1 has attempted to make some sense of why disorderly transition has taken place and appraised the status of transition through a series of reform phases. Based on this analysis, this section outlines some of the measures that may help to advance the transition process, bring order from chaos, and meet various societal objectives in a sustainable way.

9.2.1   Orderly Production and Marketing Systems

As outlined in Section 1.3 in Chapter 1, China is becoming increasingly affluent, urban, mobile and specialized, while Chinese enterprises are under pressure to shift from the production of generic to more specialised products. In this context, production and marketing systems will need to become more orderly and more sophisticated. In considering the way this should happen, a differentiation needs to be made between structures servicing higher- versus lower-value markets. More sophisticated management practices by a smaller number of larger participants is most likely and desirable in higher-value markets, while the plethora of smaller and fragmented actors may form an efficient structure for lower-value markets. Thus industry structures will change as markets develop and change. Policymakers need to incorporate such issues into industry policies and prepare for the consequences.

For high-value goods, marketing systems must be pushed in a direction where they improve the linkages between consumer and producers and accurately reflect the true values that users place on products and their attributes. Rudimentary, fragmented, localized and undifferentiated marketing systems that have proliferated in almost all sectors of the economy in the post-reform era tend to be ill-suited to the needs of modern industries and high-value markets. Competition among dealers for instance may be argued to arrive at competitive prices and the type of services demanded by other market participants. Yet few dealers have either the information or incentives

Image 9.3   The face of modern Chinese industry

Armed with modern new factories and new technologies, a new generation of young managers will steer the wool textiles industry into the future. They will bring formal management training, high-level technical skills and entrepreneurial capability to the industry. These skills will be needed in order for them to become more analytical in their decision making.

to perform this role. Dealers need to be aware of price differentials across regions and across product types if they are to take advantage of these arbitrage opportunities and so facilitate more accurate prices. The scale of these intermediaries and the limited scope of their activities in terms of regional and market segment coverage influences their ability to relay accurate price signals along the marketing chain. Furthermore the increased number of intermediaries has increased the potential for the disruption of the flow of information among these intermediaries.

Conversely, small intermediaries may be the more appropriate organizational structure in low-value markets. The short, unsophisticated marketing chains in low-value markets are well suited to the small, low-cost, intermediaries. Problems arise when the larger companies attempt to offload the surpluses they cannot sell on premium markets onto these lower-value markets, and subsequently find these exchanges are unviable and succeed only in crowding out the smaller participants in these low-value markets. Given the social benefits the small intermediaries provide in terms of a diverse local economy, and so a more vibrant and wider choice of employment opportunities, it would seem desirable to encourage participants to play an active role in these low-value markets and to discourage larger participants from "unfairly" competing in them.

Market integration and efficiency can also be influenced through proactive support services. Discovering accurate and efficient prices in industries characterized by heterogeneous products requires a range of supporting market services such as market reporting, standards, grading and product description systems. For many industries, these systems remain either rudimentary or duplicated. Modernization requires that effective, trusted and accurate distribution systems apply, involving increased testing and inspection capacity and more pressure on dealers and traders to operate according to these standardized systems. In this regard, strengthening the legal framework for trading and marketing, including the adoption of contractual relations and ensuring that dealers and traders are registered, is crucial.

Although small intermediaries are likely to remain prevalent in most industries, especially in lower-value markets, they will become increasingly bypassed in higher-value market segments. As more precise products are produced, proactive enterprises will develop closer and more direct trading relations with inputs suppliers and product customers. Ownership transition has also seen the incorporation of enterprises that perform particular functions (such as early-stage processing, later-stage processing, marketing, or input procurement) within larger structures, including group companies, shareholder companies or holding companies. In some cases there has been amalgamation between enterprises, which further shortens the marketing chain. The trend toward vertical integration also applies to the agricultural sector.

Rationalization of production structures could also be expected to continue as a result of ownership reform and greater exposure to market forces. As emphasized throughout the book, only those enterprises able to be flexible, proactive and that implement more sophisticated management practices will survive – at least in high-value markets.

9.2.2 Industry Drivers and Coordination

With the demise of planning instruments and government administrative coordination, a vigorous debate has occurred in China about who should be leading industries forward. Many industries have developed from a supply-side push under the assumption that additional capacity and output will find a market. The development of many new industries in the post-reform era in this way has led to excess industry capacity and a surplus of unwanted low-value generic products. Over time, and as some of these new industries have emerged, there has been some change in attitudes. Waldron et al. (2003) highlight how the beef industry has passed through phases of rapid development in cattle numbers, followed by a phase of developing processing capacity, to a more circumspect and mature phase of industry adjustment and market development and promotion. Other industries follow similar development pathways. For instance the dairy and sheepmeat industries exhibited enormous growth in the late 1990s and early 2000s but already show signs of underlying pressures to restructure.

While awareness that establishing market linkages and developing higher-value segments of the market is a crucial aspect of industry development, many of the problems of excess production capacity and surplus products remain. Thus the major problem is not so much an awareness of the need for linkages, but how to establish these market linkages. Developing production capacity has proved much easier than developing markets. Industry policy must be based on at least some perception of where industries may be heading. However the relationship is often tenuous and most investment projects proceed without having firm market outlets in place. A modernization of this aspect would involve a more rigorous analysis of markets and market segments, and the establishment of specific customer relationships (for individual firms) and specific market development strategies for the industry as a whole.

Participants in the final stages of the supply chain must be highly proactive in understanding consumer demands (and capitalizing on latent demand), and opening up new marketing channels if they are to lead the industry toward maximizing opportunities. However this does not always occur in China, and participants in other stages of the supply chain may need to take on a more active role in leading the industry. Because of the unclear responsibility for leading industries forward, the leading is often not done in a concerted way, and closer coordination between participants in different industry segments is required. Part of this process requires highly motivated managers willing to take initiatives and accept the risks involved in coordinating closely with other actors.

At another level, coordination also requires some changes in the way that Chinese enterprises interact with one another. Industry coordination will not necessarily result from the development of more autonomous and unencumbered enterprises operating in a profit-seeking way. Indeed as discussed throughout the book, the transition has led to industry actors pulling in different directions in an uncoordinated way. Thus industry coordination in the new market environment is of key concern.

One of the cornerstones of business practice in China has been *guanxi*, or the development of a network of business and political relationships. The analysis in this book suggests this networking of contacts may be as important if not more important in the new environment. That is the disaggregated market environment calls for higher levels of coordination or cooperation as well as strategic alliances between enterprises. These connections need to be based on, and developed from, a much more informed position. Relationships can still be used to identify and explore opportunities, but are complemented by rigorous analysis of alternatives to ensure that the options are viable and the best available. Thus trust and long-term relationships will still form an integral part of successful business practice in the future, but will need to be kept dynamic and robust by all parties to the relationship being better informed.

Institutions also have a strong role to play in promoting industry coordination. Several industry associations discussed throughout the book contribute significantly through activities such as publishing magazines and statistical sources, organizing conferences and trade shows, and coordinating policies and services. There is scope and the need to consolidate and expand the role of such institutions, but several obstacles must first be overcome. Existing institutions need to be better resourced, ideally through industry actors that can see the benefits of membership and so sustain the levels of funding and interest. To attract sufficient membership and funds outside of government sources, these institutions will need to provide services perceived as relevant by their potential members.

Discussion throughout the book highlighted the need for enterprises to embark on a series of operational and management reforms. Enterprise managers are often aware of this, but lack the required resources and skills. Services that assist enterprises in these particular transition tasks would appear a worthwhile area for these institutions to become involved in and also to attract membership and funding. Given that there will also be society or industry-wide benefits associated with this transition, the case for governments to help these institutions develop these services also appears strong. Examples of services that facilitate the transition include training programmes to encourage the use of management tools, and steps to develop an awareness of international purchasing channels and systems. There is also a need for at least some industry groups to engage in activities that span industry segments to promote industry integration.

9.2.3 Internationalization

China has sought to modernize its export-oriented and import-replacement industries in recent years so as to improve their competitiveness on world markets. Part of these efforts relate to the lead-up to, and in the wake of, World Trade Organization accession. However as Section 1.2 Chapter 1 indicated, the measures relate more to the broader integration of China's domestic economy into the world economy.

Despite the growth in China's domestic markets, China continues to play a pre-eminent role in the world trade of many commodities and products. Thus the task of integrating China into the world trading system and the institutions and arrangements that govern world trade have been of importance not only in China but in other countries as well. This aspect of modernization has involved securing access to institutions such as the World Trade Organization and establishing more rigorous and detailed protocols governing the trade of specific commodities. However these legal protocols are only one aspect of smoother trade flows between China and other countries. As Chapter 6 highlighted, more fundamental or systemic factors and characteristics of the wool textile industry influence the flow of inputs and outputs across China's borders. Many of these factors remain little changed despite the magnitude of transition in other industry segments. The apparent adoption of new trade protocols may give a distorted impression of the extent to which trade flows have been facilitated.

Considerable scope exists therefore to modernize China's internationalization process by addressing these systemic factors. Although this may not necessarily change the overall size of the trade sector, it may increase the sophistication of what China imports and exports and the way it goes about international trade.

Even in sectors where China is a dominant world player – as in the case of wool imports and wool textile exports – participants do not have a full awareness of technologies, consumer preferences, industry developments or input specifications in other countries. Several examples in the book relating to integration in textile fashions and the procurement of particular wool supplies reveal that significant improvements can be made. Thus Chinese industries, and overseas industries dependent on these Chinese industries, have not taken full advantage of the opportunities afforded by the world market. The next phase in the modernization process requires a move beyond perceiving export markets as a residual market and import markets as a generic source of supplies. In future, Chinese industries will need to actively pursue policy intelligence as well as market intelligence of these overseas markets to identify how to make best use of them.

Part of the efforts to improve international competitiveness has been to raise the size and scale of operation of export-oriented or potential export-oriented firms and industries. Despite the emergence of large, modern, sophisticated enterprises in some sectors, many are still reluctant to pursue their own marketing or branding strategies. Although well-known exceptions arise in electrical goods markets for example, Chinese garment makers stɪ. rely heavily on alliances or joint ventures with established overseas companies to sell their products. The strategy may suit the current stage of transition and the current relative costs and benefits of pursuing more aggressive and independent stance in global markets. Nevertheless Chinese enterprises may need to take a more pronounced role in not only following but leading global market developments. Once again, such a transition may involve innovative alliances both within and across industry segments to garner the knowledge and wherewithal to pursue this approach.

9.2.4 Social Development

The complexities of addressing the effects of industry development on social development often require an industry-segment or region-specific analysis. Outcomes and strategies vary significantly by industry, and so the analysis below focuses on the wool textile industry in particular rather than generalizing across industries as in other parts of Chapters 1 and 9.

Industry development can be expected to have net benefits for more progressive wool textile mills, most of which are located in eastern areas of China. Mills in eastern China – particularly around the Yangzi River Delta – not able to make the transition generally do not pose a major social problem because of the alternative employment opportunities available in other nearby mills or industries. However to the extent that rationalization in the wool textile industry mirrors what is happening in other low-skilled, labour-intensive industries, the aggregate impact can be large, especially if the displaced workers cannot easily find new employment or make the transition to a new occupation. Furthermore it is overly simplistic to argue that industry development and employment opportunities are the same throughout eastern China. Large tracts of eastern provinces – such as some areas of Shandong and Hebei – struggle to develop alternative "pillar" industries of the size of the current textile industries, which means that re-employment opportunities have to be more closely targeted.

Problems associated with industry rationalization are more pronounced in western China where there is a less diverse and robust industrial sector. There are several examples of progressive mills in the more remote parts of eastern China and in western China that constitute a major source of local employment. Intensifying efforts to assist these particular mills in the transition phase of improving management and operational practices may yield substantial benefits from a social perspective.

Rationalization may also be less of an issue for entrepreneurial textile and garment traders in the Yangzi River Delta and Guangdong where alternative employment is widely available. In the case of wool trading, most of the windfall gains flow to traders based in eastern China which are involved in a range of other trading activities. Furthermore measures to localize and consolidate wool marketing channels may generate significant off-farm employment opportunities in western China and also benefit wool growers.

The need for higher-quality and more precisely defined inputs into wool textiles processing would seem to provide opportunities for fine-wool producers in western China. Yet internationalization and some of the other mega-forces place increasing competitive pressure on wool growers in western China who are not competitive in the fine-wool sector. Nonetheless Chinese herders appear to have a comparative advantage in coarser wool when produced in association with mutton which has experienced significant price increases.

Efforts to revive fine-wool production in western China are well intentioned and involve household producers in one way or another. Realizing benefits to household wool growers requires better marketing and management structures within larger marketing organizations (the so-called Dragon Head enterprises) that lead the push into fine-wool markets. In the process, households will surrender some independence and flexibility with far-ranging social implications. Given that Dragon Head enterprises are a top-down, indirect approach to raise incomes of some of the more marginal members of Chinese society, the government has a responsibility to ensure that the contractual arrangements associated with the Dragon Head enterprises focus foremost on these social objectives. Without careful design, Dragon Head enterprises may crowd out smaller players and become competitive with marginalized members of the community either directly or indirectly, leading to a less-diversified rural economy. Operating within a more competitive market economy, Dragon Head enterprises are also turning away from operating as non-profit organizations that distribute profits back to small households in the form of higher prices or better services.

9.3   TOWARDS A SMOOTHER AND MORE COMPLETE TRANSITION

The transformation of the wool textile industry mirrors the experience of many other Chinese industries. The transition experience has largely been a positive one, especially in periods that offered opportunity for greater social participation in industry growth. Even periods of industry rationalization have given rise to more efficient and modern structures and have not interrupted the flow of new investment and resources into the industries.

At the same time however, detailed examination in this book shows that industry transition has not always been aligned with government and societal objectives, and that there have been many incomplete, suboptimal and adverse aspects of the transition. In the Central Planning era – as highlighted in the left-hand side of Figure 1.1 in Chapter 1 – the government acted as a check and balance when industry transition became too disorderly or when societal objectives were not being met.

With the move away from a command to a more market-oriented economy, the feedback and adjustment mechanisms have changed. Figure 9.2 aims to depict a more contemporary set of checks and balances. In the current environment, it is the market rather than the government that corrects imbalances, brings order to the system and moulds industries so that they can achieve society's goals. Markets reward firms able to adjust to changing technologies, consumer preferences and societal demands, and force the exit of enterprises unable to adjust. The rigour of financial markets replaces planners in evaluating the worth of particular investment proposals and provides incentives for managers to employ more efficient operation and management practices.

For markets to operate in this way requires a particularly strong set of assumptions, including: extensive and symmetrical information flows; political markets operating alongside commodity markets to reveal and implement the preferences of society in relation to regulation of the markets; and the absence of size economies and external effects. As might be expected, when these assumptions do not hold the operation of markets alone will fail to act as an effective check and balance and lead to a chaotic situation. Therefore markets need to be augmented by a series of policy responses to achieve societal goals and a successful industry transition.

As highlighted in Figure 9.2, the policy adjustments can take the form of a direct response (as in the case of an environmental edict) or a more indirect or facilitative approach to influence the way markets operate and adjust. However just as markets fail, so too can the policymaking process. In either case, the market- or policy-induced transition may have adverse consequences which over time will elicit a new set of market and policy responses.

The systems of checks and balances and the associated feedback mechanism are highly dependent on the nature of the industry structures and processes that are depicted in the central box at the top of Figure 9.2. Industry participants have to be in a position to be able to clearly interpret and respond to market and policy signals in order to generate beneficial outcomes. Interpretation and responses are often clouded – for good reasons. As discussed throughout the book, the pace of change in the first transition phase (ownership reform) and the second transition phase (technical reform) can be overwhelming. New competitors, partners, markets, policies and institutions come and go at a rapid rate. Chinese managers are consumed by the need to respond to these fast-changing, immediate pressures to capitalize on short-term opportunities – or just to survive.

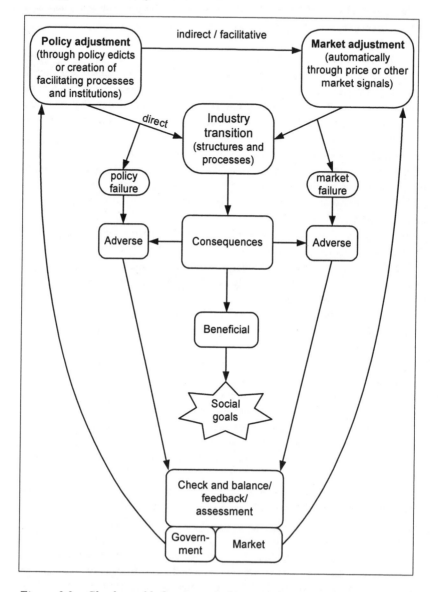

Figure 9.2   Checks and balances on industry transition

The systems of checks and balances and the associated mechanism are highly dependent on the nature of the industry structures and processes that are depicted in the central box at the top of Figure 9.2. Industry participants have to be in a position to be able to clearly interpret and respond to market and policy signals in order to generate beneficial outcomes. Interpretation and responses are often clouded – for good reasons. As discussed throughout the book, the pace of change in the first transition phase (ownership reform) and the second transition phase (technical reform) can be overwhelming. New competitors, partners, markets, policies and institutions come and go at a rapid rate. Chinese managers are consumed by the need to respond to these fast-changing, immediate pressures to capitalize on short-term opportunities – or just to survive.

One cannot help but be impressed by China's capacity in this regard. Yet perhaps modernization and the transition process have come to a stage where it is time to take stock and proactively plan for the longer-term future. Facilitating and encouraging enterprises and industries to tackle the third phase of economic transition (operational and managerial reform) has been identified in this book as a key element of developing this proactive and strategic planning capability. This involves adopting a more analytical approach to development, increased coordination between actors, and the development of enabling institutions. Tangible steps toward achieving these objectives include the use of management tools, product and brand development, market services, and the development of and participation in more independent and stronger industry associations.

References

AWI (Australian Wool Innovation Pty Ltd) (2004), 'The Australia–China Wool Trade, Submission to the Australian Government Department of Foreign Affairs and Trade on the China–Australia Free Trade Agreement Feasibility Study', Sydney, Aust.: AWI, www.wool.com.au/attachments/Trade_Markets/AWITradeSubmission_ChinaFTA.pdf

Becquelin, N. (2000), 'Xinjiang in the Nineties', *China Journal*, **44**, 65–90.

Brown, C.G. (1997), 'Chinese Wool Auctions: Failed Agribusiness Reform or Future Marketing Channel?' *China Economic Review*, **8** (2), 175–90.

Brown, C.G. and J.W. Longworth (1992), 'Reconciling National Economic Reforms and Local Investment Decisions: Fiscal Decentralization and First-Stage Wool Processing in Northern China', *Development Policy Review*, **10** (4), 389–402.

Brown, Colin G., Scott A. Waldron, John W. Longworth and Yutian Zhao (2005), 'Building Economic Decision-making Capabilities of Chinese Wool Textile Mills', *ACIAR Technical Report*, **60**, Canberra, Aust.: ACIAR (Australian Centre for International Agricultural Research), http://www.aciar.gov.au/web.nsf/doc/ACIA-6CF756

Burns, J.P. (1997), 'The Civil Service System of the People's Republic of China', paper presented to Civil Service Systems in Comparative Perspective, Bloomington, US, 5–8 April.

Chai, Joseph C.H. (1997), *China: Transition to a Market Economy*, Oxford, UK: Clarendon Press, and New York, US: Oxford University Press.

Chen, Hongyi (2000), The Institutional Transition of China's Township and Village Enterprises: Market Liberalization, Contractural Form Innovation, and Privatization, Aldershot, UK and Brookfield, US: Ashgate Publishing.

Chen, Chien-Hsun and Hui-Tzu Shi (2004), Banking and Insurance in the New China: Competition and the Challenge of Accession to the WTO, Cheltenham, UK and Northampton, US: Edward Elgar.

Chen, S., Z. Deng and F.Y. Wang (2001), 'Jinxing Yangmao Xiandaihua Guanli, Nuli Jianshe Xinjiang Youzhi Xiyangmao "Sapale" Pai Shengchan Jidi (Promote the Modernization of Wool Management, Conscientiously Build the Production Bases of Xinjiang's Quality Fine Wool Brand "Sapale")', *Caoshi Jiaxu (Ruminant Livestock/Supplement)*, 27–8 and 49.

Chen, W.D. and X.T. Chen (2002), 'Xinjiang Yangyangye de Xianzhuang he Duice (The Situation and Countermeasures Toward the Current Situation in the Xinjiang Sheep Industry)', *Caoshi Jiamu (Ruminant Livestock)*, **4**, 8–10.

China Textiles Association (2001), Zhongguo Fangzhi Biaozhu Huibian – Maofangzhi Zhuan (China Textiles Standards Collection – Wool Textiles Edition), Beijing: China Textiles Press.

ChinaOnline (2000), 'China to Rein in Textile, Steel, Coal and Sugar Production in '01', www.chinaonline.com, 20 December.

CNTIC (China National Textiles Industry Council) (2003), *China Textile Industry Development Report 2002/2003*, Beijing: China Textiles Press.

Colby, H., X. Diao and F. Tan (2001), 'China's WTO Accession: Conflicts with Domestic Agricultural Policies and Institutions', *Estey Centre Journal of International Law and Trade Policy*, **2** (1), 1–17, http://128.233.58.173/j_html/colby2-1.html

EBACTI (Editorial Board of the Almanac of China's Textile Industry) (2000), *Almanac of China's Textile Industry, 2000*, Beijing: China Textiles Press.

EBCAY (Editorial Board of China Agriculture Yearbook) (ed.) (various years), *China Agriculture Yearbook*, Beijing: China Agricultural Press.

Groenewold, Nicolaas, Yanrui Wu, Sam Hak Kan Tang and Xiang-Mei Fan (2003), *The Chinese Stock Market: Efficiency, Predictability and Profitability*, Cheltenham, UK and Northampton, US: Edward Elgar.

Hannan, Kate (1998), Industrial Change in China: Economic Restructuring and Conflicting Interests, London, UK and New York, US: RoutledgeCurzon.

Holloway, Jane (2002), 'Impact of World Trade Organisation Accession on China's Wool Textile Industries', presented to 2002 International Wool and Wool Textile Conference, Shanghai, China, Canberra, Aust: AWI (Australian Wool Innovation Limited), http://www.wool.com.au/attachments/Trade_Markets/CWTAJHolloway.pdf

IWS (International Wool Secretariat) (1995), 'Raw Wool Importing and Early Stage Processing: Impediments to Business', Parkville, Aust.: IWS.

IWTO (International Wool Textile Organisation) (2004), *Wool Statistics, 2002–03*, Brussels, Belgium: IWTO.

Ji, Xu-Dong (2001), *Development of Accounting and Auditing Systems in China*, Aldershot, UK and Burlington, US: Ashgate Publishing.

Kwan, Yum K. and Eden S.H. Yu (2005), *Critical Issues in China's Growth and Development*, Aldershot, UK and Burlington, US: Ashgate Publishing.

Laurenceson, James and Joseph C.H. Chai (2003), *Financial Reform and Economic Development in China*, Cheltenham, UK and Northampton, US: Edward Elgar.

Lieberthal, Kenneth (1995), *Governing China: From Revolution Through Reform*, London, UK and New York, US: WW Norton.

Liew, Leong (1997), *The Chinese Economy in Transition: From Plan to Market*, Cheltenham, UK and Lyme, US: Edward Elgar.

Longworth, John W. and Colin G. Brown (1995), *Agribusiness Reforms in China: The Case of Wool*, Wallingford, UK: CAB International.

Longworth, John W., Colin G. Brown and Scott A. Waldron (2001), *Beef in China: Agribusiness Opportunities and Challenges*, St Lucia, Aust.: University of Queensland Press.

Longworth, John W. and Gregory J. Williamson (1993), *China's Pastoral Region: Sheep and Wool, Minority Nationalities, Rangeland Degradation and Sustainable Development*, Wallingford, UK: CAB International.

Lu, Ding and Chee Kong Wong (2003), *China's Telecommunications Market: Entering a New Competitive Age*, Cheltenham, UK and Northampton, US: Edward Elgar.

Lyons, Ben (2000), 'Southern Jiangsu Township and Village Enterprises Engaged in the Wool Textile Industry: An Industry Specific Study of Institutional Change in a TVE Model', Honours thesis, Department of Asian Studies, St Lucia, Aust.: University of Queensland, 121 pp.

Lyons, Ben (2003), 'Risk Management and Contractual Issues in Sino-Australian Wool Trade in the WTO Era', in B. Coate, R. Brooks, I. Fraser and L. Xu (eds), *Proceedings of the 15th Annual Conference of the Association of Chinese Economic Studies Australia*, **1** (2), Melbourne, Aust.: RMIT (Royal Melbourne Institute of Technology) Business Research Development Unit, http://mams.rmit.edu.au/b4wok6v9whnr1.pdf

Lyons, Ben (2005), 'Obstacles that Persist: Sino-Australian Wool Trade in the WTO Era', PhD dissertation thesis, School of Natural and Rural Systems Management, St Lucia, Aust.: University of Queensland, forthcoming.

MOA (Ministry of Agriculture – People's Republic of China) (various years), *China Agriculture Yearbook*, Beijing: Zhongguo Nongye Chubanshe (China Agricultural Publishing House).

Niu, R.F. (1997), 'Nongye Chanye Yitihua Jingying de Lilun Kuangjia (A Theoretical Framework for Agricultural Vertical Integration Management)', *Zhongguo Nongcun Jingji* (*Chinese Rural Economy*), May.

NTIBSC (National Textile Industry Bureau Statistics Centre) (various years), *Fangzhi Gongye Tongji Nianbao* (*Textile Industry Statistics Yearly Report*), Beijing.

People's Daily (*Renmin Ribao*) (2003), 'Five Major Points Concerning State Council Restructuring', 7 March, http://english.peopledaily.com.cn/200303/07/eng20030307_112882.shtml

Qi, Luo (2001), China's Industrial Reform and Open-door Policy, 1980–1997: A Case Study from Xiamen, Aldershot, UK and Burlington, US: Ashgate Publishing.

Quirk, R. (2002), 'WTO and Sino-Australian Wool Trade', Proceedings of International Wool Textile Conference, Shanghai, China: China Wool Textile Association.

Redding, S. Gordon (1990), *The Spirit of Chinese Capitalism*, New York, US and Berlin, Germany: Walter de Gruyter.

Schak, D.C. (1995), 'The Spirit of Chinese Capitalism: A Critique', *Qinghua Xue Bao (Journal of Qinghua University)*, **13**, 86–104.

SMCCFB (Supply and Marketing Co-operative Central Finance Bureau) (2002), 'Wen Jiabao Jixu Shenhua Gongxiaoshe Gaige Zuochu Zhongyao Pishi (Wen Jiabao Issues Important Written Instructions on the Continuation of Deepening the Reform of Supply and Marketing Co-operatives)', *Shanye Kuaiji (Commercial Accounting)*, **3**, 3.

Steinfeld, Edward S. (1998), *Forging Reform in China: The Fate of State-owned Industry*, Cambridge, UK and New York, US: Cambridge University Press.

Tian, W.L. (2001), 'Mianyang Guojia Biaozhunzhong de Jige Wenti (Problems with Standards for Merino Sheep Wool)', *Neimenggu Zhiliang Jishu Jiandu (Inner Mongolia Quality, Science and Technology Inspection)*, **6**.

Tong, Donald D. (2002), The Heart of Economic Reform: China's Banking Reform and State Enterprise Restructuring, Aldershot, UK and Burlington, US: Ashgate Publishing.

Unger, J. and A. Chan (1995), 'China, Corporatism, and the East Asian Model', *The Australian Journal of Chinese Affairs*, **33**, 29–53.

Waldron, Scott A. (2003), 'State Sector Reform in China: The Diverging Path of Agriculture', paper presented to Association for Chinese Economic Studies Australia, Melbourne, Aust., 2–3 October, http://mams.rmit.edu.au/1y5iyuz4m59p.doc

Waldron, Scott A., Colin G. Brown and John W. Longworth (2003), *Rural Development in China: Insights from the Beef Industry*, Aldershot, UK and Burlington, US: Ashgate Publishing.

Waldron, Scott A., Colin G. Brown and Cungen Zhang (2004), 'Analysis of Agribusiness and Policy Developments in China's Sheepmeat Industry of Relevance to the Australian Industry – Report prepared for MLA (Meat and Livestock Australia)', Brisbane, Aust.: University of Queensland, July, unpublished report.

Wei, Shang-Jin, Huizhong Zhou and Guanzhong J. Wen (eds) (2002), *The Globalization of the Chinese Economy*, Cheltenham, UK and Northampton, US: Edward Elgar.

Weitzman, M.L. and C. Xu (1994), 'Chinese Township Village Enterprises as Vaguely Defined Cooperatives', *Journal of Comparative Economics*, **18** (2), 121–45.

Zhang, J.C. (2001), 'Goujian "Xiehui + Muchang + Shichang" de Xiyangmao Chanyehua Kuangjia (Forming the Framework of the "Association + Pastoralist + Market" Model of Vertical Integration of the Fine Wool Industry)', *Caoshi Jiamu (Ruminant Livestock)*, 20–21.

Zhang, Xiaoguang and Peter J. Lloyd (2001), *Models of the Chinese Economy*, Cheltenham, UK and Northampton, US: Edward Elgar.

Zhang, Xun-Hai (1992), Enterprise Reforms in a Centrally Planned Economy: The Case of the Chinese Bicycle Industry, London, UK: Macmillan, and New York, US: St Martin's Press.

Zhang, Z.M., F.J. Kong, Y. Gao, Y. Shao and Y.J. Wang (1997), 'Humble Recommendations about the Wool Quality Situation in Heilongjiang', *Science and Technology Supervision*, 16.

Zhao, Yutian, Colin G. Brown, Scott A. Waldron, John W. Longworth and Ping Li (2005), 'Zhongguo Maofang Qiye Jingji Juece Fenxi Fangfa' ('Methods of Analysing Economic Decisions at Chinese Wool Textile Mills', *ACIAR Technical Report*, **60a**, Canberra, Aust.: ACIAR (Australian Centre for International Agricultural Research).

Zheng, Shaofeng, Scott A. Waldron and Colin G. Brown (2003), 'Cost–revenue analysis of household ruminant livestock production in China', *Agricultural and Natural Resource Economics Working Paper*, **05/03**, St Lucia, Aust.: School of Natural and Rural Systems Management, University of Queensland.

Zhu, C. (1998), 'Shenru Guanche Dang de Shiwuda Jingsheng: Quanmian Tuijin Gongxiaoshe Gaige yu Fazhan (Deepen the Implementation of the Party's 10th Five Year Plan Report Spirit: Comprehensively Carry Out Reform and Development of Supply and Marketing Co-operatives)', *Shangye Jingji yu Guanli (Commercial Economics and Management)*, **1**, 26–7.

Index